Y0-CAY-131

Rewrite Man

[ALISON MACOR]

Rewrite Man

THE LIFE AND CAREER OF
SCREENWRITER WARREN SKAAREN

University of Texas Press AUSTIN

Requests for permission to reproduce material from this work should be
sent to:
　　Permissions
　　University of Texas Press
　　P.O. Box 7819
　　Austin, TX 78713-7819
　　http://utpress.utexas.edu/index.php/rp-form

♾ The paper used in this book meets the minimum requirements of
ANSI/NISO Z39.48-1992 (R1997) (Permanence of Paper).

LIBRARY OF CONGRESS CATALOGING-IN-PUBLICATION DATA

Names: Macor, Alison, 1966–, author.
Title: Rewrite man : the life and career of screenwriter Warren Skaaren /
　　Alison Macor.
Description: First edition. | Austin : University of Texas Press, 2017. |
　　Includes bibliographical references and index.
Identifiers: LCCN 2016033835
　　ISBN 978-0-292-75945-9 (cloth : alk. paper)
　　ISBN 978-1-4773-1201-8 (library e-book)
　　ISBN 978-1-4773-1202-5 (non-library e-book)
Subjects: LCSH: Skaaren, Warren, 1946–1990. | Screenwriters—United States—
　　Biography. | Motion picture authorship.
Classification: LCC PS3569.K33 Z76 2017 | DDC 813/.54 [B]—dc23
LC record available at https://lccn.loc.gov/2016033835

doi:10.7560/2759459

For my parents

Contents

INTRODUCTION   *1*

CHAPTER ONE. From Hallingdal to Houston   *15*

CHAPTER TWO. Hollywood on the Colorado   *38*

CHAPTER THREE. Breaking Away   *61*

CHAPTER FOUR. Highway to the Danger Zone   *80*

CHAPTER FIVE. Hollywood Gothic   *110*

CHAPTER SIX. One Hit After Another   *131*

CHAPTER SEVEN. Batmania   *150*

CHAPTER EIGHT. The Man Hollywood Trusts   *175*

CONCLUSION   *188*

Acknowledgments   *205*

Notes   *209*

Select Bibliography   *235*

Index   *239*

Rewrite Man

Introduction

He is a magician and a telepath who has only to mumble and to imagine and the world turns to his desires.

ERNEST BECKER, *THE DENIAL OF DEATH*

The memorial service for Warren Skaaren was held at the Paramount Theatre in downtown Austin on a bleak January afternoon in 1991. The day began with temperatures in the fifties, but as the afternoon wore on the thermometer dropped, signaling the return of a polar front that had chilled the city in the final weeks of December as Skaaren lost his battle with bone cancer.

As family members, friends, and associates filed into the Paramount's rows of velvet-covered seats, babies' cries and the murmurs of young children could be heard throughout the theater, which seemed fitting given Skaaren's lifelong ability to connect with children of all ages. Indeed, he and his wife, Helen, had fostered seven babies of various races in the early years of their marriage. The memorial's master of ceremonies that day, film producer Ron Bozman, even joked that an initial plan for the service featured a "stageful of babies of mixed race, just crying and googling" in front of an audience. Despite Skaaren's affinity with young people, however, he remained deeply ambivalent about having children of his own throughout his life, even into his final months.

"How do you sum up a man and a man's life?" Bozman asked.[1] A longtime producer who a year later would win a Best Picture Academy Award for his work on *The Silence of the Lambs*, Bozman had met Skaaren in 1966, when they were both sophomores at Rice University. "Words cannot begin to do it all, but they can begin," he continued, describing Skaaren as a child during the Korean War and, later, "an ardent and vocal opponent of Vietnam" who would "not have enjoyed the events of the past week, as none of us have." Bozman was referring to the U.S. government's decision to ramp up its military activity in the Persian Gulf. Iraqi president Saddam Hussein had ignored the United Nations' January 15 deadline to pull his army out of Kuwait. In the hours leading up to Skaaren's memorial, U.S. Patriot missiles began shooting down Iraqi missiles.

"It's a shame he didn't go into politics though it was available to him," continued Bozman of Skaaren, who had first moved to Texas's capital city in 1969 to work on then-Governor Preston Smith's staff. Skaaren had leveraged a position in the governor's urban development program into overseeing the state's first film commission, which he helmed for four years before leaving state politics behind. "He could have [gone into politics] and had he done it, I think, we might not be in the Middle East today." Suggesting that Skaaren could have prevented the country's involvement in the Middle East seemed like a bold statement, particularly given Skaaren's tremendous success in an altogether different field—as a screenwriter and script doctor, or "rewrite man," on four of the top-grossing films of the 1980s. Bozman's comment, however, was typical of how people reacted to Skaaren. With his engaging personality, commanding baritone, and 6′2″ stature, not to mention his sharp analytical and active listening skills, Skaaren gave the impression to nearly everyone he met that he could do just about anything. With his myriad abilities, some friends wondered why he was spending (wasting, even) his talents rewriting other writers' scripts when he could be running for public office, working as a metal sculptor, writing and performing music—the list went on and on and seemed to say more about Skaaren's relationship with each person than about what Skaaren's true calling was meant to be.

"The man was never what you would call predictable," Bozman said drily. Skaaren's friends were often surprised at the twists and turns his life took, such as his decision to leave the film commission in 1974 and try his hand at writing, or the fact that prior to his death, he had been seriously ill for six months without telling the majority of those closest to him. Bozman worried aloud that the memorial itself, which the producer had organized at the request of Skaaren intimate and attorney W. Amon Burton, would be far more conventional than Skaaren might have wanted. And yet Bozman made sure to include performances and people that may have struck some in the audience as unusual, such as the excerpt presented by Heloise Gold. Skaaren had collaborated with the dancer and performer less than a year earlier on her one-woman show titled "Maggs, the 10,000 Year Old Woman." Gold's ten-minute performance at the memorial centered on what she would later claim was Skaaren's favorite line from the show: a fart joke.[2]

Prior to Gold's performance, Bozman called to the podium Tom Viola, who was Skaaren's brother-in-law and married to Helen Skaaren's sister, Liz. Viola spoke warmly about Skaaren, saying that they shared a family life for two decades that was "active and extended." What Viola didn't say but many in the audience knew was that Warren and Helen had been separated since August 1989. (Helen Skaaren did not respond to multiple requests to be interviewed for this book.) Skaaren's reasons for not divorcing his wife before his death were as complicated as he was and reflected a deeply rooted ambivalence about women and the demands he felt they made on him.

Next, Bobby Bridger strode onto the Paramount stage carrying a guitar and wearing a fringed suede jacket. Bridger was a musician well known for his celebration of the West in his nationally acclaimed one-man shows. Bridger described Skaaren as his "closest male friend" in the 1970s. The relationship functioned, Bozman would tell another friend privately, as a way for Skaaren to act out vicariously.[3] Although Skaaren never performed music publicly beyond high school, he thought seriously about pursuing songwriting as a career and took steps to do so in the spring of 1988, when the twenty-two-week writer's strike sidelined his screenwriting projects. Accompanied by Bill Guinn on piano, Bridger performed "Heal in the Wisdom," his best-known song. "Let's hear you sing it," Bridger encouraged the audience, most of whom joined in on the final lines: "One day together we'll heal in the wisdom and we'll understand." The lyrics were eerily poignant and seemed to refer to the fact that so many of those attending the memorial service hadn't even known that Skaaren was sick, let alone dying of terminal cancer, which had been diagnosed in July of the previous year. Rumors had begun swirling by the late fall, but together Amon Burton and Skaaren's assistant, Linda Vance, worked overtime to honor Skaaren's vehement request that no one outside a shrinking circle of friends and caregivers be told of his condition. Even Mike Simpson, Skaaren's representative at the William Morris Agency, was kept in the dark until two weeks prior to his client's death. He was told only after Burton convinced Skaaren that his secrecy could be adversely affecting Simpson's own reputation in Hollywood.

As Bobby Bridger exited the stage, an older, balding man in a dark suit stepped to the podium. Robert Wise had known Skaaren when he still lived in Rochester, the Norwegian town in Minnesota that was home to the renowned Mayo Clinic. "The Warren I first knew was really a boy," recalled a somber Wise, who had met the eighteen-year-old Skaaren in his capacity as dean of student affairs at Rochester Junior College (RJC), where Skaaren enrolled following high school graduation. Wise became Skaaren's mentor and friend, assuming something of a paternal role in the younger man's life. The affection that Skaaren felt for Wise could be measured in the number of times that the screenwriter returned to the college's annual freshman camp to speak enthusiastically to the students about Wise and the school itself. "The life he led here in Austin and Hollywood was not actually comprehensible to us back in Rochester," said Wise at the memorial. "But it touched us nevertheless." Indeed Skaaren's visits, often sandwiched between his writing gigs on high-profile projects like *Beverly Hills Cop II* and *Beetlejuice*, dazzled the new freshmen, many of whom probably felt as lost and alone as Skaaren had on the day that he first ran into Wise on the junior college campus. For Skaaren, these visits and the thoughts he shared with the young people there justified what to him sometimes seemed like indulgent and shallow work. "In a life which is so utterly self-centered, it is rare and healthy exercise to share the energy and the memories with others," Skaaren wrote to Wise following what would be his final trip to the camp.[4]

"I'm told that in certain African villages, the storyteller wears a ring of white chalk around his eye, because it's the storyteller's fate to look and to look again.... Our Warren has the storyteller's steadfast gaze," Sherry Kafka-Wagner began as she recounted the time that she and Skaaren had worked together on a documentary about the San Antonio River Walk. Finding themselves hopelessly lost while on a location scout, the pair stopped the car in the middle of an empty road, turned up the radio, and sang and danced to Marvin Gaye's "I Heard It Through the Grapevine." While Skaaren was known for his ability to connect deeply with women and men alike, women in particular responded to his unique combination of attractiveness, attentiveness, and nurturing. Skaaren, who had struggled with his weight and self-confidence since childhood, reveled in this kind of female attention, particularly in the last year of his life during his marital separation. Flush with the commercial and professional success of *Batman* (1989), for which he shared screenwriting credit with first writer Sam Hamm, Skaaren wrote about several flirtatious encounters during that time.

Kafka-Wagner's remembrance was followed by Heloise Gold's performance as Maggs and Bill Jeffers's spoken-word piece about a snake shedding its skin. The two performances represented what some of Skaaren's longtime friends jokingly called his "woo woo" side. A lifelong seeker and voracious reader, Skaaren had always been interested in a variety of subjects. He routinely passed out to friends copies of two of his favorite books, *The Denial of Death* and *A Pattern Language*. He maintained a macrobiotic diet to varying degrees throughout his marriage and embraced this aggressively as an alternative to traditional Western treatment of cancer, first in 1987 and then again when his cancer metastasized in 1990.

Mike Simpson, Skaaren's agent of six years, was the afternoon's final speaker. Senior vice president and co-head of the motion picture division at William Morris, Simpson already had strong Austin ties before he agreed to represent Skaaren in 1984. He had done graduate work at the University of Texas and first met Skaaren in 1975, when he interviewed the newly departed film commissioner about his behind-the-scenes role on *The Texas Chain Saw Massacre*.

Notified of his client's condition only two weeks before Skaaren's death on December 28, Simpson seemed, like so many others at the memorial, still to be coming to terms with his friend's absence. He also was struggling to understand the way that Skaaren had handled his illness and subsequent treatment as well as his decision to tell so few people. Later Simpson would say privately, "That's the one thing for me that's puzzling in all this. He was such a spiritual guy, and I learned a lot from him in that area, and I would have figured him to be an expert at his own dying. A real pro at it."[5]

At the memorial, however, Simpson stuck to the script, so to speak. His job was to present his client in the best light possible and to remind those in attendance why Skaaren was highly successful and in demand in an industry that was so fickle, especially when it came to hiring writers. Simpson read from letters written by two of Skaaren's favorite collaborators, the actors Tom Cruise and Michael Douglas. "Warren was an easy person to like, warm, friendly, with a good sense of humor," wrote Cruise, who had first met the writer when producers Jerry Bruckheimer and Don Simpson hired Skaaren to save a floundering *Top Gun* script. A skittish Cruise had thought his character, Lieutenant Pete "Maverick" Mitchell, was an asshole. Skaaren provided a humanizing backstory and a more challenging love interest, among other changes, that kept Cruise from bailing on the project. "He was very hardworking and dedicated to his craft, something I respected in him," continued Cruise's letter, and indeed Skaaren was the first writer Cruise trusted with his five-page treatment about a race-car driver that would become the film *Days of Thunder* (1990).[6]

"Never in my professional life have I had a more enjoyable working experience than with Warren," Michael Douglas said of their time together on what was to be the third film in the *Romancing the Stone* trilogy. The project sent Skaaren around the world, from New York and San Francisco to London and Hong Kong, where he visited the stalls of the animal black market and hung out in the high-end karaoke clubs favored by the Chinese mob. "Warren would always get the work done, yet still had time to share a personal experience, to learn some new facet about life and always had time for a good dry laugh. I'll miss you, Warren," Douglas's letter continued.[7] Indeed, the two men had spent the better part of a year on the project, meeting in Douglas's penthouse apartment in New York, in various hotel rooms around Los Angeles, and in Warren and Helen's modest home in the hills overlooking downtown Austin. Douglas's marriage to his wife Diandra was in flux at the time, and Skaaren was privy to intense conversations and highly personal details.

The way Skaaren handled himself in these situations, said Mike Simpson, was partly the secret to his success. "The community felt this sense of honesty and discretion from Warren and fully embraced in bringing him into its inner circle." Simpson recalled the start of Skaaren's rewrite career, which began with his work on a midbudget romantic drama for Jeffrey Katzenberg and Dawn Steel at Paramount Pictures. Steel in particular connected with Skaaren, and it was she who recommended him to Simpson and Bruckheimer for *Top Gun*. "In the craft of high-level production rewrites, Warren had no equal. He possessed a unique ability to walk into chaotic situations where directors, producers, stars, studio executives would be at odds with each other over a troubled script of a movie that often seemed like a train barreling out of control toward a start date," said Simpson, offering a description that fit nearly all of the blockbusters that Skaaren had worked on. He described Skaaren's ability to bring focus to these situations and clarity and fresh insights to the scripts themselves. "His ability to deliver the goods practically overnight and ready to shoot was legendary," said Simpson. He neglected to mention the toll this might have taken on Skaaren. He set a precedent with *Top Gun*, delivering a first draft in an astonishing ten days (writers typically take three weeks), but it left him wearing an eye patch and with hands too calloused to type.[8]

Although Skaaren achieved his greatest financial and professional success with the release of *Batman* in 1989, it was *Beetlejuice* (1988), said Simpson, that gave the writer the most professional satisfaction. Both projects paired Skaaren with Tim Burton, who also was a client of Simpson's. Burton had traveled to Austin for the memorial, in fact, but did not speak publicly. Bobby Bridger recalls taking a cigarette break in the alley behind the Paramount Theatre, where he stood alone with another somber smoker who, he realized later, was Tim Burton. After Simpson finished speaking, a montage of clips from Skaaren's films began to play. "It's showtime!" crowed Michael Keaton's character in *Beetlejuice*. Excerpts both dramatic and comical followed for more than ten minutes, highlighting some of Skaaren's best work in *Top Gun*, *Beverly Hills Cop II*, *Beetlejuice*, and *Batman*. The memorial concluded with *Beetlejuice*'s zany dinner party sequence, in which spirits possess a group of guests and force them to dance and sing, conga-line style, to Harry Belafonte's "Day-O."

The memorial offered Tim Burton, for one, insight into aspects of Skaaren's life and personality that the writer never revealed to him during the years that they worked together. "I realized that we actually were more alike than I even thought," said Burton later. "As a director you make a movie and you make it yours. 'It's my movie.' It's the process you go through. It needs to be this and this . . . I pushed a lot of that. But the feeling I got from the memorial, and seeing pictures and actually just thinking about time past and our relationship, there is a lot of him in it, and his spirit." Continued Burton, "When you're working with someone, when you can't delineate who did what, that's the sign of a good relationship."[9]

[   ]

By the time of Warren Skaaren's premature death, in December 1990, he was one of the highest-paid writers in Hollywood—although he rarely left Austin, where he had lived and worked since the late 1960s. He was an in-demand script doctor—rewriting and polishing screenplays by other writers—on some of the most successful blockbusters of the 1980s. His industry profile had risen to such an extent with *Batman*, in fact, that Skaaren himself became the subject of a series of articles and magazine profiles beginning in 1989. The glossy entertainment magazine *Premiere* had been planning to run a profile of Skaaren in early 1991. Instead, the article became a two-page obituary titled "Death of a Screenwriter."[10]

Yet Skaaren remains largely unknown today. His anonymity is

partly the result of his early death, but it also reflects the contested role of screenwriters and script doctors, especially in contemporary filmmaking. Skaaren's struggle to claim authorship of four hit films is a struggle that for screenwriters and their union, the Writers Guild of America (WGA), has only become more intense, more litigious, and more public since the 1980s. In 1987, writer Gore Vidal sued the WGA and screenwriter Steve Shagan, who had received sole credit for *The Sicilian*, a film based on a script that Vidal had rewritten. Vidal took issue with the Guild's arbitration itself, a confidential and anonymous process involving three WGA writers who volunteer as arbiters and whose job it is to read through every draft of the screenplay and supporting documents to determine authorship of the final film. Vidal's suit alleged that the arbitration proceeding that awarded sole credit to Shagan was "unfair" because a "fundamental" document had been "withheld" from the arbiters.[11] Vidal's suit asked that the ruling be overturned, and he eventually won his case.[12] Vidal is one of the few writers (and members of the Guild) to sue the organization (writer Larry Ferguson's suit regarding *Beverly Hills Cop II* followed a few months later), but other notable arbitration cases include *The Mask of Zorro* (1998) and *The Hulk* (2003). *The Hulk's* contentious arbitration involved eight writers, including James Schamus, who received a story credit ("a lesser credit often awarded to those who lay out the basic plot and theme") and shared screenplay credit with John Turman and Michael France.[13] "The studio's internal summary of my script was, substantially, the movie," said Turman, who thought his work on *The Hulk* warranted a story credit as well.[14] Schamus was the last writer on the project; typically story credit is awarded to writers responsible for the earliest drafts. "Only in Kafka-meets-Orwell Guildland could you get this result. It's an advertisement for how screwed up the system is," said Schamus of the WGA Arbitration Committee's 2–1 decision.[15] Added Turman, "I get comments like 'Great credit!'—as if I had won the lottery. The arbitration process is seen as divorced from writing itself, and if you win everyone thinks you just got lucky."[16] Battles over screenwriting credit continue to make the front page of trade publications like *Variety* and are frequently covered in the arts sections of the *New York Times* and the *Los Angeles Times*, not to mention recounted and analyzed on the hundreds of film and screenwriting websites that exist today. The arbitration concerning *Jurassic World* (2015), for instance, pitted two writing teams against one another and was in the news for months. Although Colin Treverrow, one of the team's writers (and the film's director), admitted that he and his writing partner

Derek Connolly disagreed with the Guild's final credits determination, he acknowledged that both writing teams "share a disdain for the arbitration process and the ugliness it often breeds. Though I will remain a proud member of the WGA, I encourage my fellow members to work together to find alternative ways to evaluate our contributions."[17]

This issue of authorship, while always a tortuous subject in Hollywood, became increasingly complicated around the time Skaaren began working as a rewrite man. By the 1980s, the process of motion picture development (which includes everything from the initial idea, often expressed at a pitch meeting, to a screenplay that has been rewritten and polished by multiple writers) had grown more complex within an industry run by executives increasingly focused on making blockbuster films. "One reason screenwriters are so often replaced is that the script is the element of a project that's easiest for studios to change," explains writer Tad Friend of the development process. "They would rather replace a five-hundred-thousand-dollar writer during pre-production than lose a twenty-million-dollar star who hates the script after production has begun."[18] As film historian Tom Stempel writes, "By the mid-eighties, the major companies combined were investing between thirty and forty million dollars a year in the development process. Most of the scripts in development were not made."[19] Those that were made, however, were often scripts that had been rewritten by numerous writers with input from any number of producers and executives, in addition to the director and stars, a trend that began to dominate the industry during that decade. This trend had its precedent, of course, in earlier periods in film history, such as the 1930s and 1940s, when, notes journalist Beverly Walker, "moguls put [screenwriters] in cubbyholes, demanded a precise number of pages per day, and often assigned several writers to the same project, unbeknownst to each other."[20] But in later decades as large corporations began to purchase the major film studios, the conglomeration of Hollywood took hold and created "layers of bureaucracy" that included agents, attorneys, and "various levels of studio executives" in addition to producers and stars. As Walker observed in 1987, "The 'developed movie' is *the* motion picture for this time, as valid as the style or genre of any previous era."[21]

As a result, disputes over the assignment of writing credit—which could make or break a screenwriter's career—became commonplace as well. By 1980, the Writers Guild of America was being asked to arbitrate such disputes more than 150 times per year.[22] Arbitration is an issue, according to screenwriter Stephen Gaghan (*Traffic*), that is "ultimately going to split the Writers Guild apart. The small group of name writers who fix every film is being arbitrated by—and discriminated against by—a bunch of guys who last wrote an episode of *The Rockford Files*," he says of the "class-war dimension" of the arbitration process.[23]

Arbitration in general, notes attorney Shawn K. Judge, offers a method of "alternative dispute resolution," but the type of arbitration process employed to assign screenwriting credit in the film industry is a process far different from a typical arbitration, which does not require anonymity of its arbiters or conceal the process of determination regarding its decision.[24] Echoing the comments of many screenwriters, Judge observes that the Guild's credit arbitration process "is a potentially flawed mechanism in which the pursuit of fast resolution of disputes and preservation of anonymity may at times lessen the degree of justice achieved."[25] But these conditions are necessary, he argues, to ensure that films (and thus profits) are not threatened by a theatrical release delayed by lengthy litigation over credit, as well as to preserve interpersonal relationships within a relatively small industry. "Preservation of the integrity of credit entails quantifying a fundamentally abstract, inherently immeasurable creative process; there is no system that could satisfactorily resolve such an analytical paradox beyond a doubt," observes Judge.[26]

More often than not, and as demonstrated through its screen credit determinations, the WGA defines the author of a screenplay as the first writer or team of writers on a project. As the Guild's own manual states, "Fewer names and fewer types of credit enhance the value of all credits and the dignity of all writers."[27] But as Skaaren's arbitration experiences reveal, authorship of a film script is a highly complicated and multilayered issue often dictated by elements inscribed at various points throughout a film's journey from script to screen. Exploring Skaaren's well-documented experiences as a writer battling for shared credit on a potential blockbuster also yields a new understanding of the secretive screen credit arbitration process during the New Hollywood, a time in which the industry's embracing of development led to a greater number of screenplays necessitating the Guild's involvement via the arbitration process. The development and eventual arbitration of Skaaren's screenplays for films such as *Top Gun* and *Beverly Hills Cop II* also offer some insight into the roles of various players—the producers, directors, screenwriters, stars, the studio executives, even the Guild itself—within the overall process.

For a relative newcomer like Skaaren, this trend toward development and the tendency of studios to hire multiple writers for a single project clearly worked to his advantage. The downside to this situation, as he would experience firsthand on *Top Gun*, was that the assigning of story and writing credit on such projects often resulted in arbitration, a process of mediation that rarely favored anyone but the first writer or team of writers. In addition, the arbiters' decisions regarding story and writing credit frequently denied, or at least glossed over, the complicated process by which a film script gets written. Obscured are other, less tangible elements of the screenplay's development, such as the power a top star like Tom Cruise has over the writing and rewriting process and how this affects the screenwriters' work. Cruise's involvement in *Top Gun* and what it meant to the project also reveal another important element of the filmmaking formula that flourished in the 1980s: Cruise's star power was "bankable." As Tom Stempel explains, by the 1980s this did not mean that Cruise's involvement would translate into money from the bank to fund the production as much as it guaranteed that the film would be distributed into theaters. In turn, argues Stempel, a star such as Cruise would also function as a producer even if he did not receive screen credit as such. This further affected the development of the screenplay. "The stars' decisions influenced what scripts were written, how they were re-written, and if they were produced at all," writes Stempel.[28] This was the state of American filmmaking in 1985, when Skaaren was hired to re-write the script for *Top Gun*, his first major Hollywood project.

With the exception perhaps of his agent, Mike Simpson, Skaaren rarely talked to others about his arbitration experiences in Hollywood, but each one influenced how he negotiated and approached successive film projects. He often wrote about these experiences privately, where he vented about the process and each outcome. This tendency to keep things to himself seemed to be with Skaaren from childhood, when as an only child of somewhat older parents he began to seek solace in writing, draw-ing, and music. The memorial in January 1991 brought together all aspects of Skaaren's complex life, one that had become increasingly compart-mentalized in his final six months. Skaaren thrived on keeping separate the various parts of his world—professional and personal, friends and lovers, business and pleasure—so the concept of the memorial itself and the size of the audience it drew might have unnerved him. The event also revealed what his girlfriend Julie Jordan described as "an enormously big private life. He wasn't a public figure, but it's almost as if his private life was the size of a public life. He was someone who met someone for every single meal, had meetings, had the phone going. He was always going somewhere or doing something with someone. All the time."[29]

Skaaren's story offers insight into two very different but similarly misunderstood subjects. While Skaaren's career sheds light on the politics of writing blockbusters in 1980s Hollywood, his life also reveals one person's experience with terminal illness and the world of alternative healthcare at that time. Skaaren's memorial marked the end of a particularly chaotic six-month period that unfolded almost like a scene out of one of his screenplays for Tim Burton. "He wrote his dying script," said his assistant, Linda Vance, of what transpired during those final six months. "His own *Beetlejuice*, with all these weird characters and parts and roles played out all around him in real life."[30] The setting was Skaaren's beloved Tuscan villa, a home whose initial acquisition was so fraught with difficulties that an anxious Skaaren sought out a friend who consulted the *I Ching* before he signed the deed to the house.

In addition to Vance and longtime attorney Amon Burton, Skaaren surrounded himself with a rotating "cast of characters" that included a young couple named Brian and Kaye Connors, who had experience in caring for the terminally ill. Mary Kett, an Irish cook from the Boston area, was flown in to prepare the macrobiotic meals that Skaaren hoped would cure him of his cancer. Sculptor and friend/counselor Tom Giebink visited often, and Diane Haug, who worked with Skaaren on his breathing and meditation, went back and forth between Austin and her home in New Mexico. Throughout his adult life, Skaaren had always explored alternatives to traditional Western medicine. As he grew increasingly panicked about the terminal nature of his diagnosis, Skaaren began to seek out more "healers," which added to the number of people who came and went at the house. "He needed all of us there. We all had a part," said Kaye Connors in the months after Skaaren's death. "It wasn't just an extravagant play that he was putting on," insisted her then-husband, Brian. "It was just what he needed to get through that experience."[31]

For Vance, the lifelong ambivalence that Skaaren seemed to feel toward traditional and nontraditional medicine revealed itself in those final months. "I don't know if he didn't have faith in either one of them or he had more faith in one and less in the other, but the fact is he was still trying to mix the two without giving either one full attention and credit," she said not long after his death.[32] The situation was further complicated by Skaaren's relationship with a number of close female friends, which created power struggles within the house. "They each had a bond with Warren and they each came into the situation thinking they were going to be the savior in healing in whatever way they knew how," said Vance. Julie Jordan, who began a romantic relationship with Skaaren in the last year of his life, supported him in his postseparation quest to examine his inner life through dream analysis, counseling, reading, and writing. He was especially interested in exploring his "internal feminine" side or self (whom he nicknamed "Ingrid") and how this affected his relationships with women. Predisposed to caregiving, Skaaren was exploring in the last month or so of his life, according to Jordan, what it felt like to be cared for. Allowing himself to be taken care of by female nurses, said Jordan, was "Warren learning how not to take care of women."[33]

The themes of romantic love and death figured largely in the last project that Skaaren wrote. Eager to capitalize on the financial success and popularity of *Beetlejuice*, Warner Bros. was interested in producing a sequel for Tim Burton to direct. Skaaren was first approached to write the script in the fall of 1989. Mired in the personal drama surrounding his separation from Helen, Skaaren felt deeply conflicted about accepting the project. Characteristically, he drew up a list of pros and cons to help him achieve clarity. Citing the project's potential to bring "camaraderie . . . fun, luxury," Skaaren also noted his fear that another demanding Hollywood experience would allow "working Warren" to take over, potentially angering the women closest to him. "I'll die of stress," he predicted of having to mediate any interpersonal conflicts.[34] Skaaren turned down the project at least once before agreeing to meet with Burton in December 1989. Gradually Skaaren warmed to Burton's two-page synopsis, which opened with a romantic proposal atop the Eiffel Tower quickly followed by an accidental death and, eventually, reincarnation. Despite ongoing back pain that forced him to use crutches to get around, Skaaren finished a first draft of the screenplay in early July 1990. A week later, he would find himself on a private plane headed to MD Anderson Cancer Center in Houston, where the back pain would be diagnosed as an indication of the widespread melanoma that had attacked his bones.

According to many who were privy to Skaaren's final months, he seemed to struggle almost to the end with the knowledge of what was happening to him. As longtime friend and former roommate Ron Bozman observed, "He didn't go easily into the good night."[35] While some attributed this to his being in denial about his death, others explained Skaaren's struggle as being culturally defined. Said Julie Jordan, who shared Skaaren's Norwegian roots, "He had a faith in his own vitality. I think there really is this belief that if you can stand up and walk and keep going, that almost, like, the circulation of your blood and your vitality can keep you alive." Skaaren spent a good portion of his final weeks struggling to get out of bed and to walk. "If he could get up and walk," explained Jordan, "he could live. It's a very Norwegian way to be."[36]

A young Warren Skaaren around the time he claimed to have had a "visitation" that he believed helped him to harness his creative abilities. Courtesy of Linda Vance.

"Power of a simple stupid sort came easily into my hands." Skaaren at Rochester Junior College. Harry Ransom Center, The University of Texas at Austin.

Skaaren (smiling, back row center) during the early 1970s, when he ran the Texas Film Commission under Governor Preston Smith. Harry Ransom Center, The University of Texas at Austin.

Skaaren, then chairman of FPS, with Leonard Katzman, showrunner for primetime soap Dallas. Harry Ransom Center, The University of Texas at Austin.

Skaaren and Tom Cruise on the set of Top Gun *in 1985.* Harry Ransom Center, The University of Texas at Austin.

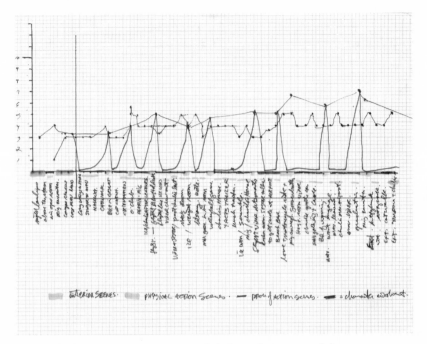

An intensity chart Skaaren created to help balance the action and character dynamics in his rewrite of Top Gun. *Harry Ransom Center, The University of Texas at Austin.*

Hollywood gothic:
Skaaren and Tim
Burton in Austin,
Texas, in 1986.
Courtesy of Linda
Vance.

Monday March 28 , 1988

George Harrison
Friar Park
Henley-on-Thames
Oxfordshire, England

Dear George;

I was very impressed that you unearthed the Bad Boys Blue discs!
Many many thanks. That's the thing about rock N roll , just like
fornication, I'm always shocked at how many obscure people do it
all over the world!

I looked around to find some way to return the favor but,
suspecting you probably had enough teapots and blenders, I
decided I'd just write you a letter describing how bloody boring
it is to be on strike and how your story about DEVIL'S RADIO led
me to a new movie idea.

The Writer's Guild of America (oppressed underclass) is on strike
against the Producers (wicked upperclass heathens). The issues
are these: the underclass wants more money so they can creep
into the upperclass.

Well I only HAVE two kinds of friends:
1. Hippie artists, and 2. Upperclass heathens.

Heathen Tom Cruise and I were in the middle of a scheme which
was to go into production on August 1st. And we can't do it now.

Jane Fonda, noted upperclass heathenette, and I were planning a
film with Tina Turner and I can't do nothin' there neither. As a
matter of fact, since I am producing this film with Fonda, I AM an
UPPERCLASS HEATHEN. I must take special care not to discuss this
film with myself.

1

*A dedicated correspondent, Skaaren often sent chatty letters to friends and
acquaintances. Here he thanks former Beatle George Harrison, whom he met on a
plane, for a gift of albums.* Harry Ransom Center, The University of Texas at Austin.

Skaaren (foreground) and close friend Amon Burton, hobbyist beekeepers. Copyright by Carol Cohen Burton.

Sean Young photographed this table read at Pinewood Studios during rehearsals for Batman: *(left to right around table) Skaaren, Robert Wuhl, Jon Peters, Mark Canton, Michael Keaton, Tim Burton, and Jack Nicholson.* Harry Ransom Center, The University of Texas at Austin.

Skaaren with Jack Nicholson getting made up as the Joker. Harry Ransom Center, The University of Texas at Austin.

Original art for Sam Hurt's "Eyebeam" comic strip, a gift to Skaaren that captured the mania surrounding Batman's *release.* Harry Ransom Center, The University of Texas at Austin.

FAX 4-11-88 ONE PAGE
CONFIDENTIAL

TO: MICHEAL DOUGLAS-BEL AIR HOTEL
FROM: WARREN SKAAREN

Dear Mikey;

On behalf the Board of Directors out at the college Give 'em heck tonight!

I was gonna' be there at the Bel Air but we got Spring lambs dropping like popcorn out in the Shelly Winters sheep meadow so I cancelled. We dragged the old Hitachi 19" out to the shed and we'll be there with our giant sack of potato chips and a gallon of Pepsi with every appendage of our bodies crossed for you.

On a personal note. Be especially careful around that Jack Nicholson. One of the vets out here says he thinks Jack's got an advanced case of the red eye and the stuff spreads like fire ants.

Warren Skaaren
President
Micheal Douglas Junior College

END OF FAX

Skaaren sent this fax to friend and former collaborator Michael Douglas on the day of the 1988 Academy Awards, when Douglas's film Fatal Attraction *was nominated in several categories.* Harry Ransom Center, The University of Texas at Austin.

Jerry Bruckheimer, Tom Cruise, and Don Simpson in Palermo, Italy, where they spent a week with Skaaren trying to salvage the Days of Thunder *screenplay. It would be the only project Skaaren walked away from.* Harry Ransom Center, The University of Texas at Austin.

Skaaren in 1990, at the height of his success. Copyright by Jeff Cannon. Harry Ransom Center, The University of Texas at Austin.

ONE

From Hallingdal to Houston

Two hours after a meeting, Warren comes up with a list of fifteen ideas. Once he called me at midnight, after a meeting that broke up at ten p.m. I said, "Can't it wait till morning?"

PRODUCER JERRY BRUCKHEIMER

What's a bogey?" Warren Skaaren asked the dark-haired twenty-two-year-old standing in front of him.

"Bogey is the enemy aircraft," replied the young man, fixing thirty-nine-year-old Skaaren with an intense gaze.

"And six?" continued Skaaren.

"Six is the rear end of your aircraft," the younger man answered.

Skaaren paused for a minute. "Is it true that you guys lose consciousness for a few seconds after you take off a carrier?"

With a confident smile, the young man said, "Yeah, but we get SHOT off . . . by a catapult. That's why we lose consciousness. The G force rolls our eyes back and the blood drains out of the brain."

"Sounds . . . like . . . sex," Skaaren said thoughtfully.

The young guy rolled his eyes. He was a happy man.

"Some . . . sex. GOOD sex."

The room erupted into laughter as Skaaren and actor Tom Cruise finished reading the scene that Skaaren had scripted days earlier for an action movie about elite naval flight school candidates. The script was called *Top Guns*, but its name would later shorten to *Top Gun* to emphasize the movie's focus on Maverick, played by Cruise.

The group that was gathered on the Paramount Pictures lot that May afternoon in 1985 included producers Jerry Bruckheimer and Don

Simpson and director Tony Scott. It was Skaaren's first time in the office that Simpson and Bruckheimer shared at Paramount, a studio that Don Simpson was running just two years earlier. Skaaren had been talking to the producers for weeks by phone from his home office in Austin, Texas, but he insisted that they hold off on meeting in Los Angeles until he submitted his first rewrite of the script. A month earlier Chip Proser had written the original scene in the Officers Club between Maverick and Charlotte "Charlie" Blackwood, an astrophysicist whom Maverick propositions. But it was Skaaren's idea to recast the characters' first meeting to start with a bit between Maverick and Goose, his best friend and wingman, in which they serenade Charlie with the Righteous Brothers hit "You've Lost That Lovin' Feelin'." The group who assembled in Simpson and Bruckheimer's office loved Skaaren's gag and the provocative dialogue he had written for Maverick and for Charlie, whose lines Skaaren read during the run-through. Simpson, known for his story sense, commandeered the meeting, which had started at 3:30 in the afternoon. "Don was in charge but drank a few beers and wasn't as much," Skaaren recalled later, writing notes to himself after the nearly seven-hour script session. Later he would drive with Scott and Cruise in Scott's newly leased Jeep to meet the producers at an Eddie Murphy concert. From there, the *Top Gun* group headed to an after-party at Carlos 'n Charlie's, a popular L.A. club where Murphy held court while Bruckheimer introduced Skaaren to Hollywood insiders like 20th Century Fox president Sherry Lansing.

Refining the character of Charlotte to make her more of Maverick's equal had been one of Skaaren's priorities in rewriting the script. In one late-night phone call with Cruise, Skaaren had been impressed by the rising star's eloquence in describing his character's need for a smart, equally ambitious love interest. To that end, Skaaren had created new scenes that showcased the couple's intellectual rapport while building sexual chemistry, later explaining to Cruise and the others that he wrote the relationship to unfold like a chess game throughout the film. He even sketched a new backstory for Charlie, writing a couple of lines of dialogue that attributed her no-nonsense delivery to her Scandinavian roots. "I talk like you fly," she tells Maverick. "If I see it, I say it. Got that from my Norwegian Grandad."[1]

Warren liked to poke fun at his Norwegian family's industriousness. He would tell friends about his father, Morris, who after working all day as a welder at Quarve & Anderson in Rochester would come home, change clothes, and power up the riding mower so that he could tend to the two and a half acres of rural property on which the Skaarens lived just outside the city. Distant cousin Clyde Skaaren was only four years younger than Warren and spent time with him at family gatherings during their youth. (His grandfather was one of Morris's two brothers.) "My grandfather Lewis always took time to rest, and he always took his breaks, lunches. But the brothers were of a nature that they never actually let up because if they had more energy to expend, they would," says Clyde of the family's penchant for long hours and hard work.[2]

Like Morris Skaaren, Lewis worked with his hands, earning a living as a woodworker. Their brother Julius chose a more contemporary career as an executive for the Stran-Steel Corporation. Little is known about the Skaaren brothers' family tree other than that it took root in Vestre Slidre, a municipality tucked into one of the most picturesque valleys on the southwest coast of Norway. A local cemetery includes a number of headstones for members of the "Skaren" family, which feature the original Norwegian spelling of the surname, pronounced SCAR-en.

Approximately seventy-five kilometers to the southeast of Vestre Slidre is the broad river valley of Hallingdal, where Warren's maternal ancestors, the Rauk family, farmed their land along the Hallingdal River in the mid-1800s. According to a Rauk family history, residents of the East Country region where the Rauks lived depended on agriculture and forestry for their livelihood. One bad farming year could spell disaster for the entire region, and since the Rauks' land had few trees or wooded areas, they relied almost exclusively on farming. As with many emigrants, the family's decision to leave Norway for the United States was fueled by money.[3]

In 1859, Hans Knudtson Rauk and his wife, Sigrid, left Hallingdal with members of their extended family en route to Wisconsin. The Rauks were part of a wave of Norwegians who had begun to arrive in the United States in the late 1840s. Approximately 850,000 Norwegians immigrated to America between 1825 and 1928. And while the Rauks initially settled in Wisconsin, they soon found their way to Minnesota, where the rich, fertile land and plentiful acreage enticed more Norwegians than any other state.[4]

Once the Rauks arrived in the United States, most likely in Buffalo, New York, or in New York City, they would have journeyed west by boat or on the more expensive and relatively new railroad. Primary Norwegian settlements in the Midwest included Rock Prairie, where the Rauks lived for approximately two years; two colonies near Spring Grove, Minnesota, where Warren's mother, Pearl Rauk, was born, in 1907; and the

Claus Clausen colony near Decorah, Iowa, the birthplace of Pearl's future husband, Morris Skaaren. "Although the Rauk family weren't the first arrivals," wrote Kaye Rauk, "they were pioneers."

And while Hans Rauk and his family didn't understand the language or the customs of their new home, they knew soil and had mastered basic farming principles. What they didn't know about American crops and farming practices they picked up while laboring for more established farmers in the first few years. Hans eventually moved his family to the rolling hills of southeast Minnesota, traveling by oxcart. They grew to respect, if not appreciate, the stark beauty of the area's tall-prairie grasses, which often grew at least to eye level and were once described as rolling in the breeze "like a sea of stiff, wire waves."[5] An "exceedingly thrifty" individual much like his parents, Hans purchased a farm in 1862, and the land remained in his family for more than a century, being recognized by the state in 1976 for its "continuous agricultural operation . . . signifying more than 100 years of service and contributions to the community, state, nation, and world." Younger brother Ole Rauk also bought a large parcel of land after moving near Spring Grove and eventually sold a portion of the twenty-acre family farm to his fourth child, Edward, who would marry Pauline Pederson in 1901. Together they had eight children—four girls and four boys—of whom Pearl was the third eldest and firstborn girl.

The details of Pearl Rauk Skaaren's Spring Grove childhood are lost to time, but family and the Lutheran church clearly were institutions to be revered, as they were for most Norwegian immigrants. From about the age of twelve, Pearl assumed many of the Rauk household duties. Pauline Rauk was sick, Pearl would tell her son years later, and as the eldest girl it was her responsibility to take over her mother's role to some degree. When Warren asked if Pearl minded the extra work, she brushed off the question, saying that she did what needed to be done.[6] During a period of deep introspection after his first cancer scare in 1987, Warren reflected on his mother's family history, noting that his maternal grandfather, Edward, was a handsome, quiet man—"stern but not harsh"—who liked to joke with his grandchildren. He also observed that Edward was devoted to his wife, Pauline, who often appeared "rundown."[7] This dynamic—a man caring for a wife who was physically or emotionally fragile—would color Warren's own life and relationships with women almost until the day he died.

In the late nineteenth and early twentieth centuries, extended families like the Rauks tended to stay close not just to one another but to other

Norwegians, associating very little beyond school or work with other ethnic groups like the Swedes or the Danes.[8] Places like Spring Grove and Decorah in Iowa—two of the primary Norwegian settlements in the Midwest, as well as the respective birthplaces of Warren's parents—nurtured their Nordic ties through the publication of Norwegian-language newspapers and magazines well into the 1900s. Rochester, where Morris and Pearl would raise their only son, was home to two of these newspapers for many years.

Although Warren made fun of his familial roots over the years, he embraced a number of traits valued by his ancestors. His commitment to work, particularly once he signed on to a project like the *Top Gun* rewrite, which he turned in before his contracted deadline, clearly set him apart among script doctors in the 1980s. And the careful way he managed the huge sums of money that began rolling in after *Top Gun* resulted in an estate valued in the millions of dollars at the time of his death. Skaaren even journeyed to Norway in June 1977, spending two weeks soaking up the country's culture and history for an unproduced screenplay titled *Cleng Peerson*, about the Norwegian-American pioneer who eventually settled in Texas.

At best he maintained a bemused attitude toward some of the other aspects of his Norwegian Lutheran upbringing, writing to a friend in the mid-1980s about the strange pull that he felt concerning his birthplace and its people, which he described as "attractive and stifling all at once. The potato slowness, the commitment to some kind of conservative standard, a protectiveness, which if you want to relax into it can be seductive . . . but on the other hand . . . viewed from outside, it can be molasses in the brain."[9] As he grew older he struggled more with the religion of his youth, turning away from it completely, even angrily, in the final months of his life. While some friends attest to Skaaren's disavowal of his parents' Lutheran beliefs, distant cousin Clyde Skaaren views his reaction differently. "I don't think he grew away from it. I think he was trying to grow into it. He was a 'what if' kind of guy and a questioner of every given point of view. He really had to come to an absolution, should I say, in himself before he could outwardly attest to anything. He was a deep thinker."[10]

Warren's parents had known each other for many years before their marriage and shared a commitment to the Lutheran church in addition to their Norwegian heritage. Morris was a skilled metalworker, a quiet but sweet-natured man not unlike Pearl's father, Edward. Pearl "laughed easily and often," according to her son, but she also had a darker, even depressive side that may or may not have been part of her DNA given her mother Pauline's fragility.[11] Pearl and Morris married in 1938 and made their home in Rochester, which was named after the city in upstate New York that boasted the country's first Norwegian settlement. Founded in 1854, just a few years prior to the Rauks' arrival in the United States, Minnesota's Rochester had always appealed to immigrants and attracted entrepreneurs, according to historian Harriet W. Hodgson.[12] Its location in a valley along the Zumbro River and its heavy rainfall helped to create an especially rich topsoil that produced abundant crops, such as wheat, that eventually became big business. But perhaps the most significant development in Rochester's history occurred in the spring of 1863, when English transplant Dr. William Worrall Mayo arrived to begin his service as an examining surgeon for the Union Army during the Civil War. Mayo came to like the town, and he relocated his family there shortly before the end of the war. The Mayos—especially Dr. Will's sons, William and Charles, who followed their father into medicine—would have a significant impact on Rochester's future development. Their renowned Mayo Clinic grew out of a collaboration in the late 1800s between Saint Marys Hospital, founded by the Sisters of Saint Francis, and the Doctors Mayo, who established such medical practices as wearing rubber gloves and whose staff pioneered the use of iodine and cortisone, among other medical breakthroughs.

As Hodgson observes, the Mayos' wealth "generously supported the beautification and development" of Rochester over the years. It is no small irony, then, that Warren Skaaren was born and raised in a city famed for its cutting-edge medical institution and yet he and his family, in particular his mother, had a deep distrust of Western medicine. By the time of Warren's birth, in 1946, Rochester had grown to be a city of approximately 30,000. "Rochester looks a lot bigger than it really is," says Herb Sleeper, who attended junior high and high school with Warren. "And that's mainly because of the Mayo Clinic."[13] By the 1940s, the clinic had expanded to the extent that it became a campus located in the heart of downtown. The influx of out-of-town patients required that the rather crude airport (first built by the Mayo Association in 1928) be upgraded with paved runways and floodlights around 1940. In addition to the Mayo Clinic and Rochester's agricultural expertise, the city was becoming a manufacturing hub that included many businesses, such as Quarve & Anderson, a road construction company where Morris Skaaren worked as a heavy equipment welder. In other words, the Norwegian settlement was growing quickly, as were other towns around the state, particularly in the postwar era when Warren was born. "By 1950," historians observed of the state's immigrant population, "the Norwegian American of 1914 was no longer clearly visible in Minnesota."[14]

Thirty-eight-year-old Pearl Skaaren gave birth to her only son on March 9, 1946. The healthy baby weighed around "seven pounds something," according to his mother, who despite her general distrust of medicine delivered Warren at Saint Marys Hospital.[15] Morris, the proud father, had recently celebrated his birthday. He had turned forty-four, the age his newborn son would be at the time of his own death.

While the quiet and reserved Morris put in twelve-hour days at the construction company, the more outgoing Pearl stayed at home with Warren, keeping house and tending to her young son. She read to him daily, while he was still crawling, a habit that she began to regret because he eventually wanted to be read to constantly. Pearl felt justified, however, when Warren started school and his teachers commented that despite being an only child "he was quite well adjusted," so he must have been read to and doted on.[16]

It is unclear whether the Skaarens hoped to expand their family. One copy of Warren's birth certificate indicates that Pearl had previously given birth, but the document appears to have a few mistakes (i.e., Morris's age is incorrect) and may simply have recorded Pearl's medical history inaccurately as well.[17] Both Morris and Pearl grew up with siblings, most of whom continued the Skaaren and Rauk tradition of having several children of their own. Holidays among the extended families were raucous, which Warren loved. He and his parents spent many Christmases with Pearl's mother and father, her seven siblings, and their children. These gatherings often boasted more than twenty-five people, and Warren was often in the thick of things, commandeering the kids in the planning of a new game or activity in which everyone could participate.[18]

At some point during his childhood, Warren's parents moved into and assumed management of a log cabin–style motel located on the rural outskirts of Rochester.[19] Morris continued to work at Quarve & Anderson and tended to the motel's upkeep in his off-hours. Pearl handled the administrative and day-to-day needs of the motel. One of the motel's key attractions was an old-fashioned wood-fired sauna. Psychiatrist Bob Rynearson first met an adolescent Warren when Rynearson, then a medical resident in Rochester, and his father went to the motel to use its sauna. Two decades later, Rynearson and Skaaren would meet in Texas, where an artist friend introduced them. "You know, I've heard the name 'Rynearson' before," Warren told Bob. "In fact, I think I have a sweater with the name 'Rynearson' in the collar." Pearl Skaaren bought many of her son's clothes at a local secondhand shop, and the green cashmere pullover turned out to have first belonged to Bob Rynearson.[20]

The city itself continued to grow up around the Skaarens. In the mid-1950s, thanks in part to Rochester's manufacturing profile, IBM chose the city for its Midwest headquarters. Finnish architect Eero Saarinen designed the sprawling blue-paneled facility, and construction began amid the vast cornfields in 1956. Although the city prospered, the Skaarens themselves remained a family of fairly modest means. Their lifestyle was relatively simple. On most summer Sundays during Warren's childhood, the family would attend church services. Pearl would prepare lunch at home, then send Warren and Morris off to spend part of the afternoon at a nearby fishing hole.

Shortly after her son's death, Pearl recalled for one of Warren's friends a relatively uncomplicated childhood and teenage years that were marked by avid learning and achievements related to what she described as Warren's natural leadership ability. From an early age her son was creative, a "doodler, always drawing things" and writing. He composed songs, things that made sense only to him, and kept a journal of stories. He joined the Boy Scouts and eventually became an Eagle Scout and junior scoutmaster. "Whatever he went into, he was always playing as a leader," his mother said with pride, crediting an inherent fairness that she felt others responded to in him. Even at a young age, however, the responsibility seemed to weigh on Skaaren. After one scouting trip in which he was chosen to lead the group, he returned home and sighed, "Now I can go and be a kid just like everyone else." He also spent five years as a school safety patrol leader, and he entertained himself on the long walk to school by keeping an eye out for speeding drivers. A Rochester policeman once told Mrs. Skaaren that her son was so observant that he could remember their names and license plate information better than some of the officers on the force.[21]

Warren's version of his Rochester years was much different. College roommate and longtime friend Ron Bozman would remark that Warren's being the only child of older parents had left a "unique mark" on him. Warren believed that the differences in his parents' personalities and the dynamic that resulted took a toll on him as a child. Years later, when Warren confided to his mother that he and Helen had separated, Pearl admitted that she and her husband had had their differences, too. "I lived in a little world and always wanted a big world," she told him. "But maybe I should have quit the marriage and gone after it."[22] Warren described his mother as someone who "told me scary stories of the world to keep me close to her, to shore up her world view, to make me rescue her." He felt that even their presumably close, happy times together—when his mother was baking, for instance, and let him lick the mixing bowl—were actually colored by the darkness he sensed in her. "I came to love the sugar event in place of love," he wrote years later. In his journals Skaaren confided that his mother was a woman prone to rages and greedy for his attention. He would awaken anxious, uncertain of how she would behave toward him on a daily basis. He longed for more of a connection with his gentle but reserved father. He admired Morris's skill as a welder and spoke warmly about him into adulthood. "He's a very creative guy, and watching him was the most inspiring thing in my life," Skaaren told his hometown newspaper while promoting Top Gun in 1986. However, an adult Warren would reflect privately that "I felt deeply understood but unprotected against my mother." As he put it, "I felt he chickened out against her and abandoned me to her. . . . He tapped out at night from fatigue and ignored her. I was left being her mate."[23]

As Bob Rynearson and Skaaren became friends as adults, Skaaren occasionally talked to the psychiatrist about his parents and his struggles as an adolescent. "His father was not able to manage his mother. She was very controlling," recalls Rynearson. Skaaren confided that his mother was mentally ill. Rynearson concluded, based on her son's description of her dramatic mood swings and other symptoms, that she could have been schizophrenic. "Part of what Warren was worried about growing up was his own rage about a lot of things, particularly, I think, his mother's mental illness." As a youngster, Skaaren agonized about the repercussions if his rage took over. He spoke about having anxiety that he would be sent to "the Wing," or the Minnesota Correctional Facility at Red Wing, a state-run institution for troubled adolescents.[24]

"If your mother is disturbed, and can't really appreciate you as an individual, there's a wound, a kind of emptiness that the child has to blame on him- or herself, and that's a lot of what Warren had to process," says Rynearson, who gained experience treating schizophrenic patients while head of the psychiatry department at Scott & White Hospital in Temple, Texas. "His father wasn't close enough to him to even tell him about his own metal work. His father had to 'leave' the mother because she was crazy. He just created enormous distance. That's the only thing he could do."[25]

At the very least, Skaaren's older parents seemed to respond to their son as more of a peer than a child, occasionally signing letters to an adolescent Skaaren away at summer camp using their first names. "He never really had the parented childhood," mused sculptor Tom Giebink shortly after his friend's death. "He was an adult within that, sort of expected to measure up as an adult."[26] Giebink and others interpreted Skaaren's early creative efforts at drawing and writing (described by his mother) as something of an outlet or a response to the troubling situation he was experiencing at home.

Around extended family during holiday gatherings, however, the Skaarens appeared to have a warm relationship with one another. "Warren was as close to his parents as any child could be," insists his cousin Clyde. "He had a real reverence for his folks."[27] Aside from longtime friends like Amon Burton, Ron Bozman, and Bob Rynearson, with whom Skaaren shared confidences about his parents over the years, a number of the people who characterized Skaaren as having deep-seated rage toward his parents, his mother in particular, were those who were around him in the final months. One of these was a relatively new friend named Lee Walker. Skaaren and Walker met at one of Amon Burton's parties. Having survived a major health scare himself, Walker was encouraged by Burton to talk with Skaaren. Shortly after Skaaren's death, Walker was careful to interpret the anger Skaaren expressed toward his parents in light of his terminal diagnosis. "Warren did not hate his parents. I think hatred is too strong a word for his parents. He was angry, and I think the anger at his parents could probably be construed as anger toward death," said Walker.[28]

Over the years Skaaren spoke openly about another formative childhood experience. On a number of occasions, he shared with one friend or another the details of what he could only describe as a "visitation." When he was around eight or nine years old and living with his parents in Rochester, Skaaren recalled being awakened by a light from the hallway that was so powerful that it had penetrated around and underneath his closed bedroom door. Skaaren talked about being drawn to the light, which felt to him like a presence that was neither friendly nor malevolent but powerful enough to summon him. "Warren had done so many miraculous things," says Kaye Connors, to whom he described the visitation in spiritual terms. "I think that he really felt that that spiritual experience with the lights and everything, he felt that that had given him something in some way." To friend Diane Haug, Skaaren explained it as a kind of life force through which he had learned to harness particular abilities, such as his creative success. "I think he really felt that he had been visited and empowered by this force," said Haug not too long after

Skaaren's death. "I think he in essence felt that his life had been graced by something that he couldn't understand."[29]

If Skaaren had shared the experience with his parents, his mother likely would have explained it as a kind of religious awakening. When Skaaren and a friend were involved in a serious auto accident in high school in which their car slid underneath a semi-trailer truck, his mother attributed their survival to the "guiding hand" of the Lord. She described Warren's talents in general as "God given." She boasted about her son's facility for learning, which prompted his teachers in elementary school to suggest that he could skip a grade or two. Having read an article that hinted this could be detrimental for a young boy, Pearl decided against the move.[30]

As an adult, Skaaren would sometimes describe himself as a miserable teenager to friends like Bob Rynearson. He struggled with his weight, his anxiety in social situations, and his presumably troubled home life. And yet outwardly, Skaaren seemed to flourish in high school. Classmate Herb Sleeper barely recalls Skaaren in junior high, but by the tenth grade, when they started as sophomores at the newly built John Marshall High School, Skaaren was becoming more actively involved. Many of Skaaren's classmates were the children of doctors who worked at the Mayo Clinic or of fathers who relocated their families after being transferred to IBM's newest facility. Herb Sleeper's family had moved from upstate New York in 1957 to join his father, who had relocated a year earlier to help IBM open the development and manufacturing facility.[31]

Skaaren may have felt out of his league among the doctors' kids and the children of white-collar workers. His family managed a motel on the outskirts of town, and his father worked as a welder. In a speech he wrote in adulthood, Warren referred to his younger self as a "rural" student somewhat overwhelmed by high school and everything it entailed. Of all his courses, Skaaren was most interested in psychology. He loved his teacher and told his mother that he hoped one day to become a psychologist. Although his focus would shift once he arrived at Rice University, this early exposure would instill in Skaaren a lifelong interest in the study of the mind. His fascination with Jungian concepts, for example, would find its way into character sketches and dialogue for *Beetlejuice* (1988) and *Batman* (1989). His interest in the subject made sense to his mother: "Kids at school would always come and ask him what they should do about certain problems they had, so he probably would have made a good psychologist."[32]

Herb Sleeper remembers a similar capacity in his classmate. "He was a real easygoing guy, and he was pretty receptive to listening to people," says Sleeper. But he also observed a reticence in Skaaren, noting, "He didn't talk too much. He wasn't a very bold person." A list of Skaaren's extracurricular activities at John Marshall, however, reveals that the quiet kid from the outskirts of town was fairly involved in sports and, by his senior year, beginning to explore student government. He played baseball during his first year and suited up as a guard on the football team all three years. Dressed in his uniform for his football photo, Skaaren appears trim and clean-cut. With his slight smile, deep-set eyes, and closely cropped hair, he is at once wholesomely good-looking and somewhat mysterious. He ran track beginning in his junior year, and he lettered in wrestling as a senior. Skaaren's high grades in English and science classes gave him honors standing by the time he graduated, in the spring of 1964.

Skaaren also began to work part-time in high school, earning pocket money at the local Dairy Queen during the spring and summer months, driving a bakery truck for a local grocery store, and selling menswear at M. C. Lawlers' Squire Shop on South Broadway Street in downtown Rochester. From his sales position at the men's shop Skaaren developed an appreciation for fine fabrics like cashmere and silk and a tailor's eye for cut and fit. It was not uncommon, for instance, for an adult Skaaren to mention in his journal when someone—whether man or woman— was nicely dressed in clothes that flattered in color and style. Years later, upon Skaaren's graduation from college, the Squire Shop manager approached him about running the store, but Skaaren was not interested. He was burned out, his mother later said, on the customer service demands of retail.

Skaaren also nurtured his love of music during this time, forming a folk group with two classmates. With Skaaren on lead vocals and playing guitar, their Kingston Trio sound became fairly popular. Morris bought his son a used car, and the group was able to book paying gigs at school dances and other events around the state and in nearby Wisconsin. Throughout his high school career Skaaren also maintained his involvement in scouting, rising to the rank of Eagle Scout. Only about 6 percent of Boy Scouts succeed in reaching this highest level, which requires scouts to earn twenty-one merit badges, assume a leadership role for at least six months, and conceive of, design, and implement a community service project, among other criteria. In his junior year, Skaaren participated in a series of public speaking competitions and eventually was named the state radio speaking champion for 1963. This acknowledg-

ment of Skaaren's skills and abilities seems in keeping with the successful adult he would become, but it also suggests how focused and disci-
plined the high-schooler must have been to overcome his self-described
internal strife and to achieve such external validation.

Decades later Skaaren would describe his younger self as "dazzled
by the urban social whirl of the high school seniors."[33] To some extent
he seems to have become a part of that world: active in sports, president
of the student council, publicly recognized for his musical talents. His
nickname at this time, according to classmate Herb Sleeper, was "Horny
Warny." It was chosen more for its rhyming potential than anything else,
but Skaaren was "livid" about its suggestiveness, so classmates rarely
used it.[34] While it is highly unlikely that the quiet and self-conscious
Skaaren would develop a reputation as a ladies' man, he did have at least
two romances while in high school. He described one girlfriend, a pretty,
outgoing brunette, as a "sexual athlete" who had a drinking problem that
would lead to her death in an auto accident years later. The other was
a young woman named Suzanne, whom Skaaren spoke about to close
friends like Bob Rynearson and Tom Giebink as someone who loved him
unconditionally and gave him the attention and support that he felt was
missing from his life at that time. They were involved when Skaaren decided to move from Rochester to attend Rice University, in 1966, and she
came to represent to him the road not taken.[35]

If high school gave Skaaren opportunities to come out of his shell,
college helped him to focus his energies and talents. Skaaren graduated from Rice University after having earned an associate's degree from
Rochester Junior College (now Rochester Community and Technical
College). In an essay Skaaren published to promote Community College
Month in 1989, he describes his transition from high school to RJC in
practical terms: "College sneaked up on me like a Thanksgiving fog, the
way it did for a lot of rural students. . . . Cash was short and although my
grades were good, my foresight had yet to appear."[36]

Skaaren had enrolled at RJC in 1964, a year before the school celebrated its fiftieth anniversary. By then, approximately 1,700 students
from thirty-one states and nations were attending the school. Robert O.
Wise Jr., then associate dean of students, took an interest in the bright
yet shy eighteen-year-old. "He schemed and cajoled until I attended a
freshman camp in the forests of Wisconsin and there won the first thing
I'd ever won in my life: a leg wrestling contest," wrote Skaaren of his
mentor years later. In actuality Skaaren had won at least one award, for
public speaking, prior to his leg-wrestling victory. Whether he tweaked

his own narrative because it made a better story or because the physicality of the contest meant more to a young man who struggled with his weight and self-esteem, he regarded the achievement as "the first thing I won . . . really on my own."[37]

Robert Wise became one of Skaaren's earliest mentors and something of a father figure for the teenager. Wise shared with Skaaren his philosophy that one's life could be organized around projects that reflected one's passions and curiosities. Skaaren embraced this approach, jumping headlong into the RJC community over the next two years. He ran for and won election as president of his freshman class, claiming to a RJC audience years later that he defeated his opponents only because "all the other candidates had enemies."[38] By the end of his first year he was included in the "Who's Who of Junior Colleges." A year later he became president of the entire student body. He joined the drama club, oversaw the design and implementation of a campus coffeehouse and community center, and worked part-time for the school's television station. Skaaren also worked part-time outside of school. He continued selling men's clothes at the collegiate Squire Shop and spent a summer working alongside his father at Quarve & Anderson, where he learned about road-grading and developed his welding skills.

Skaaren entered RJC intent on becoming a premed major. In addition to courses in psychology, which he still enjoyed, he took a number of classes in chemistry and other sciences and gradually realized that premed wasn't where his passion lay. His success in student government suggested that Skaaren had a knack for politics. With the help of Associate Dean Wise and the "small, safe environment" of RJC, Skaaren had gained confidence and overcome a poor self-image. Indeed, the local Chamber of Commerce recognized Skaaren's community involvement and enormous potential by naming him Champion Citizen of Rochester during this period. Clearly it was, as Skaaren wrote more than twenty years later, "the right place at the right time for a farm kid without a plan."[39]

A nearly full-page advertisement in the *Rochester Post Bulletin* from late August 1967 features ten nattily dressed young men touted as "The Campus Board" at the Squire Shop, where Skaaren had worked since high school. His photograph appears alongside the Squire Shop's manager, identifying Skaaren as a student at Rice University, a small, distinguished private college in Houston.[40] Although it is unclear how Skaaren ended up choosing Rice as his transfer school, those close to him suggest that it was his Uncle Julius, Morris's brother, then export manager for Stran-Steel in Houston, who suggested his nephew consider the university. Years later Skaaren told producer Don Simpson that the character sketches for the various tech types he outlined for early drafts of *Top Gun* drew on memories of the bright, driven classmates he had met as a chemical engineering major at Rice. Skaaren would eventually change his major to sculpting, however, and take classes in art, philosophy, theater, and English literature. He also explored French language and literature classes and continued to study psychology, although he gradually moved away from an academic interest in the subject.[41]

For most of his time at Rice, Skaaren lived in Hanszen College, one of the university's four original dormitories, or colleges. The university was known, then as now, for cultivating colleges with distinct personalities and traditions. Nicknamed the "Gentleman's College," Hanszen boasted an all-male student population who dressed for meals in suits and neckties. By the late 1960s, when Skaaren lived in Hanszen, its residents wore at most a string around their necks if they wore anything formal at all in the dining hall. At one such meal Skaaren met fellow Hanszenite Ron Bozman, who would become his roommate and lifelong friend. The pair shared a "trust level," said Bozman, that was built on experiences at Rice both profound and absurd. Recalling a time when a milkshake Bozman was making exploded in his face midconversation with Skaaren, Bozman described the therapeutic power of their endless laughter. They could share such experiences, said Bozman, without exploiting one another's vulnerability.[42]

To say that Skaaren threw himself into college life at Rice would be something of an understatement. Buoyed by his successes at Rochester Junior College and invigorated, perhaps, by the freedom of being thousands of miles away from his parents for the first time, Skaaren made the most of his three years at Rice. As Natasha Waxman has written of this period, "There was a ravenousness to Skaaren's collegiality . . . a will to wring every drop from the experience of Youth."[43] Intramural sports, the campus literary magazine, original theatrical productions, community service projects, student government—Skaaren engaged in them all. Writing to mentor Robert Wise shortly after arriving in Texas, Skaaren boasted about being invited to dine and converse with Hanszen College's master, Dr. Ronald Sass, and a few upperclassmen. "I knew that sometime soon I would have the opportunity to say something so I had somewhat organized my thoughts and let fly with both barrels."[44] Skaaren, the perpetual Boy Scout, was prepared for the moment, and his idea to convert the dormitory's underused attic into a coffeehouse surprised and thrilled his listeners. Skaaren oversaw the renovation of the seventy-foot space, which was transformed with fourteen wooden telephone cable spools converted into tables, 150 old classroom chairs, a movable stage, and a piano. The Rice Coffee House, nicknamed the "Corner of the Dreaming Monkey," became a popular campus hangout. "We have lost an attic, but we have gained a place where it's proper to do the most human of all things, to dream," Skaaren told the campus newspaper.[45]

Having decided to switch out of chemical engineering, Skaaren declared as an art major with a focus in sculpting. His primary area of interest was metalwork, like his father. Although, curiously, he never had a show of his own work while at Rice, Skaaren did open and manage a private, off-campus art gallery called Richmond Art Forum in his junior year. His involvement in the local art scene brought him in contact with Dominique and John de Menil, a wealthy Houston couple who were amassing what would become one of the world's largest private collections of modern art. Through the de Menils, who had moved to Houston from Europe in the 1940s, Skaaren met international celebrities like Roberto Rossellini and Andy Warhol. By 1969, when Skaaren graduated, the de Menils had helped to create the university's Institute for the Arts, which introduced a multimedia focus to Rice's art offerings through courses, lectures, and exhibitions.

As much as Skaaren wanted to nurture and explore his artistic side, he seemed equally drawn to the opportunities that his leadership and organizational skills made possible. He was a senator representing first Hanszen College, and then the campus Student Association. In 1968, toward the end of his junior year, he decided to run for student body president. Skaaren's activism was in keeping with the times. Like many of his contemporaries, Skaaren was adamantly opposed to the Vietnam War. Years of dealing with a nervous stomach had earned him 1-Y draft status, which meant that he was available for service only in times of national emergency. A lifelong seeker himself, Skaaren appealed to his classmates' own search for identity in his campaign platform, describing it as a "common goal" that would guide him in his leadership. Detailing this platform for the student newspaper, Skaaren struck a confident tone that mentioned his years of prior experience in student government, but in an offhand way, suggesting that something bigger was at stake in electing a student body president. "My platform is an attitude, one it has taken me twenty-two years to form," he wrote in the *Rice Thresher* a couple of weeks after his birthday. "This attitude is not political; it is my lifestyle and it works well. The techniques of leadership are learned and they help, but are worthless without timing and patience." He promised change, but not at the expense of a collaborative approach: "The priority is people."[46]

At the age of twenty-two, Skaaren was coming into his own. It was during this period that Skaaren met Helen Griffin, a University of Houston art major who worked in the library at Rice. She had expertise in running a technical library with charts and maps, and she was conversant in German. Griffin had a willowy dancer's body and pretty, delicate features. She was almost exactly two years older than Skaaren. Their attraction was intense. "Seductive, untamed, exotic . . . she was very powerful," Skaaren wrote in a journal entry decades after their first meeting.[47] And like Warren, Helen had had a difficult family life. According to Skaaren, "hers was crippled by an autistic brother and a chronically home-bound ill father. Her mother worked two jobs. Her caregiver was no one." He described their relationship as one of "instant bonding and ancient attachment" and of feeling understood "after years of yearning." They felt united by their troubled childhoods and even by the fragility that resulted from those experiences. "Us together," wrote Skaaren. "Fiercely."[48]

In the fall of 1968, Skaaren entered his final year at Rice buoyed by his relationship with Helen and energized by his triumph in the previous spring's student government election. Skaaren took his role as president of the Rice student body very seriously. With roommate Ron Bozman as his vice president, he was excited to work with the university's president, Dr. Kenneth Pitzer. Skaaren considered Pitzer a kindred spirit. A California native and professor of chemistry who had served as director of research for the Atomic Energy Commission after World War II, Pitzer was, in Skaaren's mind, a scientist who was also a humanist. During his seven-year tenure, Pitzer had been instrumental in integrating the all-white campus and had paid special attention to improving the university's humanities and social sciences departments.[49] Before the 1968–1969 school year had even begun, however, Pitzer accepted an offer to become president of Stanford University.[50]

Although Pitzer announced that he would remain at Rice through December in order to ensure a smooth transition for his successor, Skaaren was tremendously disappointed about Pitzer's decision. One of Skaaren's first acts as president was to meet with H. Malcolm Lovett, chairman of the Rice University Board of Trustees, to urge the trustees to involve the campus community in appointing a new president at Rice. In September, Lovett announced that a search committee formed by the

Board of Trustees would be assisted by a faculty committee. "No plans have been made, however, to enable students to have a voice," reported the student newspaper.[51]

"A large group of students . . . thought there was no hope, absolutely none, for any kind of student involvement in this thing. It became very important to me at the beginning of the year to make sure that the students did get involved," Skaaren said at the time.[52] His efforts paid off, and the Presidential Selection Committee made up of six faculty members, two undergraduates, and one graduate student was formed before Pritzer departed for Stanford at the end of Fall semester. (Skaaren was not a member of the committee.) Coordinating with the Board of Trustees to discuss the committee's list of sixty potential candidates was a more challenging issue, however. A meeting was scheduled for December and canceled, then rescheduled for January and canceled again. The committee assumed the trustees were moving slowly on the decision. The committee pared its initial list to five candidates and submitted it to the board on February 10, 1969, acknowledging that the five names were "tentative suggestions." Chairman Lovett thanked the committee for its list and acknowledged that three of the board's top candidates were on the committee's list as well.[53]

Four days later the board unanimously agreed to appoint Dr. William H. Masterson, then-president of the University of Chattanooga, as the next president of Rice University. Masterson had strong ties to Rice. He received a bachelor's degree from the university and returned in 1951 to teach in the Department of History. For the next fifteen years he also held various administrative positions at the university, including master of Hanszen College, the dormitory Skaaren moved to in 1966. (Masterson had left Rice that same year to assume leadership at Chattanooga.)

The Board of Trustees announced its decision to the student-faculty Presidential Selection Committee six days later on Thursday, February 20. While some members of the university community worried that a candidate "from within" wasn't in Rice's best interests (Masterson's name hadn't even been included among the student-faculty committee's original list of sixty candidates), Trustee Herbert Allen stated Masterson would offer "a firm hand on the tiller in these troubled times."[54]

The Trustees had planned to make public their decision two days later, on Saturday, February 22, when Masterson was scheduled to arrive at Rice for a press conference. News of the announcement began to spread, however. "By noon Friday," wrote the editor of the *Rice Thresher*, "the campus was alive with rumors."[55] As president of the student body,

Skaaren felt disheartened: despite his best efforts to ensure student involvement, a new university president had been chosen without the input of the wider campus community. He attended a concert that evening, where he felt exhaustion and anxiety give way to a general feeling of doom. "It had no connection really with Masterson," he told an interviewer months later, "just a feeling that there was [going to be] an amazing catastrophe with the next couple of days at Rice."

The very next day, as rumors began to circulate around the Rice campus, both the faculty and the student association scheduled separate emergency meetings. The faculty drafted and circulated a petition protesting the procedures used to select Masterson, specifically objecting to the fact that the Presidential Selection Committee was not consulted on the final decision. Skaaren led a campus-wide meeting of approximately 450 students in the auditorium of the physics building. Despite the size of the meeting and the free-floating tension and anxiety circulating around campus, the student group was unified. According to Ron Bozman, serving at the time as student body vice president, it was Skaaren's idea that the students should organize a protest to occur during the Masterson press conference scheduled for the following day. But unlike many of the student protests erupting across the country and in other parts of the world that spring, this convergence would be peaceful. Dean of Students Paul Pfeiffer, who attended the meeting, encouraged students to act but reminded them that "disruptive tactics are not dissent." Rice sophomore Bryan Williams suggested that the men in the group dress not in jeans and army jackets but in coats and ties "to present a unified, respectable appearance." The idea was discussed—and a consensus was reached. For as much as the student body wanted to confront the administration on the issue, Skaaren, for one, believed that mediation might be a more effective strategy. "We have to realize the tremendous naiveté on the part of the board members here. They will listen, but they must have time to convince themselves of the depth of the discontent," Skaaren told the group.[56]

Skaaren had been nominated by the students at Friday's afternoon meeting as their official press representative. KOWL, the university's AM radio station, had begun sending news reports along the Associated Press wire, which were picked up by several local radio and television stations. Reporters at Houston's two newspapers began covering the story, which made the city papers' front pages. The next afternoon, more than 700 students and faculty—women in dresses and men in coats and ties—assembled at the gymnasium on the southwest part of campus. From there, the group "marched in an orderly fashion" eastward to the Masterson press conference at Cohen House, Rice's faculty club. The group's protest was civil; they listened as Masterson spoke publicly for the first time about his controversial appointment. The president-elect acknowledged the tense situation in his remarks to the assembled students, faculty, and administrators. He said that he had not inquired of the Board of Trustees whether they had consulted the Presidential Selection Committee before accepting the position. Masterson observed that he was caught in the middle, but that he "did not foresee any circumstances which would force him to resign."[57]

Masterson spent the rest of Saturday afternoon meeting with various groups, including members of the faculty, the Presidential Selection Committee, and student government. The meetings dragged on for nearly four hours. After a two-hour dinner break, discussions resumed until about midnight. Skaaren was among those who met with Masterson, who in turn promised to visit again with him and the full Presidential Selection Committee before returning to Chattanooga the following day. On Sunday morning, however, Skaaren received a phone call from Masterson, who said that he had decided not to meet with the committee. Within hours, the students who had been present at Saturday's meetings with Masterson made a public announcement. Given Masterson's actions and unwillingness "to consider the issue of due process," they had concluded that he was "unacceptable as president."[58]

Skaaren met with various department heads and Dr. William Gordon, CEO of Rice, to convey the extent of the student body's discontent. Together they came up with a plan to poll the entire university community about its opinions concerning the procedure used in selecting Masterson and the choice of Masterson himself as president. The meetings and protests of the previous two days had been focused on dissatisfaction with the methods used to select the new leader. Masterson's visit and his subsequent remarks to the campus community did little to quell this dissatisfaction, however. With the inclusion in the poll of a question regarding the Board of Trustees' choice of Masterson, it was becoming clear that the focus was shifting from due process to concerns about the president himself.

Skaaren spent the remainder of Sunday, February 23, presiding over more campus-wide meetings and preparing for the next day's vote. An itemized list from that period reveals the careful thought and planning that went into preparation for the event. Walkie-talkies, vote counters, transformers, and other tools were gathered. Student volunteers were en-

listed to answer phones, gather the necessary paperwork, and "solicit local support" from area schools and even the regional arm of the American Civil Liberties Union.[59] Balloting began at 8 A.M. the next morning.
Turnout was high among Rice's nearly 3,000 undergraduate and graduate students, its faculty, and its staff. By 6 P.M. Monday evening the votes
had been tabulated. Skaaren and CEO Gordon communicated the results to two members of the Board of Trustees, who in turn shared the
information with the remaining Trustees and, eventually, with Masterson. Although the results were never revealed publicly, one faculty member who participated in the vote counting described the message conveyed as "unmistakable" in its sentiment against Masterson.[60]

By Tuesday morning Masterson had resigned. Board of Trustee
chair H. Malcolm Lovett formally announced Masterson's resignation
and said the Trustees had accepted it "with regret." The four-day crisis,
the university's first major such event in more than a decade, had come
to an abrupt and decisive end. At 7 P.M. that evening, Skaaren read a prepared statement broadcast over the campus radio station. Observing that
the "real job" had just begun, Skaaren encouraged each member of the
Rice community to take responsibility and to consider how "to make
a university in fact now from the university that we've formed in spirit
within the last four days."[61]

The Coat and Tie Rebellion/Masterson Affair, as the controversy
came to be known, has been described as a "watershed event" in the
history of Rice University. Its impact was so significant, in fact, that a
committee of professors and staff archivists formed within two weeks
to sponsor an oral history project to document the details of the event.
Certainly the controversy was a turning point for Skaaren, whose leadership during the four days prior to Masterson's resignation was recognized and lauded across campus and beyond. W. S. Dowden, an English
professor at Rice, wrote to Skaaren the day after Masterson's resignation.
Calling the event a "grave crisis," Dowden wrote, "The University community, the city of Houston, and the nation are in your debt for this remarkable demonstration of responsibility and decorum in student action."[62] The city's newspapers continued to cover the crisis, devoting a
page to Skaaren and other student leaders in the Sunday edition following Masterson's resignation. The Student Association gave Skaaren the
Rice University Service Award that year, noting that "in a student body
where intelligence, commitment, and initiative run high, he has frequently provided the integrating and unifying influence which has made
the efforts and services of many others more effective."[63]

During those final days of February 1969, Skaaren presided over a whirlwind of phone calls and hastily called meetings, the successful Coat and Tie Rebellion, the polling of the university community, and myriad other details. In September of that year, Skaaren reflected that "it was exactly the kind of show I like to run."[64] His tone is confident, even a bit arrogant. This and other comments, made during an interview for Rice's oral history, reveal Skaaren's strong sense of duty as president of the student body coupled with a finely tuned sense of the emotional tenor and political dynamics of the situation as it developed. Decades later, Skaaren looked back at his younger self, a college student who had become "a public official" in his twenties, and observed, "Power of a simple stupid sort came easily into my hands."[65]

Less than two weeks after the controversy, Warren Edward Skaaren, twenty-two years old, married Helen Harriet Griffin, twenty-five. They obtained their marriage license on Wednesday, March 5, which was also Helen's birthday. Two days later, the Reverend John D. Worrell "solemnized" their union in a small ceremony. A photograph from the day captures the couple in a private moment as Helen, dressed in a delicate white dress, reaches up toward Skaaren's smiling face.

Skaaren, who turned twenty-three a few days later, began spring break of his senior year as a married man. He and Helen lived on Banks Street, which was just a few blocks from campus and on the edge of Houston's museum district. They shared an apartment on the top floor of a two-story rental. Looking back on that time, Skaaren would write of their early dynamic, "We were in a box even then." He blamed himself, or at least his ambition, noting, "I was on a star-making trip as a student leader."[66] That spring, in fact, Skaaren had participated in a program sponsored by Preston Smith, the governor of Texas. Once a month or so, a small group of student leaders from colleges around the state were invited to spend the weekend in Austin as guests of the governor's office. Events would include an intimate dinner hosted by the governor's staff and a two-hour coffee klatch with the governor. "The idea was to get these college students to understand a little bit more about government, plus the fact that it was good P.R. for Preston," explained Jerry Hall, Smith's press secretary.[67] Hall, who emceed the Friday night dinner for the visiting students, was impressed by Skaaren's intensity and professionalism. Governor Smith also noted Skaaren's potential, and his office eventually offered the graduating senior a job. Skaaren's official title was impressive: Program Analyst, Human Resources, Division of Operations Analysis, Office of the Governor of the State of Texas. His duties would include analyzing budgets and initiating cost-benefit studies for various departments, such as Public Welfare and Mental Health and Mental Retardation.

Despite his professed passion for sculpting and a degree in fine arts, Skaaren seemed intent on pursuing another path, one inspired by his role in the events surrounding the Masterson controversy. "I am gravely concerned with the lack of confidence expressed by many Americans in the established institutions," Skaaren noted in a résumé written around this time. He wanted to understand the institutions, he wrote, and then do what he could to restore confidence in them by making them "responsive" to those whom they served.[68]

The newlyweds packed up their Houston rental and were in Austin by July, when Skaaren began his new job in state government. Initially they leased a small house in a residential area just north of the downtown area. Helen, who had earned a degree in fine arts from the University of Houston, began looking for a library job similar to the technical positions she had held at Rice and her alma mater. Outwardly, at least, the couple expressed excitement about the new opportunities awaiting them in Austin. Even before they settled in the capital city, however, Skaaren was already sensing how the demands of real life, including marriage, work, and the stress that results, were hastening "the fading protective light of student life."[69]

TWO

Hollywood on the Colorado

Warren was like a Wizard of Oz *character that was very
mysterious and able to do these magical things, like suddenly
showing up at the airport with Steve McQueen. He was moving in
a world that none of us could even imagine. He just made things
happen.*

SCREENWRITER BILL BROYLES

Jerry Hall and Bill Parsley were enjoying a few drinks one evening in the fall of 1973 at The Quorum Club, a popular hangout
for Austin's political crowd. Located about five blocks northeast
of the Capitol, The Quorum had a big corner table that was barely visible
beneath the dim lights and the cloud of smoke that hovered near the ceil-
ing. Power players of the time frequented the watering hole, which was
once written up in *Texas Monthly*'s restaurant guide with the following
caveat: "Plain décor. Good bar. We think a little more care in the housekeeping area would be in order."[1] Hall and Parsley, who were sitting toward the back of the club, had been friends since their days at Texas Tech
University. Hall started as a political reporter before becoming Governor
Preston Smith's press secretary. Parsley was an attorney by trade, and he
became vice president of public affairs at Texas Tech in 1965. Based in
Lubbock, Parsley was in Austin checking on one of his investments, a
low-budget horror movie called *Leatherface* that had been filmed in and
around the city the previous summer. Its director, Tobe Hooper, was fe-
verishly cutting the footage with editor Larry Carroll over on the west
side of town. They had blown the film's $60,000 budget (much of it sup-

plied by Parsley) and were behind schedule, and Hooper had been dodging Parsley's phone calls.

Hall and Parsley looked up as The Quorum's front door opened. Warren Skaaren walked in, looked around briefly, and spotted the pair. He made his way over to their table. He had something to show the men, he said, having to do with Hooper's film. Skaaren insisted that the group adjourn to The Quorum's narrow restroom, which raised a few eyebrows among the bar's good 'ol boy patrons. As the trio shuffled into the cramped lavatory, Skaaren produced a sheet of white paper that read, "THE TEXAS CHAIN SAW MURDERS 1973." Alongside the words, in the top right corner of the page, was a sketch of an arm holding a chainsaw. Below the drawing were a couple of questions ("WHO DID IT? WHERE ARE THEY NOW?") and the provocative declaration, "THE MOST BIZARRE MURDER IN AMERICA."[2]

By the fall of 1973, Skaaren was the executive director of the Texas Film Commission, a state entity that he had helped to create nearly three years earlier. "Warren was not supposed to, under the commission, participate in an individual film," said Hall of Skaaren's covert involvement in the horror film as producer's representative. "But Warren had a poster and a title." While the Texas Film Commission may have seemed like an odd segue for a programs analyst with a potential future in politics, Skaaren's first exposure to the film industry actually happened at Rice when he was rooming with Ron Bozman, who had begun working on local productions. During that same time, Skaaren had also become interested in multimedia productions through his growing friendship with Dominique and John de Menil, who were supportive of Rice University's efforts to develop a media center on campus.[3]

Once Warren and Helen moved to Austin, in July 1969, Skaaren threw himself into his job as a programs analyst. Within six months, he had established a vocational rehabilitation program in Texas for heroin addicts, initiated a statewide campaign against rubella, and begun a task force to investigate the state's population explosion and tease out its connection to "agricultural development and land use control." Skaaren also was charged with finding funds to support various projects throughout the state. He was learning how to approach foundations and, by extension, learning about foundation law. "I really enjoy this particular part of my work," he wrote to John de Menil in early 1970.[4]

Skaaren had warmed to his new home as well. With a population of just under 245,000, Austin had a reputation as a laid-back city despite being the state capital. Future Texas governor Ann Richards, who had moved to Austin the same year as Skaaren, observed the effect the every-other-year schedule of the Texas Legislature and the academic calendar of the University of Texas had on the city. "To its benefit, Austin has never had a 'solidified society' because the power structure changes. It goes in, it goes out. It waxes, it wanes. It comes and it goes with the student body. It is a 'live and let live' city."[5] An avid cyclist, Skaaren especially loved the biking trails that looped around a reservoir of the Colorado River known as Town Lake. He often took to the trails for exercise and, once he began script-doctoring, as a way to think through thorny structural problems and challenging interpersonal dynamics.

Within ten months of arriving in Austin Skaaren was promoted to Urban Development Specialist within the Office of the Governor. His new position involved more responsibility and even some travel, but Skaaren was becoming tired of the bureaucracy and politics. In a letter to a friend, he confided that he sensed a "creeping boredom, which of late has been sleeping with me, waking me, and signing most of my letters." He had considered a graduate degree in business and also thought about law school, but couldn't bring himself to take the LSATs. What he really wanted to do, he said at the time, was to be creative. He had many interests, including wanting to be involved in the film industry (acting, writing, directing); writing fiction, poetry, and songs; and sculpting. He was tired of wearing a suit to work, and he longed for time to himself.[6]

By October 1970, Skaaren had received another promotion. In his new position as Community Development Coordinator in the Division of State and Local Relations, Skaaren was approached by Jerry Hall and Governor Smith to write a proposal that would "lead to a vehicle" to develop the state's film industry.[7] In early February of that year, Governor Smith had spoken at the National Association of Theatre Owners of Texas convention being held in Dallas. Smith, a former theater owner himself, promised to support the state's film industry and to do what he could as governor to cultivate its growth. According to Hall, the original impetus for the Texas Film Commission came from Bill Parsley, who had read about the success New Mexico was having with its newly formed film commission and encouraged the governor's staff to look into it. Hall knew Charlie Cullen, a former newspaperman who had become head of the New Mexico Motion Picture Industries Committee. Within its first year, New Mexico had attracted $40 million in productions to its state. *Butch Cassidy and the Sundance Kid* and *Easy Rider* shot there, as did a couple of Walt Disney films.[8] Hall and Cullen had a series of conversations about the nuts and bolts of running such a committee, then Hall called Parsley, and they arranged a meeting with the governor.

Hall may have drafted an initial prospectus, but at some point in October 1970 he approached Skaaren to do more research and write a formal proposal that could be shared with the governor. On November 17, Skaaren presented a fourteen-page report to Governor Smith and members of his staff.[9] Comprehensive in scope, Skaaren's research reviewed the state of the national and international film industries. What Skaaren discovered about American film, for instance, was that the structure of the industry had changed dramatically in the previous decade. Studio production had been greatly affected by a shifting political climate, the introduction of television, and the Paramount Decrees, a series of legal decisions that forced the top studios to divest of their theater chains, thus eliminating a significant source of revenue. Major companies, such as Paramount Pictures and Warner Bros., were trying to stay solvent and relevant amid such changes. The heavy-handed Production Code, which for decades had restricted on-screen content such as sex and violence, had been replaced in 1968 by a seemingly more flexible ratings system. Independent productions made outside of the major studios had been on the rise since the mid-1950s, and shooting on location, often outside of California, was becoming an industry norm. In addition to proposing a "citizens advisory group" to attract feature film productions to Texas, Skaaren's report emphasized the need to cultivate other aspects of the film industry, such as documentaries, industrial and commercial filmmaking, and related industries, including transportation and hotels.[10]

Skaaren's thorough research and quietly persuasive style impressed the governor. Plans were set in motion to create a film commission that would attract films to shoot in Texas and nurture the state's indigenous filmmaking. By all accounts Skaaren was eager to run the proposed film commission. Although still a state job, it would put him in contact with an industry that offered the potential, at least, for more creative work, something he wanted desperately. Carlton Carl was Smith's assistant press secretary and around the same age as Skaaren. He had grown up in Houston and interned at the *Houston Chronicle*, which had covered Skaaren's triumphant role in the Masterson Affair at Rice on an almost daily basis. He encouraged Hall to appoint Skaaren as the film commission's first executive director.

On December 9, 1970, Governor Smith signed the official appointment that commissioned Skaaren as the state's first executive director of what was then called the Texas Film Communication Commission.

("Communication" would be dropped from the title by May 1971.) Encouraged by Skaaren's report, Smith and Hall tasked him with the job of assessing the state's profile in Hollywood. Beginning in early 1971, Skaaren traveled back and forth to Los Angeles for meetings with "motion picture industry leaders." Skaaren laid the groundwork for several discussions between the governor and a number of producers who encouraged the idea of the Texas Film Commission and expressed interest in shooting in Texas. On May 24, 1971, Governor Smith held a press conference to officially announce his executive order to create the Texas Film Commission (TFC). Producer Martin Jurow joined Smith to publicize the commission's first production, a 20th Century Fox film tentatively titled *Sunday Morning*, which would begin shooting in Texas later that year. The film's star, Karl Malden, was also on hand to accept Governor Smith's official Texas welcome.[11]

The Texas Legislature had agreed to a budget of $100,000 for the TFC's first year. Skaaren's first major expenditure was a 35mm still camera so that he could document the state's variable geography. Skaaren asked colleague Joy O'Dil (now Davis) to become the commission's first secretary. "We were dealing in Urban Development with things like solid waste and mass transit, so it took me maybe 10 seconds to say okay," says O'Dil Davis.[12] Together, they set up the TFC's office in the penthouse of an apartment building a few blocks west of the Capitol on 12th and Guadalupe Streets. The address may have seemed posh, but the reality was not. Worn carpeting, cast-off furniture, and a stack of boxes decorated the otherwise bare space. The office's one nod to its former penthouse luxury was a crystal chandelier suspended from a gold velvet rope, which hung over O'Dil Davis's desk. When Skaaren wasn't in the office handling the day-to-day details with O'Dil Davis, he was crisscrossing the state and taking photographs to build a location file that could be shared with potential clients. Skaaren's trips to Los Angeles earlier in the year had paid off to some degree. *Bonnie and Clyde* screenwriter and Waxahachie native Robert Benton, along with producer David Newman, had committed to shooting Benton's directorial debut in Texas. The Western-themed period piece starred Jeff Bridges, who had spent time in Archer City a year or so earlier while working on *The Last Picture Show*. "With the production of Paramount's *Bad Company* beginning in the second week of November, the entire budget for the year 1971 will have been returned into the Texas economy," Skaaren boasted in a memo to Dan Petty, executive assistant to Governor Smith. Still, recalled O'Dil Davis, "the phone didn't ring a whole lot in those days."[13]

Speaking to a reporter at the time, an expansive Skaaren described the post of executive director of the new film commission as "ripe with fantasy."[14] That fantasy collided headlong with reality in December of that year when a drunk Sam Peckinpah landed in Texas to scout locations for *The Getaway* (1972), a $3 million action movie featuring Steve McQueen and Ali MacGraw as married bank robbers on the lam. Don Guest, the film's production manager, waited with Skaaren at Dallas's Love Field airport to greet Peckinpah and his Los Angeles entourage, which included assistant producer Gordon Dawson, assistant director Ted Howorth, and cinematographer Lucien Ballard. If Skaaren was anxious about meeting *The Wild Bunch* filmmaker, who had a reputation as a "wild, two-fisted beer guzzler" and had been known to plunge a needle full of B-12 vitamin complex into his own rear end in full view of others, he didn't let on even in private.[15] Instead, Skaaren summoned his best diplomatic skills and turned himself inside out to ensure the filmmakers had everything that they needed, including access to the Texas State Penitentiary in Huntsville. As *Getaway* producer David Foster recalled years later, "Skaaren was like a bulldog, but in a nice way. He had great style and great taste and was a real gentleman. And yet he knew, we needed that prison, goddammit, and he was going to get us that prison."[16]

What Skaaren did reveal privately was his impression of Peckinpah and the production, such as it was, at that first meeting in mid-December. "We make flix, Warren—and if you're going to be with us remember that nothing else matters," the inebriated Peckinpah told him.[17] As was his habit, Skaaren wrote about the event after it happened, analyzing the players and their behavior in an attempt to figure out their needs and, perhaps, how he could best satisfy them. In Peckinpah, he sensed a wounded soul beneath the macho posturing and the cruelty, but he also respected the director's single-mindedness in regard to the film.

David Foster, who had only recently become a producer, was also Steve McQueen's publicist. For years McQueen had been encouraging Foster to transition into producing. Agent Mike Medavoy passed him Jim Thompson's 1958 novel *The Getaway*, and Foster could easily envision McQueen as the mercurial lead character Doc McCoy. McQueen, who had been voted top male star by *Photoplay*'s readers in 1968, was in a bit of a slump by 1970 after a trio of his films received only lukewarm returns at the box office. He was eager for a hit and wanted to model the *Getaway* character along the lines of Humphrey Bogart's gritty yet vulnerable Roy Earle in *High Sierra* (1941).[18]

McQueen had worked with Sam Peckinpah on *Junior Bonner* (1972) a year or so earlier, and he developed a respect and fondness for his director during shooting. Peckinpah felt the same about McQueen. He also liked Thompson's novel and needed a job, so he agreed to helm *The Getaway*. With Peckinpah in place, Foster and the others began discussing McQueen's female costar. The romantic drama *Love Story* had opened the same day that Peckinpah touched down in Dallas, and while critics didn't love the film, audiences certainly did. Ali MacGraw, who played the lead, became a sensation. In a few short weeks *Love Story* would set box-office records. According to a number of sources, it was Foster's idea to pair McQueen and MacGraw on *The Getaway*, not only because of MacGraw's trending star power but also because of the alliterative draw the stars' names would have on theater marquees and posters.[19]

Principal photography on *The Getaway* began in Texas in early February 1972. The shoot itself was grueling, with filming on location in six different Texas cities over the course of sixty-two days. With Skaaren's help, Foster had secured permission to film at the Texas State Penitentiary in Huntsville for three days. McQueen had shown up prior to the first day of shooting on February 7 so that he could spend time at the Huntsville unit, learning its routines, taking part in required outdoor work details, and making license plates in the prison shop.[20]

The Getaway would become Skaaren's trial by fire as the new film commissioner. Before production began, McQueen, who liked to race cars in his spare time, told Skaaren that he also liked to learn his lines while driving at high speeds. "If I get speeding tickets," said McQueen, "can you take care of that?" Skaaren told the star he could not. "We are not here to help you circumvent the law of the state of Texas," he explained to McQueen. "But I will help you find a lawyer."[21] Within hours of Ali MacGraw's arrival in Texas, she and McQueen began a torrid affair that would attract intense interest from the press. McQueen was newly divorced. MacGraw was married to Paramount executive Robert Evans, who was back in Los Angeles overseeing postproduction on Francis Ford Coppola's *The Godfather* (1972). MacGraw was the top female star, and Evans wielded considerable power at Paramount. They were a Hollywood golden couple and new parents to a baby boy barely a year old. As news of the MacGraw-McQueen affair leaked from the Texas set back to Los Angeles, the ensuing media response was cataclysmic for its time, akin to the 2005 media circus that surrounded Brad Pitt and Angelina Jolie after Pitt's separation from Jennifer Aniston. Skaaren found himself in the middle of the maelstrom, having to usher McQueen, for instance, through the Dallas airport as they were being trailed by a growing number of female fans described by one bystander as having "that pinched, reckless look some women get when they're after something."[22]

The production moved on to San Antonio, shooting scenes there and briefly in nearby towns like San Marcos and New Braunfels. By late spring *The Getaway*'s cast and crew had relocated to El Paso, where Governor Smith visited the set for a photo op with the film's stars. Assistant producer Gordon Dawson, who had become friendly with Skaaren during the production, described the visit in a letter sent from the Holiday Inn in downtown El Paso. "Dear High Mucky-Muck," Dawson began as he set the chaotic scene unfolding just prior to the governor's arrival. It included a high-stakes craps game taking place at the entrance to the Holiday Inn, a visit from "the El Paso/Juarez Chief Mafioso," and "an actor about to go on a psychotic freak out." *The Getaway* was scheduled to wrap its Texas sets on May 6. Before production ended, Skaaren posed for a photograph with a laughing Peckinpah and smiling Mac-Graw. Skaaren is grinning as well, but he is also noticeably heavier than in years past. He was self-conscious about any weight gain, which he associated with his lonely childhood, and the extra pounds may have been a sign of the stress he was feeling in his demanding new job.[23]

When Skaaren wasn't putting out fires on *The Getaway* that spring, he and Joy O'Dil Davis were putting together the first issue of *Film Texas!*, the official semimonthly newsletter of the film commission. Assisting them was another Rice graduate named Diane Booker. Skaaren and Booker had known each other in college, where Booker was a year behind him. She wrote to Skaaren in the fall of 1971, asking him to consider her for an interview if a position at the newly formed commission were to become available. With the arrival of *The Getaway* and the work that the TFC was doing behind the scenes to attract more projects, Skaaren got in touch with Booker.[24]

Years later, after his first cancer diagnosis in 1987, Skaaren described the effect Booker had on his life at the time. "My work was intense and cut badly against the grain of my deeper personality," Skaaren wrote about the stress he was feeling as head of a state agency at the age of twenty-four. Booker's arrival not only eased the workload at the TFC but also rekindled what Skaaren referred to as the "protective light" of his college days that had for a time masked the difficulties he and Helen were having in their young marriage. Booker became a familiar presence in the Skaarens' lives. "Although there was a relationship growing between me and [Booker], the great majority of it was shared openly with Helen. We ate together, travelled together, were constant companions. I was cruel to Helen and cruel to the woman too."²⁵

Skaaren ultimately sought counseling, declaring, "I am in love with two women and I need help in understanding what is happening." In the process of trying to strengthen his marriage with Helen, Skaaren promised that if they both sought help through therapy, he would agree to have a child, something he claimed Helen wanted desperately. Coincidentally or not, it was around this time, in mid-1972, that the couple began taking foster babies into their home. They had moved out of their Austin rental and purchased a modest cottage in West Lake Hills, a wooded enclave west of downtown that boasted plenty of deer and other wildlife that scampered among the area's winding roads. For a man who wrote prodigiously about most events in his life, Skaaren mentions this familial experience very little, aside from acknowledging that in the early 1970s he and Helen fostered seven infants of mixed race over an eighteen-month period. It is unclear why the Skaarens never had biological children, although paperwork in Skaaren's medical files reveals that he had his sperm tested around this time, so perhaps conception was proving difficult.²⁶

By the fall of 1972 Skaaren's energies were focused on convincing the state legislature, which convened in Austin every other year, to support the TFC for the next funding cycle and to keep the commission within the governor's office and away from excess bureaucracy. The film commission bill, known as SB 30, passed by a 26–1 vote and was sent to the appropriations committee in mid-October 1972. The release of *The Getaway* in December of that year no doubt helped to polish Skaaren's reputation and that of the TFC. In the film's final credits, in large type that spanned the width of the movie screen, the producers offer their thanks to Skaaren and the commission. *The Getaway* eventually made $36 million worldwide and became the seventh largest grossing film of 1972. The top-grossing surprise of that year was a "nonlegitimate" (industry-speak for pornographic) film called *Deep Throat*. It had earned $600 million by the time *The Getaway* opened in theaters that holiday season. Little did Skaaren know that he would soon become intimately involved with *Deep Throat*'s New York–based distributor.²⁷

The year 1973 got off to a strong start for the film commission when Universal Pictures came to Texas to shoot an action movie called *The Sugarland Express* (1974) in and around Houston and San Antonio. Starring the comedienne Goldie Hawn, the film would mark the feature de-

but of a young director named Steven Spielberg. Skaaren's biggest head-
ache on the production was mediating between the state's Department
of Public Safety (DPS) and the film's producers, Richard Zanuck and
David Brown. The story, about a DPS officer (*The Getaway*'s Ben Johnson) kidnapped by two fugitives played by Hawn and William Atherton,
ended in a spectacular finale that featured two hundred police cruisers.
The DPS took issue with various aspects of the screenplay, and Skaaren
stepped in to finesse the situation.[28] Shortly after production wrapped
that spring, an advertisement appeared in *Variety*. The open letter was
signed by Zanuck, Brown, and Spielberg and read, in part: "The energy
and enthusiasm that your commission offered were only equaled by
Warren Skaaren's thorough knowledge of the film maker's problems and
his generous solutions."[29] Recalled *Getaway* producer David Foster, "A
lot of guys just do the job and try to con you into working in their state.
Warren actually knew the business of making movies." More important,
perhaps, was the fact that Skaaren seemed to understand the people who
made up the business. "Hollywood is based on some very expensive fan-
tasies. Stars are intelligent like Mother Nature. They just aren't very linear people," he once said. It was his job to help them connect the dots.[30]

Skaaren tried to do just that for a local filmmaker later that spring.
Tobe Hooper was a few years older than Skaaren and had developed
something of a reputation as a promising director with an artistic style.
A native Austinite whose father owned a local hotel, Hooper had grown
up going to the movies. He was remaking horror classics like *Dracula*
and *Frankenstein* on 8mm when he was barely out of elementary school.
As an adult, Hooper shot commercials and industrials and the occasional documentary, such as *Peter, Paul, and Mary: Song Is Love* (1970),
about the popular folk trio, that aired nationally on PBS. Members of the
Academy of Motion Picture Arts and Sciences had seen Hooper's 1965
comedic short *The Heisters* and invited him to enter it into the Oscars'
short subject category. But it was the psychedelic feature *Eggshells* (1969)
that had received the most attention. This "American freak illumination"
loosely followed two young hippie couples and the otherworldly presence that takes root in the basement of their communal home. *Eggshells*
featured an aspiring writer and University of Texas student named Kim
Henkel in one of the lead roles. Henkel and Hooper developed a friendship based on a shared love of movies and storytelling. Shortly after *Eggshells* wrapped, the new friends began writing a feature-length script for
a horror movie.

Although *Eggshells* was never picked up for distribution, it won the top prize at the Atlanta International Film Festival. Skaaren noted this and more in a three-page letter to an industry colleague that May. Weeks earlier, Hooper and Henkel had approached Skaaren with the draft of their horror film, which they were calling *Leatherface*. Hooper in particular was keen to make a second feature that would be more commercial than *Eggshells*, and he knew that as head of the film commission, Skaaren had valuable film industry connections. For his part, Skaaren wanted to become more creatively involved in the industry. In his letter written on behalf of the project, Skaaren also revealed that his initial plan was to offer whatever guidance he could to Hooper and Henkel, but "as I read the script and talked with [Hooper] regarding his concept for the picture, I began to see the tremendous exploitational potential of the film."[31]

Skaaren's letter went to great lengths to extol Hooper and the marketing possibilities of *Leatherface*. He asked questions about the profit potential of the title ("Does BLOOD in the title increase box office?"), the film's possible rating (PG versus R), and whether the letter's recipient, a colleague named Norman, would consider distributing the film. Skaaren's letter exudes an easy confidence and at times is almost boastful, as when he assures Norman that because of his involvement, Hooper won't make the marketing mistakes that he made on *Eggshells*, noting, "I, for one, won't let him." Skaaren also revealed that he had agreed to be involved in the project in exchange for "a nice portion of the producer's share," although his name would not appear in the credits or be publicly associated with the film. It is clear from Skaaren's letter that while he was excited to work behind the scenes on *Leatherface*, he was also quite aware of the potential conflict of interest posed by his involvement on a feature film in a for-profit role while he was executive director of the state's film commission.[32]

While Skaaren massaged his Hollywood connections on behalf of Hooper and Henkel's film, he also mined his Texas ties by introducing the young filmmakers to Bill Parsley. The Lubbock businessman, who over the years had invested in various projects related to oil, ranching, and the like, agreed to produce *Leatherface*. He proposed a deal in which he would either raise the film's $60,000 budget through other investors or provide the funds himself. In exchange, Parsley would own half of the film, with Hooper and Henkel retaining ownership of the other half.[33]

Within months, the filmmakers had assembled a cast and crew made up of locals and a few relatively experienced out-of-towners, like Ron Bozman, Skaaren's Rice roommate. Since their graduation four years earlier, Bozman had worked as a production manager on a number of independent features, such as *The Windsplitter* (1971), which introduced him to Hooper, acting in a supporting role. Production on Hooper's horror film began in mid-July 1973, when the temperatures in Austin typically hover around ninety-five degrees. Many of the early scenes took place in an un–air-conditioned Victorian-style home located on a bluff just off a farm-to-market road north of Austin. As with most independent productions, *Leatherface* had its share of problems, such as a week's worth of footage ruined because of a faulty camera lens. Parsley, the primary investor on the project, was a familiar visitor to the set. His presence put pressure on Hooper and Henkel, and the others felt the tension. "When we were dealing with Bill Parsley," recalled Henkel three decades later, "I definitely felt like it was his intention to keep us under his thumb. I don't respond too well to thumbs."[34]

Skaaren, by contrast, kept his distance from the set and from any discussion of the production itself. "I never got to talk too much about the film commission's connection with [the film] because we weren't supposed to connect them," said Governor Smith's press secretary, Jerry Hall, of the film, which Skaaren would help to rename *The Texas Chain Saw Massacre* before the year was out. Still, Skaaren continued to work diligently behind the scenes, making phone calls and writing letters in an effort to secure distribution for the horror movie.[35]

The production limped to a close by the end of September. On October 9, Henkel sent a letter to Skaaren at the film commission's downtown office. "I wanted to thank you for your most able and efficient assistance in the production of this film," wrote Henkel in his capacity as president of Vortex, *Leatherface*'s production company. "It is reassuring to know that such aid is available from the Governor's Office. Without your cooperation, many aspects of our production would have been more difficult, if not impossible."[36] Henkel may have been referring to Skaaren's introduction to Bill Parsley and thus the funding for the film. The extent of Skaaren's involvement on *Leatherface*, such as the feelers he was putting out in Hollywood regarding distribution, was still a closely guarded secret. It was around this same time, in fact, that Skaaren pulled Parsley and Jerry Hall into the men's restroom at The Quorum Club to show them his initial marketing concept and a potential new title for the film, which he eventually suggested renaming *The Texas Chain Saw Massacre*.

Hooper and editor Larry Carroll (and, later, Sallye Richardson) had begun cutting the footage that same month. Hooper had budgeted four weeks for the process, which would ultimately take more than a few months. As *Chain Saw*'s editing dragged into 1974, Hooper had to find a new location for the footage and his Steenbeck editing table. He had been cutting after hours at Shootout Films, a downtown freelance production company co-owned by local filmmaker and producer Richard Kooris, editor Carroll, and a few other members of *Chain Saw*'s crew. The project had overstayed its welcome, so Skaaren arranged a move into the second floor of Encino Press, a local publishing company owned by aspiring screenwriter Bill Wittliff. Skaaren and Wittliff had become friends over the years, and at the end of 1973 they had set up The Skaaren Corporation to pursue "the production of high quality motion pictures and television programming," according to the company's corporate filing. Together Wittliff and Skaaren planned to solicit screenplays, develop and write their own scripts, and package projects for "sale, joint venture, or production and distribution."[37] It was one of a few signs that Skaaren had grown tired of his position at the film commission and longed for a more hands-on role in media production. His growing involvement in *Chain Saw* was another.

Once editing was finished, in early 1974, Hooper and Henkel discovered that the negative of the film was out of sync due to some cutting errors. It was, said Henkel, an "expensive error" that stood in the way of their finishing the film.[38] They approached Parsley for more money in exchange for an additional 19 percent of the film, but Parsley declined.[39] Once again, Skaaren stepped into the breach. He assembled a group of Austinites that included Wittliff and his University of Texas fraternity brother, attorney Joe Longley; banker Richard Logan; state legislator Tommy Townsend; businessman Richard Haney; and Tom Viola, Skaaren's brother-in-law. Gathering downtown one night in a boardroom at City National Bank, where Logan was vice president, the potential investors watched a "sizzle" reel of *Chain Saw*'s most compelling moments. In exchange for 19 percent of Vortex's net profits (Vortex owned half the picture, with Parsley's company MAB owning the other half), the investors contributed a total of $23,532 to the budget. They finalized the deal in late February, jokingly naming their investment group P.I.T.S., which stood for Pie in the Sky.[40]

Days later, in the March 1974 issue of *Film Texas!*, Skaaren officially announced his resignation as executive director. Skaaren framed his success as head of the commission as success for Texas's burgeoning media industry: "And for top-flight pros from Texas, access is success, and one Texan's success is access for ten more." He also noted the challenges facing the state's industry: "But being in the spotlight isn't easy. It means

that Texas must perform and improve. As always, that is the challenge."
He could have been writing about himself, hinting at the demands of
such a high-profile job. Privately, Skaaren had been documenting his desire to "write to live" and his growing disenchantment with what was essentially a bureaucratic position. "The office I go to everyday is a card-
board place, the air even tastes like paper," he wrote around this time.[41]

Skaaren's resignation took effect on March 1. A few weeks later, Kim
Henkel, Bill Parsley, and other key shareholders of *The Texas Chain Saw
Massacre* met to discuss appointing Skaaren as "sole agent" to negotiate the film's distribution. Henkel had floated the possibility to Skaaren
in February, and it was essentially making official what he already had
been doing on behalf of the film for nearly a year. The terms of Skaaren's
contract, however, would take another eight months to finalize and
would eventually include ownership of 10.5 percent of the film through
The Skaaren Corporation, his newly formed consulting company. He
would also receive $5,000 in deferred compensation and reimburse-
ment for all expenses related to his position as producer's representative.
Without putting any money into the production, Skaaren's stake in the
film was roughly equal to that of Hooper and Henkel, who were banking on his Hollywood connections. As Skaaren told an interviewer in
1982, "Tobe and Kim needed a distribution deal and they wanted me to
go out and utilize some of the contacts I'd made as director of the film
commission."[42]

Skaaren worked the phones on behalf of *Chain Saw* from his new office on the second floor of Wittliff's Encino Press. The publishing outfit
operated out of a Victorian-style house located in Clarksville, a neighborhood just west of downtown Austin. One of the first people Skaaren
called was *Getaway* producer David Foster. Skaaren told him about
Hooper and Henkel and explained his involvement with the film. "It's
kind of a scary, frightening movie. They don't know how to get a release
on it," said Skaaren. "Can you help them?" Foster told Skaaren that he'd
have to see the movie himself, so Skaaren and Parsley flew out to Los Angeles to screen an early cut of the film. Although Foster's initial reaction
was that *Chain Saw* was a bit unpolished, he also thought it had potential. "A lot of it was innuendo, which you don't really see. I could see how
it could connect with an audience," he recalled years later.[43]

"If I get involved, it's not going to be a charity case," Foster told
Skaaren, who helped to negotiate Foster's deal of 1.5 percent of Vortex's
share of the profits and $500 in deferred compensation.[44] Throughout
the spring and early summer months of 1974, Skaaren dedicated himself

to *Chain Saw*'s distribution. With Foster's help, screenings were arranged for representatives of nearly every top studio, including Paramount and 20th Century Fox. "The general reception for the film in Los Angeles was excellent and if distributors' reactions are any indication of audience enthusiasm, 'The Texas Chain Saw Massacre' may be commercially a very successful film," wrote Skaaren in an update to the film's investors. Foster remembers the distributors' reactions differently: "Frankly, a lot of them passed."[45]

One company that did show interest was Bryanston Distribution, Inc. Based in New York, Bryanston had branch offices in several other cities, including Los Angeles and Dallas. As producer's representative for *Chain Saw*, Skaaren received a proposal from Ted Zephro, Bryanston's vice president and general manager. The previous October, Zephro had left a prominent position at Paramount as the assistant to studio president Frank Yablans to oversee operations at Bryanston, which was quickly attracting industry attention as an independent distributor on the rise. Zephro had started in sales at Paramount and had worked on the release plans for some of the top films of the 1970s, including *Love Story* and *The Godfather*. This impressed Skaaren, as did the favorable press Bryanston had been receiving since its successful distribution earlier that year of *Return of the Dragon*, an action film directed by and featuring martial arts star Bruce Lee, and *Andy Warhol's Frankenstein*, an X-rated spoof of the horror classic featuring members of Warhol's famous Factory. As with *Chain Saw*, both of Bryanston's latest releases were made for relatively low budgets.[46] And with the film industry experiencing a recession and the studios cutting back on the number of films released each year, independent distributors like Bryanston were able to gain a foothold in Hollywood.

What may not have been as readily apparent in the summer of 1974 was the real story behind Bryanston's breakout success in Hollywood. Bryanston Distribution filed incorporation papers as early as July 1971, but it wasn't until December 1972, with the release of *Deep Throat* and its tremendous box-office returns, that Bryanston was able to establish a West Coast office in Los Angeles. *Deep Throat*, which was made for approximately $22,000, was produced by Lou Perry, a pseudonym for thirty-two-year-old Louis Peraino. Lou, who also went by the childhood nickname "Butchie," was the son of Anthony "Big Tony" Peraino and the nephew of Joseph C. "The Whale" Peraino, both of whom were considered by New York law enforcement to be "made" men ("officially initiated") linked to the powerful Joseph Colombo crime family. Colombo, who had been shot in the head in late 1971 and remained in a coma until his death seven years later, led one of the five families that ran the New York–based Mafia. The late 1960s and early 1970s marked a time of diversification for the Mob, with pornography following gambling and drugs as one of the top three most lucrative new business ventures. At twenty-six, Butchie Peraino had broken into the market as the owner of a Brooklyn-based film processing plant that trafficked in pornography. This led to his involvement with *Deep Throat*, whose profits made it possible to expand Bryanston. By acquiring titles like *Return of the Dragon*, which were considered exploitation but not pornography, Peraino was able to transition into the legitimate film market.[47]

As Skaaren told a reporter in the early 1980s, the company was eager to distribute *Chain Saw*. "Right off the bat these guys were talking $100,000 up front," he recalled of Zephro's initial proposal. Back in New York, Louis Peraino screened a mere ten minutes of the film, the story goes, and immediately increased the offer to $200,000.[48] Although early agreements suggest that *Chain Saw*'s investors were hoping to secure a deal for no less than $250,000 cash and a significant portion of the film's rentals, the final agreement negotiated by Skaaren with Bryanston was for $225,000 and 35 percent of the film's gross rentals. The deal was struck in July 1974, and Skaaren and production manager Ron Bozman planned to meet with Bryanston executives in New York the following month to finalize the contract and to receive the first payment.[49]

It is unclear how much Skaaren knew at this point about Bryanston's connection to *Deep Throat* and Louis Peraino's family background. Given his scrupulous nature and tendency toward overpreparation, however, it seems likely that Skaaren had at least some inkling of Bryanston's shady history. Tucked away amid the drafts of contracts and other documents in Skaaren's *Chain Saw* files is a plain white legal-sized envelope with the words "NEW YORK" typed across the front. Inside is an undated document, a typewritten list titled "THE GRAPEVINE ON JOE AND LOU PERAINO." It contains eleven points of information, noting that both Lou and his brother Joe had been convicted in New York and had enough of a past to warrant FBI surveillance. The list also details the Perainos' connection to the Colombo family and other key Mafia figures, such as Robert Lino. Finally, the document notes that the Perainos' "trade has been stolen goods and Pornography." Indeed, one New York paper writing about Bryanston during this period nicknamed Lou the "Sultan of Smut."[50]

Trouble with Bryanston began almost immediately. By mid-August, Skaaren had yet to receive any part of *Chain Saw*'s agreed-upon cash advance from the distributor. He engaged New York attorney Arthur Klein on *Chain Saw*'s behalf. Klein was a founder of Frankfurt, Garbus, Klein & Selz, a well-respected firm specializing in entertainment law. Klein corresponded with Bryanston's attorney, Philip Vitello, and may have encouraged Skaaren to come to New York to deal with the distributor in person.[51] Skaaren and Ron Bozman made the trip together. On August 28, they arrived at Bryanston's Midtown office in the Film Center Building at 630 Ninth Avenue. Its somewhat storied history no doubt appealed to Butchie Peraino's desire for business legitimacy: Warner Bros. once stored cans of nitrate film inside the Film Center's specially constructed vaults.

Arthur Klein and his partner Tom Selz met Skaaren and Bozman for the meeting. The group walked through the building's main entrance, underneath an ornate gold-toned metal grill set above triple glass doors. Everything about the building conveyed an air of sophistication. They took the elevator to Bryanston's offices on one of the upper floors and were greeted by the company's administrative assistant. They were ushered into a meeting room, where Lou and his brother Joe, who was vice president of the company, were surrounded by their "gorillas," as Bozman and Skaaren later described them. These were the Peraino brothers' "lieutenants," large men in dark suits who stood silent but alert, stationed around the room. Butchie and Joe were equally intimidating. Each brother weighed upward of 250 pounds. Lou's voice, with its thick Brooklyn accent, was ragged from his five-pack-a-day smoking habit. Even the tattoo on his left forearm was menacing: the name "ROSE" with a dagger piercing the letters.[52]

Negotiations with Bryanston lasted all day. Skaaren and Bozman were exhausted, but also triumphant. They were returning to Austin with a check for $136,000, representing Bryanston's partial payment for the purchase of the film's distribution rights. According to the agreement, *The Texas Chain Saw Massacre* would be released in Texas in early October, with a subsequent rollout in New York and no fewer than nine of the top twenty-five major markets around the country. Back in Austin, the former roommates shared details from their New York meeting, joking that it was like a scene out of *The Godfather*, released a couple of years earlier. At one point, they said, discussion ground to a halt when a Peraino associate interrupted the meeting to deliver a large diamond ring purchased by Joe as a gift for his wife. The "rock" was passed around the table for everyone to admire.[53]

A week or so after Bozman and Skaaren returned from New York,

Tobe Hooper wrote a letter to *Chain Saw*'s cast, crew, and investors informing them of the deal and explaining how the first payment would be distributed. Hooper described Bryanston as a "young aggressive organization" that was having great success with *Return of the Dragon* and *Andy Warhol's Frankenstein*. He thanked everyone involved with the film for their support, writing, "I believe we have made a highly commercial motion picture. Of course only time and the audience will determine its real strength." A memorandum included with the letter broke down the distribution of Bryanston's first payment. Glass & Caylor, an Austin-based accounting firm, had been hired to oversee *Chain Saw*'s finances, including distribution of the film's profits. More than half of the $136,000 from Bryanston went to MAB, the investment company formed by Bill Parsley to finance the film. Bill Wittliff and his fellow P.I.T.S. investors were paid back as well. After settling the film's postproduction debts and paying Glass & Caylor's fees, only $3,005.20 remained to cover the cast and crew's deferred salaries and pay those who had invested in Vortex (which included *Getaway* producer David Foster). At this point, at least, Skaaren had yet to receive any substantial monies for his efforts on behalf of the film. Perhaps this is why, around the same time, Skaaren renegotiated his contract with Vortex to include a "policeman" service to monitor the film's distribution. This would entitle him to 3 percent of the film's gross earnings, which would be subtracted "off the top" of any profits returned. In other words, he would be among the first in line, ahead of even Hooper and Henkel, to be paid as distributions became available. This clause also designated Skaaren as the point person to deal with Bryanston should any problems arise during distribution.[54]

Trouble was certainly on the horizon. In August, the same month that Skaaren and Bozman had met with the Perainos in New York, a federal grand jury in Memphis indicted Louis Peraino, his father (Anthony), and his uncle (Joseph S.) for "transporting obscene materials across state lines."[55] The charges stemmed from the Perainos' involvement with *Deep Throat* and were directly influenced by recent changes to U.S. obscenity laws. Prior to 1973, it was considered a federal crime to transport pornographic materials across state lines. In June 1973, the U.S. Supreme Court handed down a landmark decision in *Miller v. California* that gave individual states the ability to decide and regulate whether or not a work "appeals to the prurient interest in sex."[56] While the criminal trial would be delayed until March 1976, the indictment would have a more immediate effect on the Perainos' various business holdings, including the "legitimate" Bryanston Distribution company.

For the time being, however, Bryanston seemed to be riding high. In October 1974, the same month that *Chain Saw* was released, Bryanston received a bonanza of press coverage in various trade papers and magazines. "BRYANSTON BOFFO" blared the *Variety* headline, detailing the company's seemingly overnight success. According to one article, Bryanston had made $20 million in rentals since opening its West Coast office a year earlier. Bryanston employed about ninety people in nine branch offices throughout the country and at its New York headquarters in the Film Center Building. The *Hollywood Reporter* and *Box Office* also touted the company's "unique sell and an unique distribution pattern" for its low-budget titles, including the newly acquired *Chain Saw*. The press would only help the Texas-made film, which opened in Austin the same month. Weeks earlier, Bryanston had taken out a full-page advertisement in *Variety* announcing *Chain Saw*'s upcoming release. The ad featured Leatherface (played by Gunnar Hansen) brandishing a chainsaw and Pam (Teri McMinn) hanging from a meat hook. It also included the original text from the mockup poster Skaaren had drawn a year earlier, which read: "WHO WILL SURVIVE AND WHAT WILL BE LEFT OF THEM?"[57]

None of the articles about Bryanston that October mentioned *Deep Throat* or the Peraino family's connections to the Colombo family, nor did they comment on the fact that the family's involvement in pornography had been the subject of FBI surveillance since 1969. Rumors existed, of course. Fred Beiersdorf ran a family-owned distribution company called Dal-Art, which served as Bryanston's Dallas office and handled the company's distribution throughout the Southwest. Louis Peraino gave Beiersdorf a Rolex watch, and in the year after Beiersdorf's daughter was born, she received lovely baby outfits every month from Neiman Marcus courtesy of the Perainos. "I was like family to them, but I have never been around a bunch of people who could get you killed and have you killed," says Beiersdorf.[58] But as *The Godfather* producer Al Ruddy told a reporter, "There are rumors about a lot of people in this business, one or two who are very powerful and who reputedly have [organized crime] contacts all over the place, and I'm sure they do. And it doesn't impair their ability to function in this business."[59]

Ruddy's assessment was accurate, judging from *Chain Saw*'s success that fall. By the end of 1974, the film was ranked third among those with the highest national grosses. Nine months earlier, before Skaaren left his post at the film commission, he had been earning an annual salary of approximately $20,000. In a financial statement from December 1974,

Skaaren listed his ownership in *Chain Saw* as 10.5 percent, which had helped to increase his personal worth to around $50,000.[60]

Skaaren took his policeman's role in *Chain Saw* seriously. Lou Peraino had yet to pay the Texans the remaining balance on their contract. Skaaren spent the first two months of 1975 peppering Bryanston's New York office with phone calls. As of January 1, Bryanston was also expected to begin sending profit reports and disbursements to the film's investors, but Skaaren feared these payments would be delayed as well. He wrote to New York attorney Arthur Klein, asking him to check the distributor's deals for the film's upcoming releases in Japan and Italy. "I look forward with apprehension to their first report and profit division," wrote Skaaren of Bryanston. "We might be thinking of an accountant type to assist us should the report be grossly mutated." In late April, Vortex president Kim Henkel sent a letter to the cast, crew, and investors noting that Bryanston's second quarter report was "delayed" and that Skaaren would be traveling to New York to discuss the matter with the Perainos.[61]

Skaaren arrived in Manhattan on May 13. He had told the Perainos he was coming to receive the delayed quarterly reports on *Chain Saw* and to discuss Bryanston's plans for the film's spring and summer release. He was relieved when Lou Peraino handed him the requested reports, but he was shocked to discover later, while examining the report and an accompanying list of expenses related to the distribution, that the film actually lost money. With the help of attorneys Arthur Klein and Tom Selz, as well as Main LaFrentz & Co., a Park Avenue certified public accountant, Skaaren determined "that the expense list was inaccurate in many cases, and in fact, a profit should have been declared."[62]

When Skaaren confronted Lou Peraino about the discrepancies in the report, Peraino offered to pay $25,000 in cash with three additional payments of the same amount over the following four months. Skaaren negotiated for and received $56,000 up front with the remainder payable (with interest) in three installments before the end of September. He left New York feeling cautiously optimistic.[63]

That summer, when Skaaren wasn't monitoring Bryanston's handling of *Chain Saw*'s overseas distribution or keeping tabs on the film's profit-and-loss statements, he was beginning to explore the possibility of a *Chain Saw* sequel. He began working with a writer in Dallas, for instance, to draft a screenplay based on Skaaren's own rough outline. As with the first film, he seemed conflicted about his involvement. He told Arthur Klein that the investors were eager for a "quickie" follow-up film to capitalize on the original's success. "I guess I will cooperate . . . so long as I don't have to have my name near it or visit the gory set," he wrote. In other correspondence, however, Skaaren clearly is positioning himself to have a prominent role in the sequel, most likely as a producer. In one undated phone conversation with another attorney, possibly a few years later, Skaaren outlines the "parameters" of his involvement in a sequel, saying, "If I produce, it's $125,000. If it's associate produce, it's $75,000."[64]

By the end of August 1975, Bryanston was behind on paying the three $25,000 notes Skaaren had negotiated with Peraino during his visit in May. Once again Klein was brought in to put legal pressure on the company. Sometime that fall Skaaren made another trip to New York, possibly to meet with Klein and the Manhattan-based CPA who was auditing Bryanston's books with regard to *Chain Saw*'s release. The film continued to make money. Bryanston had begun distributing the film overseas in mid-1975, and in May, at about the same time that Skaaren was in New York, *Chain Saw* had played in the independent-oriented Directors' Fortnight section of the Cannes Film Festival.

The film received a dubious mention in the *New York Times* in October, when reporter Nicholas Gage's first article in a two-part series about organized crime's involvement in pornography ran on the newspaper's front page. Gage identified Lou Peraino's father, Anthony, and his uncle Joseph as the "most successful of all the Mafia figures involved in the production and distribution of hard-core films." While the article was careful to identify Bryanston as a "legitimate" distributor of motion pictures, it also noted that Lou Peraino had been named in the federal indictment returned in the *Deep Throat* obscenity case, which was still awaiting trial in Memphis. If Skaaren or any other individual connected with *Chain Saw* had doubted the Perainos' Mob connections, the *New York Times* article made them quite clear.[65]

Skaaren's efforts to collect past-due monies from Bryanston were proving futile. The latest profit reports from the distributor were again showing a deficit. Bill Parsley was ready to sue the company, but Klein and Selz advised against it. So Parsley convinced Skaaren and others involved with the film to hire Austin attorney Robert Kuhn, who was one of the film's original investors, to represent them. Skaaren, Parsley, Kuhn, and Kim Henkel flew to New York in early December to meet with Lou Peraino and his brother Joe in person. While Henkel remained behind at the hotel bar, the others headed off to face the Perainos.

Skaaren described the scene years later. On this particular visit, he was struck by a large painting that hung behind Lou's desk. It featured, he said, "Jesus in substantial physical torment." Aside from the distinctive artwork, Skaaren and Parsley by then were familiar with the scene at Bryanston's headquarters. Large men positioned themselves around the room while Lou Peraino held court from behind his desk. But it was Kuhn's first meeting with Peraino, and he took in the vaguely threatening atmosphere. He pressed Peraino to allow them to see the books on *Chain Saw*. Peraino made excuses (the bookkeeper was not in the office that day, etc.), until finally Kuhn threatened to sue. "Don't sue me," said Peraino, enunciating each word.[66]

The Texans left New York without any resolution to the matter, but they were determined to sue for breach of contract, which they eventually did five months later in May 1976. By this time, however, Bryanston had all but ceased to exist. The company's demise occurred as quickly as its rise to the top. Despite the mysterious disappearance of marketing executive Ted Zephro sometime in 1975, Bryanston earned one last bit of positive press in January 1976 when *Variety* noted the company's opening of a London-based production subsidiary called Swadevale Inc. Two months later, the *Deep Throat* obscenity trial finally got under way. "As you may or may not have heard they are under federal indictment in Memphis for *Deep Throat* and fraud, I think," Skaaren wrote of Bryanston and the Perainos to Arthur Klein in March. He mentioned that since the beginning of January, his ongoing efforts to reach Lou had been unsuccessful and that he had heard their New York offices were nearly vacant. "I fear the courts will have the mess before its [*sic*] over," wrote Skaaren of the *Chain Saw* situation.[67]

On April 30, Louis Peraino, his father, and his uncle were convicted in federal court. By the end of May, Bryanston's West Coast office had been shuttered. Exchanging letters with Klein's associate Tom Selz, Skaaren noted that Bob Kuhn had initiated *Chain Saw*'s suit against Bryanston for breach of contract. The Texans may have sued Bryanston, but the Perainos' legal situation made it nearly impossible to collect any monies due. Despite negotiating a $400,000 settlement to end the suit, Kuhn and the others involved with *Chain Saw* would not receive any further payments from Bryanston. Invoices from Klein and Selz for their legal expertise went past due, and Skaaren and Parsley had to scramble to cover the costs. Ironically, in the final week of the year, *Chain Saw* was named to the twenty-third spot in *Variety*'s year-end list of the fifty top-grossing films of 1976. A few weeks later, *Getaway* producer and *Chain Saw* investor David Foster sent a copy of the *Variety* list to Skaaren. "It isn't often that one gets a chance to make money on his participation and here we all sit with a big winner and nothing to show for it," Foster fumed.[68]

Skaaren continued to monitor the film's distribution, which became even more complicated when it was discovered that Bryanston had sub-distributed the film to another company for overseas release without the Texans' knowledge. Although he would eventually profit handsomely from his stake in the low-budget horror film, Skaaren by 1976 was eager to work on other projects as an antidote to *Chain Saw*'s tangled legal situation. He and Jerry Hall, who had left the governor's office to start his own consulting firm, would meet for monthly lunches, sharing sandwiches and driving around Austin while catching up on each other's lives. Skaaren talked to Hall about potential projects. The untimely death in 1971 of University of Texas football player Freddie Steinmark, who had lost a leg to bone cancer, became a topic of interest for Skaaren; in 1973, he had purchased the film rights to Steinmark's autobiography. He also continued to pursue the possibility of producing a *Chain Saw* sequel.[69]

"OK Skaaren," he wrote in a letter to Arthur Klein during this period. "You work inordinately hard for the boys who made the *Chain Saw Massacre*, and then you go home at night and dream about doing good movies."[70]

THREE

Breaking Away

SOMETIME IN LIFE, EVERYONE GETS THE URGE TO . . . BREAKAWAY

TAGLINE FOR THE ALASKA ADVENTURE FILM WRITTEN AND
DIRECTED BY WARREN SKAAREN

S hortly after Warren Skaaren left the film commission, in the
spring of 1974, he and business partner Bill Wittliff negotiated
a deal that gave Skaaren an exclusive option to produce Wittliff's original screenplay *The Raggedy Man*. Wittliff loosely based the
story about a World War II–era single mother trying to raise her two
young sons on his own mother, Nita, and on his experiences growing up
in the Texas Hill Country. The deal, good for one year, also authorized
Skaaren to acquire all rights for the project. In the original agreement,
Wittliff had included a clause that allowed him to terminate the contract
after five months' time at his "sole discretion." In mid-November, while
the two men were still sharing office space at Wittliff's Encino Press address, Wittliff decided to exercise this option and sent Skaaren a letter
that began, "As it now appears that serious negotiations to sell 'The Raggedy Man' have ended, I am hereby terminating our Option Agreement."

Skaaren was livid and drafted his own missive in reply, a four-pager
that chronicled his efforts to sell the project. According to Skaaren,
most of the major studios, such as MGM, Warner Bros., and 20th Century Fox, had passed on Wittliff's script, but Paramount's Frank Yablans,
president of production, showed interest. Director John Hancock (*Bang
the Drum Slowly*) liked the script, and Skaaren's old friend David Foster, together with Foster's producing partner Lawrence Turman, were interested in sharing a production credit with Skaaren. The project stalled,

wrote Skaaren, when ABC Television's Barry Diller replaced Charles Bludhorn as chairman of Paramount that year. Rumors were rampant that Yablans would be fired. Skaaren was hearing from all quarters that they should sit tight and "wait until the organization stabilizes." Wittliff, according to Skaaren, was impatient and doubtful that this course of action would benefit the project. Skaaren disagreed.[1]

In the end, Skaaren never sent his missive to Wittliff. Across the top he scrawled "drafted but unsent/no use in further involvement with greed" and then filed it away. In December, Wittliff resigned from his position as director in The Skaaren Corporation, and Skaaren eventually bought out Wittliff's shares in the company for $1,000. "I learned a painful lesson. Unfortunately, it involved the loss of an alleged friend," Skaaren wrote of the incident to attorney Arthur Klein, with whom he had consulted about the Paramount situation. (Klein had advised Skaaren and Wittliff to wait out the turmoil.) As Skaaren saw it, he had supported Wittliff's work and tried to educate him about the business. In exchange, Skaaren fumed to Klein, Wittliff "took devastating advantage of the only weak spot I had in my option."[2] After the *Raggedy Man* incident, the typically generous Skaaren surprised some friends and associates by asking them not to maintain a relationship with Wittliff. "He told me that if he ever learned that I was friends with Bill Wittliff that he would never speak to me again," says musician Bobby Bridger. Given the tight-knit nature of Austin's creative community in the mid-1970s, it was inevitable that Bridger's and Wittliff's paths would cross. When they did meet, and then struck up a casual friendship, Bridger always felt as if he were cheating on Skaaren. "I was surprised that Warren was that petty," recalls Bridger. "He didn't wear it well."[3]

Skaaren and Wittliff, according to the *Raggedy Man* writer, never repaired the rift. But Skaaren did keep tabs on Wittliff's career, filing away newspaper and trade articles that chronicled the success he would have as a screenwriter, beginning in the late 1970s with *The Black Stallion*. "Even then, Warren was thinking on a much grander scale in terms of the size of movies. I was interested in doing the smaller, more intimate character-driven things. Warren was already seeing big, kind of boffo pictures," Wittliff said more than a decade after Skaaren's death.[4]

First with *The Texas Chain Saw Massacre* and then with later projects like the short-lived *Raggedy Man*, Skaaren seemed destined to become a producer. He understood the importance of packaging projects and had something of a commercial sense when it came to evaluating scripts and treatments. (Wittliff's *Raggedy Man*, for instance, would eventually get made. Universal Pictures released the film, starring Sissy Spacek, in 1981.) But Skaaren also wanted to write. One of his earliest professional efforts was a screenplay called *Spooks*, which was based on a six-and-a-half-page treatment he had received from a friend in Houston while he was still executive director of the film commission. Together with Grant Fehr, Skaaren wrote a screenplay based on the original treatment, which focused on two "poltergeisterists" who are good at their jobs but "real sleezo dudes."[5] By August 1974, around the time that he and Ron Bozman were negotiating *Chain Saw*'s original deal with Bryanston, Skaaren and Fehr had completed a first draft.

It was unlike Skaaren to share his writing or any other kind of creative work with others before he felt that it was ready to be seen. But with *Spooks*, Skaaren seemed to understand that he needed to learn the basics of telling stories for the screen if he was to succeed in the business. Throughout the fall of 1974, he solicited advice from a range of readers, most of whom were friends with ties to the film and television industry. *Getaway* assistant producer Gordon Dawson suggested he eliminate the script's overly descriptive sections for flow and movement. Skaaren had struck up a friendship with L.A.-based writer-director Ted Flicker, whose controversial film *The President's Analyst* (1967) had angered FBI head J. Edgar Hoover. Flicker also cocreated the television series *Barney Miller*, which premiered in 1974. Flicker put Skaaren in touch with a number of his colleagues, who offered feedback on the *Spooks* screenplay. Television writer Mark Saha (*Peyton Place*, *The Mod Squad*) gave Skaaren the most useful advice, offering step-by-step instructions about story action and momentum. He also advised Skaaren to create an outline for the story and to brainstorm for effective scenes before attempting to rewrite the script, two suggestions that Skaaren would adapt and use throughout his future screenwriting career. Although Saha cautioned Skaaren about submitting *Spooks* before it was sufficiently revised, he praised the story's premise and encouraged him to keep working on it. "SPOOKS is a picture I would buy a ticket to go and see," Saha told Skaaren.[6]

Skaaren met Walter Yates in the summer of 1975. The fifty-year-old was a successful real-estate developer and entrepreneur who thrived on travel and adventure. Yates had learned to pilot an airplane a few years earlier and began taking trips to remote parts of the country. A 1973 visit to Alaska inspired Yates to make a documentary about this unforgiving but beautiful expanse of the United States, to be released to coincide with the American Bicentennial in 1976. By the time Skaaren was introduced to Yates by Ivan Bigley, who ran Texas Motion Picture Services (TMPS) in Austin, Yates's idea for the documentary had evolved. He and his wife had recently divorced. And after discovering a parcel of land along Alaska's Post River in 1974, Yates decided that he wanted to spend a year alone in the wilderness, building a log cabin by hand and living off the land. His film would chronicle this adventure. Yates approached Bigley for help. Bigley had learned to operate a film camera while serving in the Vietnam War. Relocating to Austin after his discharge, Bigley opened TMPS in 1975 to offer postproduction services to local filmmakers and Hollywood productions shooting on location in central Texas. He and Yates formed a partnership to make the film, and Yates planned to send footage from Alaska for Bigley to begin editing into a rough cut. "You really need a director," Bigley told Yates, and he recommended Skaaren.[7]

Skaaren and Yates met for lunch before the entrepreneur left for Alaska. Although Bigley suggested that Skaaren direct the project, Yates initially only wanted Skaaren's advice about its commercial potential. Skaaren was intrigued by the documentary and Yates's determination to spend a year alone in the remote North Country. Having left the safety of state employment only a year earlier, Skaaren thought he understood Yates's desire to challenge himself. The only story worth telling, Skaaren wrote to Yates after he had left for Alaska, was "one man's search for peace in a changing world."[8] In August 1975, Skaaren committed to helping Yates develop the feature, but he also requested clarification about his involvement. In addition to his role as a consultant on its distribution, would he direct or write the feature? Over the next three months, the pair exchanged several memos hammering out the details of the agreement. Skaaren negotiated for a series of deferred payments plus a percentage of the film's profits depending upon the role(s) he ultimately played in the feature's completion. Yates wanted to retain his rights to the story in case he decided to publish excerpts as articles or in book form. Skaaren, perhaps feeling cautious after his contract dispute with Bill Wittliff over *Raggedy Man*, inserted a clause that allowed him to withdraw from the project if, after assessing Yates's sample footage, he decided that the feature would not be commercially viable.[9]

Yates began sending footage back to Austin in mid-September. Skaaren liked the images of Yates toiling alone in the wilderness and began to envision the feature as an adventure film suitable for all ages. The G-rated movie *Benji*, which Dallas director Joe Dante had made for $300,000, had just passed the $17 million mark at the box office, Skaaren wrote to Yates.[10] The stark beauty of the Post River area was undeniable, and Skaaren realized that the simple images needed just the right musical accompaniment. He thought of his friend, musician Bobby Bridger, and went to see Bridger's one-man musical, *Seekers of the Fleece/Lakota* at the tiny Creek Theatre overlooking Austin's Waller Creek. After the show, Skaaren made his way backstage to congratulate Bridger. He also told Bridger that he had a film project "in development" and that he wanted to discuss it with him at some point. "Knowing Warren, I also knew to be patient, that he would reveal more when he was good and ready."[11]

Yates returned to Austin in August 1976. He, Skaaren, and Bigley began to work through the raw footage and the piecemeal rough cut that Bigley had begun assembling during Yates's year away. The existing footage provided some great scenes, but the men agreed that additional background shots were still needed. And while Yates had been able to film himself climbing part of Peaceful Peak, the more than 9,000-foot-high mountain rising majestically above the Post River, he hadn't been able to shoot footage of the entire climb on his own. The three men and Loyd Colby, an associate of Bigley's, made plans to fly to Alaska to reshoot Yates's climb and any other footage that could be used for transition and background shots. Once the group arrived in Anchorage, Yates flew everyone in his Piper Comanche to Post River.

The men based themselves at Yates's cabin, which was about four miles from the foot of Peaceful Peak. Bigley had brought a 16mm camera and accessories, including an 800mm telephoto lens with which they could follow Yates as he scaled the peak's highest point. It took around two hours for Skaaren, Bigley, and Yates to make their way up the mountain to a clearing at about 4,000 feet elevation. Once there, Skaaren and Bigley set up the camera equipment while Yates continued the rest of the way solo. After a couple of hours, he scaled the pinnacle.[12]

Skaaren was in his element. Ideas about how to edit and market the film came easily because he was so enthusiastic about its potential. He also loved being in Alaska among such unspoiled wilderness, and he enjoyed the company of the men in the group. In later years Skaaren would embrace the teachings of poet Robert Bly and his "expressive men's movement," searching for the kind of male camaraderie that he had felt was mostly absent during his childhood in Rochester. After a few more days at Yates's cabin, the group loaded up the Piper Comanche and headed back to Anchorage. Along the way, Yates piloted the plane past an active volcano. As steam rose up around them, the men sang songs and reveled in the experience.[13]

Bobby Bridger was holed up in a Colorado basement when he finally heard from Skaaren about the project. Bridger was dodging calls from attorneys and record executives concerning the rights to his latest album, but Skaaren tracked him down at a friend's house in Golden, Colorado. "We're ready to start on *Breakaway*," he said, using the title that he and the others had chosen for the film. Bridger returned to Austin, and by the beginning of 1977 he and John Inman and a number of other musician friends were spending more than ten hours each day recording guitar tracks and other musical pieces for the soundtrack.

Skaaren began to envision *Breakaway* as similar to *The Man Who Skied Down Everest*, a 1975 documentary about Japanese speed skater Yuichiro Miura's quest to ski the South Col, or pass, between Mount Everest and Lhotse. Yates's climb of Peaceful Peak in particular resembled Miura's challenge. But Skaaren also was eager to dramatize Yates's battle with loneliness in the year the newly divorced father had spent living in the remote Alaskan wilderness. These scenes especially, Skaaren told Bridger, would depend on the soundtrack to evoke the desired emotions from the audience. "Warren saw *Breakaway* as a folksy version of the Miura film with Walter going to Alaska to build this cabin and heal himself," recalls Bridger.[14]

Having taught himself to play a twelve-string guitar, which is what Bridger used, Skaaren was able to communicate fairly quickly the types of sounds he envisioned for each scene. At the same time, he trusted Bridger's instincts. When the musician thought that a fellow guitar player's style would work better for a scene than his own, Skaaren convinced the fiscally conservative Yates to spend the money to fly in Bridger's friend Chuck Pyle from Colorado so that he could play a country-blues theme behind a scene of Yates preparing cinnamon rolls on his first Christmas morning at the cabin. Similarly, when Bridger decided that an orchestral accompaniment would heighten the impact of a few of *Breakaway*'s key scenes, Skaaren once again convinced Yates to foot the bill for members of the Austin Symphony to score the scenes. "Every time there is an emotional high in a movie, it's articulated with violins," Skaaren told Yates. "It's essential to pull at the heartstrings."[15]

Skaaren wore many hats on *Breakaway*. The film's official credits list him as writer and director, but he also provided the film's voiceover narration, helped to design the marketing materials, and worked unofficially as producer's representative to book the film into as many theaters as possible. Before they four-walled *Breakaway* across the country, Skaaren and Yates decided to host its premiere at the Paramount Theatre in downtown Austin. Nearly 300 people turned out for the March 22 screening, which Skaaren arranged to benefit the Wild Basin Preserve, a local nonprofit dedicated to the protection of more than 220 acres of Hill Country wilderness and its wildlife.[16] The hometown crowd embraced *Breakaway* and all who had contributed to it. "That film was really a collective effort," says Bridger. "Walter had a very gigantic ego, and he had to be really convinced of what it took to make a movie. Warren had gotten Walter to the part that he would trust him and move forward with a notion like that."[17]

Breakaway stayed at the Paramount for a weeklong engagement before opening in theaters outside of Texas. One of its print ads called it "the perfect family film for Easter," and the feature was well received during its theatrical run.[18] It earned the Award of Excellence for Outstanding Documentary from the Film Advisory Board, a national organization formed in 1975 to call attention to "quality" family-friendly entertainment. Yates and Skaaren had had their conflicts throughout the project, particularly over money. But on a trip to Los Angeles to oversee the final edit, Yates watched Skaaren move confidently among his Hollywood friends. It had convinced him of Skaaren's talents. "I realized how lucky I was to have him working on my film," Yates recalled decades later.[19]

With *Breakaway*, Skaaren seemed to fulfill a promise to himself that he had shared with Arthur Klein at the height of the *Chain Saw* drama: he had wanted to work hard on behalf of a "good" movie, and with *Breakaway* he felt that he had succeeded. As the film wound down its theatrical release, Skaaren began to spend more time on another project also inspired by a real-life subject. While still at the film commission, Skaaren had received a screenplay by Frank Waldman titled *The Season of '69*, about the University of Texas football player Freddie Steinmark. Despite his rather small stature, Steinmark was recruited by Longhorn head coach Darrell Royal, who had heard about the teenager's exceptional speed and dexterity on the field. Steinmark accepted a football scholarship to Texas and started as a defensive back on the varsity team in 1967. Steinmark continued to distinguish himself at UT, leading the team in punt returns while majoring in chemical engineering. He played a pivotal role in UT's December 1969 win over Arkansas during a game that came to be known as "The Big Shootout" and earned UT the national championship that year. Steinmark's story turned tragic when, just six days after that game, a troubling bruise on his left leg was diagnosed as a tumor that indicated bone cancer. Steinmark lost the leg but returned to UT, determined to finish his degree. He helped to coach the football team, proposed marriage to his longtime girlfriend, and made plans to apply to law school. During this time, Steinmark also became nationally known in part because of then-President Richard Nixon's interest in the impressive young man. But Steinmark was unable to beat the cancer that had claimed his leg, and he died on June 6, 1971.[20]

In retrospect Skaaren's interest in Steinmark seems almost eerie given the similarities between the two men's experiences with cancer. Like Steinmark, Skaaren would develop a mark (in Skaaren's case, a chest mole) that would prove to be cancerous. Skaaren also would seek treatment at MD Anderson in Houston, where he would receive the diagnosis in 1990 that his cancer had returned and was inoperable. Both Steinmark and Skaaren would die of bone cancer.

At the time, however, Skaaren was simply drawn as most people had been to Steinmark's compelling personal story. By 1978, Skaaren had been working on and off for approximately five years to develop this story into a feature film. He partnered with associate Bill Downs to purchase the movie rights to Steinmark's story, which were owned by William Jamail and Dallas-based producer Martin Jurow. The project lay dormant until late 1975, when Skaaren and Downs began to investigate the possibility of attracting Texas investors to the feature. Eventually they succeeded in raising $75,000 in development funds from close to a dozen investors from around the state. An overall budget for the film was estimated at just under $3.5 million.[21]

Sometime in 1977 Skaaren began corresponding with Steinmark's family, including his fiancée, Linda Wheeler. In early September 1978, Warren and Helen traveled to Colorado to meet with the Steinmarks and to discuss the project. After another trip— four days in Los Angeles— Skaaren returned to Austin and began to work on a treatment for the film in early October. Initially Skaaren reworked Waldman's *Season of '69* script and then wrote from scratch a treatment for a new screenplay tentatively titled *Freddie*, which would highlight not only Steinmark's football career but also his personal relationship with Wheeler, whom he had begun dating in the eighth grade.[22]

Skaaren thought Waldman's script had failed to capture the "real part" of Freddie, and he believed that understanding Steinmark's relationships with his family and with Wheeler was crucial to understanding the young man's motivation in life. His treatment gave structure to Steinmark's story via a voiceover by sports columnist Blackie Sherrod, who had used his column in the *Dallas Times Herald* to closely cover the Longhorn football team and its rising star player as they advanced to the Cotton Bowl during the 1969 season. Sherrod later collaborated with

Steinmark on the athlete's 1971 autobiography *I Play to Win*. Skaaren's forty-one-page treatment also incorporated a poignant letter Steinmark had received from Chicago Bears running back Brian Piccolo, who was in the midst of losing his own battle with cancer when he wrote to Steinmark in 1970.

Skaaren believed that Waldman's script had also lacked sufficient action for a story about a college football player at the height of his career. Having played the sport in high school, Skaaren knew what it felt like to be on the field during a game and to be part of a team. In addition to Blackie Sherrod's newspaper columns and *I Play to Win*, Skaaren pored over print coverage of Steinmark's football career. He mined the research materials for insight into Steinmark's athletic prowess and special approach to the game. Months later, Skaaren would incorporate significant details from a meeting with Longhorn assistant coach Fred Akers, who worked with Steinmark during the 1969–1970 season. Akers diagrammed key plays on the back of his personal stationery for Skaaren, walking him through an explanation of Steinmark's role on the field.[23]

Throughout 1979, with the *Breakaway* project behind him, Skaaren devoted a good deal of his time to *Freddie*. In January he returned to Denver to meet with the Steinmarks. He was there to share his treatment with the family and to solicit their feedback on the project. Although his Hollywood career was still a few years in the future, Skaaren would rarely deviate from this creative process of writing a treatment and/or outline and then meeting in person, if possible, with key players associated with the project. Skaaren believed it was crucial to the success of the entire project to connect with the people involved and to be able to read their reactions not only to the work but also to one another to understand the dynamics of the situation. With *Freddie*, Skaaren understood intuitively how much the family had invested in a film about their deceased son, brother, and fiancé.

Skaaren arrived at the family home in Wheat Ridge, about twelve miles outside of downtown Denver. He had an easy rapport with the Steinmarks that grew out of their initial correspondence, begun two years earlier, and his and Helen's visit the previous fall. Skaaren began to read the treatment aloud. As he spoke the last line, he looked around the room to assess the family's reaction. After a brief silence, someone commented that it seemed different from the Waldman script, which Skaaren took to be a good sign. It was clear to him from the emotional reactions around the room that everyone had been moved by his version.[24]

Skaaren had also come with a list of questions that would help him flesh out the treatment once he began writing the screenplay. "What movie do you see most closely identified with this story?" he asked the group.[25] The obvious answer was *Brian's Song*, the 1971 ABC Movie of the Week about Brian Piccolo's friendship with teammate Gayle Sayers during Piccolo's own battle with cancer. For Wheeler, however, the answer may have been *Love Story* (1970), the romantic drama about a young couple coping with a terminal illness. She and Steinmark had seen the film over the Christmas holidays in 1970, shortly after Steinmark's leg was amputated. They went into the movie knowing little about the film given that the previous weeks had been a swirl of hospital visits and bad news. At the end they walked out of the screening, stunned. "We just watched our future," Freddie told Linda.[26]

It had been a good meeting, Skaaren thought, and he left feeling closer to the family than on his previous visit. He felt confident that he had connected with the Steinmarks and that his treatment had struck a chord with the family. He knew that he had gained Wheeler's trust because she had shared with him the love letters she and Steinmark had exchanged throughout their relationship.[27]

The following month Skaaren began to push the project in earnest. He and *Freddie* partner Bill Downs received their first serious interest from Home Box Office (HBO). Launched in 1972, the for-pay premium program service, a subsidiary of Time-Life, offered viewers new films, major sporting events, and other options via satellite (the first television network to do so continuously) without the interference of commercials. At the time, HBO probably was best known for broadcasting "Thrilla in Manila," the boxing match between Muhammad Ali and Joe Frazier. In mid-July Skaaren and Downs flew to New York to have a meeting with HBO executives. One of the people they met with was Sheila Nevins, a former news producer who had recently been hired to head up HBO's documentary programming division. Given that *Freddie* combined a compelling real-life story with a sports angle, Nevins and her HBO colleagues were intrigued by the project. The meeting went well, and as Downs later communicated to Richard Hassanein of United Film Distribution Co., the cable company indicated that they could offer between $600,000 and $750,000 for pay television and syndication rights for the project.[28]

The Time-Life headquarters of HBO was just a few minutes' walk from the Film Center Building, where Skaaren had first met the Peraino brothers five years earlier, in 1974. What had followed was more than two years of frustration, thwarted negotiations, and mounting legal bills. By

1979, Louis "Butchie" Peraino and his brother Joseph had served their time related to the *Deep Throat* obscenity case, but they were about to be indicted again as part of Miporn, a sweeping FBI investigation into the thriving pornography videocassette trade based in Miami. Only a few years separated Skaaren's New York experiences, but it may have felt like decades. On *The Texas Chain Saw Massacre*, Skaaren had been a first-time producer's representative dealing with reputed mobsters. On *Freddie*, he was a writer-producer with a couple of credits to his name, including the award-winning documentary *Breakaway*.

HBO's interest in *Freddie* was encouraging. That fall, Skaaren began working with Los Angeles–based casting director Ruth Conforte. He had first met Conforte in his relatively new capacity as chairman of FPS, Inc., a Dallas-based company that handled below-the-line services, such as electrical, script supervising, catering, and so on, for film and television projects. Founded in 1972, FPS had built a solid reputation as a reliable company with an impressive roster of film and television clients, many of them out of Los Angeles. FPS scored one of its biggest clients in 1978, when Lorimar began shooting the television series *Dallas* on location in Texas. Initially approached by FPS's Joe Pope in 1975, Skaaren signed on as chairman at a nominal annual salary of $600 supplemented by 6,000 shares of company stock. The position required that Skaaren make the short flight from Austin to Dallas on a relatively regular basis, but the demands of FPS were manageable and left Skaaren time to write and work on other creative pursuits in Austin. As chairman of FPS, Skaaren was able to flex his producing muscle, helping to put together deals and packages. The connections that he made while serving as FPS chairman were invaluable. He had met Conforte, for instance, when she began casting actors for *Dallas*.

Skaaren and Downs tapped FPS to produce *Freddie* at a budget of approximately $3.3 million. Conforte and Skaaren agreed that rising star Robbie Benson, who had recently costarred in the Academy Award–nominated romantic drama *Ice Castles*, would be a compelling lead as Freddie Joe. Skaaren devoted much of the remainder of 1979 to rewriting a completed first draft of the screenplay. HBO's distribution offer had yet to be finalized, so Skaaren and Downs continued to solicit offers for both production and distribution. The family-friendly company Osmond Television liked the project but eventually passed. Stephen Girard, of the Girard/Flaherty Agency, helped Skaaren and Downs get the project to key representatives at 20th Century Fox, United Artists, MGM, and low-budget distributor AIP. "Most everyone thought the script to be workable but generally felt the subject matter to be television fare," Girard wrote to Skaaren at the end of February 1980.[29]

As Skaaren and Downs focused on producing the project themselves, Skaaren continued to reach out to potential distributors, such as Time-Life Films. The response generally was the same: people liked the project and the script, but they eventually passed. Despite Steinmark's inspiring personal story, the clock was ticking—if not on its relevance to contemporary audiences, then on its name recognition. The final blow came just before the Christmas holidays, when Skaaren received a letter from Fred and Gloria Steinmark. They expressed concerns about the latest draft of the screenplay, which focused more heavily on Freddie's relationship with Wheeler and, to their minds, "was not acceptable to us because it did not portray the son that we knew and loved."[30] They concluded the letter by asking Skaaren to relinquish or transfer all rights to the project. Skaaren's frustration over the failed project ran deep. He had spent more than three years nurturing its development and writing multiple drafts of a screenplay that he hoped would become his first produced effort. He had enjoyed the process of getting to know the Steinmark family and researching their son's inspiring life on and off the field. He believed that the latest draft of the script, with its emphasis on Freddie's commitment to the Longhorns, his education, and his relationship with Wheeler, captured Steinmark's resilience, strength, and humanity. Still, Skaaren knew that without the family's full support, the project would be even more difficult to get made. "Our exhaustive efforts since 1977 to fund the production of the film or to sell the screenplay and supporting rights have met with no success," Skaaren and Downs wrote to their preproduction investors in April 1981. "Therefore, we are ceasing any further efforts to market this project."[31]

Skaaren's role as chairman of FPS served as a distraction. The television series *Dallas* had proved to be a tremendous boon for FPS. Created by David Jacobs for Lorimar Productions, the prime-time serial centered on two generations of a wealthy, dysfunctional oil family that lived on a sprawling ranch outside Dallas. Picked up after its initial five-week run in the spring of 1978, *Dallas* didn't become an international phenomenon until the 1979–1980 season. Thanks to a programming move to Friday nights and the ongoing use of a seasonal cliffhanger ending, *Dallas* finished that season with an episode in which the lead character, J.R. Ewing, played by Larry Hagman, is left for dead after being fired upon by an unknown assailant. The "Whot Shot J.R.?" mystery created an international mania for the television show, which finished the 1980–1981 season in first place.[32]

By the early 1980s Skaaren's monthly salary from FPS had jumped to around $1,800. He supplemented this with consulting fees, some of which he earned by traveling to Los Angeles on behalf of FPS to attend and speak at industry conferences. He and Helen had always lived frugally, which made it possible for him to continue to pursue his "bohemian" lifestyle of writing for the screen. He worked on a number of diverse projects, including writing and directing television spots for a statewide political campaign.

Sometime in late 1981 Skaaren was introduced to Fred Fox, a colorful former Marine and oil field rough hand who had gotten rich by inventing, developing, and marketing equipment for use by the petroleum industry. Fox was similar to Walter Yates in that he was a successful entrepreneur with a story to tell. He approached Skaaren about researching and writing a feature film about the Nepalese Gurkhas, who served in the British army in the late 1800s. "Fred Fox is a very unusual gentleman," wrote one of Fox's associates. "He is not a film producer by profession. He is, however, a long time friend of the Gurkhas, having been involved with them in the Second World War."[33] Fox had plenty of military contacts thanks to a tour of duty in the South Pacific as a combat flamethrower on the island of Peleliu, for which he received the Navy Cross and a Purple Heart. He also had the resources to fund the development of such a sweeping epic, which is how he viewed the Gurkhas' story. The historical and international scope of the project appealed to Skaaren. "Fred decided he would try to write the story and I would be a consultant to him," Skaaren noted in December 1981. As with Yates, however, Skaaren's quiet authority, confidence, and ability to grasp the project's scope eventually convinced Fox that he should entrust the writing to Skaaren. It was a dream proposal in a lot of ways, not the least of which was that Fox was going to pay him to write. Skaaren negotiated a fee of $50,000 to script and co–executive–produce the film. He estimated that it would take him approximately nine months to research and write a first draft of the screenplay and included a contract clause that bound him to the project for no more than three years beyond delivering the final draft. By May 1982, Skaaren had officially signed on to Fox's adventure.[34]

Skaaren approached the project with his usual zeal for research. Stacks of photocopied articles from *British History Illustrated*, *Soldier of*

Fortune, and *Smithsonian* began to accumulate in his garage office be-hind the Laurel Valley house. Military newsletters provided very spe-cific accounts of the individual battalions within the Gurkha Brigade. He was reading everything he could get his hands on in preparation for his and Fox's three-week trip to Nepal, where the British first recruited soldiers after signing a peace treaty in 1815. After World War II, Nepal entered into an agreement with India and Britain to transfer its Gurkha regiments from the Indian army to that of the British. These four reg-iments became known as the Gurkha Brigade, a group of fearless war-riors fiercely loyal to the Crown. "These short, wiry hillmen have served the kings and queens of Britain with such loyalty, tenacity, and incred-ible bravery that often the sound of their battle cry . . . has caused en-emy soldiers to flee," wrote military historian Byron Farwell.[35] Among the "toughest and most covert soldiers" in the British army, the Gurkhas had even been involved in the raid on the Iranian embassy two years ear-lier, in 1980.[36]

Fox and Skaaren arrived in Nepal in mid-May 1982, landing in the capital city of Kathmandu. During their trip they dined with some of Fox's British military contacts and their wives, and Skaaren took copi-ous notes about what was said and how it was said, careful to capture speech patterns and word choice and to note social customs and behav-ior among the British officers. He spent the trip soaking up details, such as the stark contrast between the controlled, highly civilized way of do-ing things among the British and the apparent chaos and color of the Ne-palese. He noted, for instance, that when he and Fox deplaned in Kath-mandu, they were greeted by Nepalese wearing tribal dress. "Strange silence. Strange sense of gravity," Skaaren observed, reimagining the moment for the screen as a scene in which British officers returned to Kathmandu from battle.

Skaaren returned to Austin in early June brimming with ideas for the project, which he was now imagining as a U.S.-British coproduction given the story's historical sweep. He began keeping tabs on British film news, and his research files grew thick with clippings from *Variety* and *The Hollywood Reporter* about English producers, such as David Putt-nam, whose film *Midnight Express* (1978) had won two Academy Awards. Skaaren's travels with Fox yielded additional research materials that of-fered information not readily available to the general public. A classified document titled "British Gurkhas Nepal Brief 1982" allowed Skaaren in-sight into the unique dynamic between the British military officers and the Gurkha soldiers. Skaaren's notes reveal that he was planning to develop his story around a relationship that would depict this dynamic between two young men, one British and one Nepalese, who had become friends while fighting for the British during World War II. By the fall of 1982 the screenplay had the working title *A Few Grains of Rice*. Skaaren also sought out contemporary films with similar themes, such as Bruce Beresford's war drama *Breaker Morant* (1980), which follows three Australian lieutenants as they are put on trial for orders they carried out during the Boer War. Skaaren paid particular attention to the film's camerawork and characterizations, noting how they worked together to play up each character's particular drama and conflicts. He seemed to be training himself to think beyond simply writing the screenplay and anticipating, perhaps, what a director or producer might bring to the project.[37]

Although it may have appeared that Skaaren wasn't doing much work during this period, he was actually readying himself for one of the most important projects of his career. Longtime friend Amon Burton recalls stopping by the Laurel Valley house around this time and being surprised to find Skaaren watching a movie on videocassette tape in the middle of the afternoon. "He was just watching a video, didn't seem to be doing anything. I know he wasn't making much money, and I just wondered, 'What was he *doing*?'"[38] Years later, in a letter to a young man requesting career guidance, Skaaren would sum up his approach to work: "In my view, there is no job, there are no careers, there is *only* the search," Skaaren wrote. "I can tell you where I start, every day—I sit quietly and sense my curiosity. What seems to interest me most at this moment in my life? The practical reason for this is simple. Anything worth creating takes a very long time."[39]

Skaaren spent the beginning of 1983 writing the first draft of the Gurkha screenplay. In a five-page outline that accompanied the draft, Skaaren described the story as "a Kipling style of story not written by Kipling and not written at the turn of the century."[40] Rudyard Kipling's epic poem "The Ballad of East and West" inspired the script that Skaaren initially envisioned, and he included the first stanza as a title card to precede the film's opening scene, set in 1952, of young Nepalese hillmen lining up for the chance to be recruited into a Gurkha regiment. Fast-paced and deft, the opening images quickly establish one of the film's two principal characters, an adolescent boy named Harkbahadu, or Hark, who is "to [*sic*] short and too young" and of a low caste. He sprints down the mountain to the recruiting depot and is turned away, but as the recruiting party's British colonel and his wife begin their slow departure along the rain-soaked mountain's rutted switchbacks, "around every turn, he is there saluting." Within five beats, Skaaren's outline establishes Hark's character and his conflict. The story then introduces Nigel, an upper-crust British youth with a "gamey leg" who dreams of joining the Queen's army.[41] Skaaren's first draft worked hard to draw parallels between the two young men, playing up their similarities despite cultural differences.

Skaaren revised the first draft into the summer in anticipation of his and Fox's fall trip to London to meet with potential investors and producers. Simultaneously, he was pursuing another historical epic that sparked his interest. Earlier in the year he had read a series of articles about Pancho Villa, the legendary Mexican revolutionary who had been ambushed in 1923 and, later, whose corpse had been decapitated by grave robbers. Villa's death mask, which had been gifted to the Radford School for Girls in El Paso, Texas, and for years resided in the school's vault, was by early 1983 the subject of a controversial proposed international trade between the United States and Mexico. Skaaren wrote an article, which *Texas Monthly* magazine published in December 1983 as "Pancho Villa's Last Gasp," that traced the checkered history of the death mask and its unusual connection to the Radford School and explored the ethical issues surrounding the potential trade. "It is thankless, this business of trading the artifacts of international history, and even more so when the artifact involved is of mysterious origin, associated with a person of dubious character," Skaaren wrote.[42] A devotee of the Center for Environmental Structure's *A Pattern Language*, Skaaren approached ideas based on their relational patterns to one another. His notes for the article reveal a free-form flowchart documenting themes in Pancho Villa's life, such as his psychological preoccupations. Skaaren would later use this kind of diagramming to map everything from story structure to character backstory as a screenwriter.[43]

The feature appeared in the December issue of *Texas Monthly* and was touted on its cover. Margery Graham, a Radford School graduate and one of Skaaren's sources for the piece, wrote a scathing letter taking him to task for factual errors and for constructing a potentially libelous character portrait of the school's former director. Graham accused Skaaren and the magazine of publishing a "sensational and journalistically disgraceful story." A handful of readers wrote complimentary letters about the piece, including a prestigious former student of The Radford School. "I very much enjoyed reading the article about the Pancho Villa death mask and its curious connection with Radford School. I remember the mask well from my days as a student there," wrote Supreme Court justice Sandra Day O'Connor.[44]

A biographical note accompanying "Pancho Villa's Last Gasp" identified Skaaren as a filmmaker, a writer, and the chairman of FPS. It also
revealed that he had "recently completed a screenplay about the Gurkhas
of Nepal."[45] Indeed, by December not only had Skaaren completed a revision of the script's first draft, now called *Of East and West*, but he and
Fox had also traveled to London with an ambitious, detailed budget and
casting ideas to share with potential investors. The film had been estimated to cost just under $7 million. Among the details in the fifteen-
page document was a list of proposed stunts, including the collapsing of
a house. Before they left London, Skaaren and Fox received a letter from
Bob Montgomery, a New York entertainment attorney who was helping
them shop the project. At their request, Montgomery had sent the script
to John D. Eberts, head of British production company Goldcrest Films
and Television Limited. Goldcrest worked mostly with David Puttnam,
who from the start Skaaren had hoped might be interested in the project.
Eberts passed on the script, he told Montgomery, because it "is not suited
to today's mood which does not support the glorification of war."[46] This
issue in particular would become more of a sticking point for other producers and agents, although both Skaaren and Fox viewed the story as a
cautionary tale. Tucked among Skaaren's notes and letters for this project, in fact, was one of Fox's business cards. On the back was a quote
from Robert E. Lee: "It is well that war is so terrible or we should grow
too fond of it."

While in London Skaaren and Fox met with a number of potential backers, and their reactions to *Of East and West* were varied. British producer Euan Lloyd had a knack for getting independent projects
off the ground. His most noteworthy film to date was the actioner *The
Wild Geese*, which became the fourteenth highest-grossing film of 1978.
"Goose it up a bit," Lloyd advised the Americans, telling them that he'd
be interested in producing *Of East and West* if it was rewritten to showcase more action and if financing was in place. London agent Douglas
Rae liked the story in general but ultimately thought it "too literary for
the screen." Fox and Skaaren had been introduced to Rae by producer
Beryl Vertue, who had executive-produced *Tommy* (1975) and had exten-
sive television experience, most notably with the series *The Prime of Miss
Jean Brodie*. Vertue offered the most negative feedback, according to Fox,
who wrote to Bob Montgomery that she was "clearly disappointed with
the characterization, setting, and approach we took."[47]

Fox and Skaaren returned from London down but not out. Fox
wrote to Montgomery that they realized they must fine-tune their sales

approach, emphasizing to prospective producers and investors alike that the script was still an "early" draft and future versions would be "responsive to the direction chosen by the producer." Additionally, Fox and Skaaren agreed that their goal was to find an established producer who could put together a creative team and "complete the production."[48] Together they were hopeful that this producer might be David Puttnam, who had recently returned from shooting *The Killing Fields* in Asia. Although Skaaren and Fox were unable to meet with Puttnam while in London, they were successful in getting a copy of *Of East and West* into his hands before they returned to Austin.

A month later, Montgomery wrote to Fox. "Here's bad news from David Puttnam," he began, and included Puttnam's response to the screenplay, which was mixed at best. While Puttnam took issue with a few of the characters, whom he thought were stereotypes of their class or group, the biggest obstacle, he wrote, was the "fundamental premise of the screenplay, the notion that man has an instinctive relationship to combat, that I found untenable." Puttnam did add, however, that Skaaren's screenplay was "in almost every other respect . . . a real pleasure to read amidst so much 'dreck.'"[49]

Montgomery's letter urged Fox and Skaaren to "rethink how this film is to be done." Montgomery, who had initially envisioned the story as a television miniseries, raised the point again, suggesting that future drafts focus less on the friendship and military careers of Nigel and Hark ("which does not seem to be working well with potential producers/financiers") and more on the Gurkhas themselves.

But Skaaren, for one, didn't seem ready to leave behind the sweeping story of Nigel and Hark's friendship, which took the characters from the jungles of Burma to the sprawling estates of Sandringham and finally back to Nepal and the remote hilltop village from which Hark had come. Skaaren had had Montgomery send it to producers David Brown and Richard Zanuck in New York, whom he first met a decade earlier while running the Texas Film Commission. He suspected that Brown in particular, whose previous films included *Jaws* and *The Sugarland Express*, would appreciate the dramatic nature and epic scope of Hark and Nigel's story. A response arrived in early January 1984. "Both Richard and I were so taken with the script OF EAST AND WEST that we held it an inordinately long time," wrote Brown. "Regrettably, and alas, we don't think we would be successful with this."[50] Fox suspected that while Brown was interested in the project, Zanuck "questioned the overall profitability of

BREAKING AWAY [79]

the movie . . . and its appeal to the majority of American moviegoers; 14–18 year olds who affect 55% of the world's box office receipts."[51]

Montgomery, who had forwarded Brown's letter to Fox and Skaaren, included a note of his own. "I am sorry to enclose this letter. We came close. Call me and let's discuss the next step."[52]

FOUR

Highway to the Danger Zone

*Once a film comes out, they say, "Oh, of course, that's why he took
it. It's a commercial movie—it's a hit! Why wouldn't he want to do
that?" People don't understand the risk factor. [Top Gun] didn't
start out as a commercial movie.*

TOM CRUISE

Sometime between David Puttnam's rejection of *Of East and
West* and The Zanuck/Brown Company's passing on the project, Skaaren decided to take matters into his own hands. In
December 1983, he sent a letter with a copy of his *Texas Monthly* article
about Pancho Villa's death mask to William Morris agent Mike Simpson,
whom he had met a decade earlier. After sketching out the terms of his
deal with the magazine regarding future articles (which never came to
pass), Skaaren mentioned his screenplay about the Gurkhas and a number of other projects such as a book deal with Random House, which
may or may not have been résumé-padding on Skaaren's part. "I have
some material which I am very certain is excellent film material, some of
which I will write for *Penthouse* or *Esquire* first, but I really want someone sharp in Los Angeles to augment my contacts in the studios and net-
works," he wrote to Simpson. "Let's talk at your convenience. I'll come
out there, or if I or FPS has anything interesting going on here, we'll
fly you down to Dallas." As Natasha Waxman has observed of the letter,
Skaaren's tone is so self-assured and "muscular" that it is not readily apparent that he is seeking representation.[1]

Skaaren had first met Simpson a decade earlier, when the agent, then
a graduate student at the University of Texas, had interviewed him for

a magazine article about the making of *The Texas Chain Saw Massacre*. "The filmmaking scene in Austin was a small pond at that time, but Warren was the very apex. He was like the guy no one could ever talk to," said Simpson of Skaaren's reputation during the film commission years. "He was very different from all the other film guys. They were one step out of the hippie syndrome, and he was a businessman, already successful in the field."[2] Simpson had transferred to UT from USC, where he was majoring in international economics. Once at UT he changed his major to film and focused on documentary production. He graduated in 1973, spent a year in Colorado, and returned to Austin to earn a graduate degree in film production.

Simpson moved back to California and decided that what he liked most about film production was putting packages together. It took him six months to get an interview at the venerable William Morris Agency, where he started in the mailroom in early 1979. Within two months he was promoted to messenger, and after three more months he seized an opportunity to become Stan Kamen's assistant. Kamen was head of the film department and was known as the agent who turned Steve McQueen into a movie star. Within two years of starting in the mailroom at William Morris, Simpson himself had become an agent.

Simpson recalls getting a phone call from Skaaren sometime in early 1984. "I'm next door. I'm staying at the Beverly Wilshire," Skaaren told the agent. Simpson agreed to meet him for a drink at the hotel, where Skaaren told him about Fred Fox's Gurkha connection and *Of East and West*. "I was the go-to guy because I was the Texan," recalled Simpson of his early years at William Morris. "I'd get all these calls and letters from Texans who'd written a screenplay that they were sure was going to be the next Oscar winner. And about 100 percent of the time they were just awful."[3]

But Simpson liked *Of East and West* and thought it showed promise. Still, he asked a fellow agent for a second opinion. That agent's assessment was equally positive. Simpson then asked Skaaren if he wanted to work together, and he said yes. The whole exchange was so laid-back and their rapport so effortless that the two men never signed a contract. A simple handshake sealed the deal.

Simpson immediately went to work, sending around Skaaren's screenplay as a way of introducing him to the Hollywood community. By early June 1984 the Australian filmmaker Bruce Beresford, who had been on Skaaren's wish list to direct *Of East and West*, had received the script. Beresford had directed *Breaker Morant*, whose story Skaaren had

studied in preparation for writing about the Gurkhas, and had just released *Tender Mercies*, written by Texan Horton Foote. "All of the characters are well developed and many subtle intricacies are drawn between
relationships," wrote Beresford's reader, Karen Glasser. "Mr. Beresford's
stark realism could be just what this picture needs. It has very good commercial potential (in the vein of 'Chariots of Fire') but remains at the
same time unusual and original."[4]

Producer-director Norman Jewison also received a copy of the
screenplay. Although Jewison's reader admitted to some reservations
about the story's commercial potential, the report was overwhelmingly
positive: "One of the nicest scripts I've read in a long time. It's exciting
and different, moving and at times funny."[5]

While Simpson continued to shop *Of East and West*, he also actively
pursued script-doctoring opportunities for Skaaren. Rewriting or "doctoring" a screenplay was a time-honored tradition in Hollywood that
dated back at least to the heyday of the studio system in the 1930s and
1940s. It was not uncommon for a script to have gone through multiple
iterations before it went before the cameras. Once production began, specific scenes received further rewrites, polishes, and tweaking by everyone from studio executives, worried about potential ratings issues with
language or love scenes, to the producer and the star. But by the time
Skaaren began his Hollywood writing career in mid-1984, the process of
motion picture development had grown increasingly complicated. A studio film's development often began with a germ of an idea, either based
on an original concept or adapted from a book, a magazine or newspaper article, or a similar story in the news. A writer or writers would
be assigned to develop the idea into a synopsis or outline and then into
a full-length screenplay. From there, the script might go through multiple drafts before it was even considered for production, or "greenlit," by a
studio. As film historian Tom Stempel has observed, most of the scripts
in a studio's development pile were never made.[6] Those that were made
were often scripts that had been rewritten by numerous writers with input from many other individuals, such as studio executives, producers,
the director, and the star or stars. As Skaaren's agent, Simpson knew that
the fastest way to get his client work was to offer his services as a script
doctor. A successful first project could lead to others and, eventually, the
opportunity to write an original screenplay for a studio or star. Given
Hollywood's culture of writing by consensus, sustained by tens of millions of dollars within each studio's budget, the chances were good that a
strong writer like Skaaren, repped by a top agency, could find work fairly

quickly. "It was a time of unbelievable spending. It was such a seller's market. He was in a really extraordinary situation," recalls *Divergent* producer Doug Wick, who would work with Skaaren during this time.[7]

In early May 1984 Skaaren flew to Los Angeles for a series of sit-downs with various studio heads. "MEETINGS: Hollywood lives on them. Because they need to find ideas. And they don't have much else to do," Skaaren noted in preparation for his trip.[8] He had read screenwriter William Goldman's recent bestseller *Adventures in the Screen Trade* and memorized the differences between an audition meeting (you're hoping to get hired) and a creative meeting (you're already hired, you've written the script, and now the studio wants changes). "Never be desperate. Look Prosperous," he reminded himself ahead of his first audition meetings with executives such as Paramount Pictures' head of production Jeffrey Katzenberg.

Katzenberg was one of the first executives to whom Mike Simpson had sent *Of East and West,* and the Paramount chief then shared it with Dawn Steel. One of the few female executives at Paramount, Steel had a reputation for being as tough as—if not tougher than—most of her male colleagues. Recently promoted to senior vice president of production, Steel had successfully shepherded slick, soundtrack-driven hits like *Flashdance* and *Footloose* into theaters. Skaaren, distinguished and even a bit conservative in his tailored jacket and pressed khakis, hit it off with Steel, whose sleek Armani pantsuit contrasted with her wild mane of chestnut hair. Her tendency to swear like a sailor didn't bother the former Eagle Scout. "I like her. . . . I don't know why but I have such empathy for her in that role," Skaaren observed in a journal entry.[9] Steel thought of him two months later when she needed a script doctor for a romantic drama about star-crossed teenagers called *Captive Hearts.* Steel express-mailed the script to Skaaren on a Thursday, and within twenty-four hours he had read the material and prepared four pages of typed notes.[10] "He called Dawn and said, 'These are the things that are wrong with it, and these are the things I would do to fix it.' He had a very specific take on it and the whole thing mapped out," says Mike Simpson. "It just blew her away."[11]

Skaaren's observation that an audience needed to know more about *Captive Hearts*'s young lovers' frustrations in order to care about their conflict assured Steel that he could handle characterization. But it was his rather bold suggestion to flip the characters' personalities ("girl is 'tough' one, boy is quiet") that may have really impressed the studio executive. Steel also took note of Skaaren's laser-like ability to read a script, zone in on its problem areas, and propose multiple solutions. The combination of his speed, his focus, and his creativity set Skaaren apart—and Steel respected him for it. She would become an ally, and her support would be crucial in the coming years.

Skaaren's entry into writing for the studios was no overnight success story. By 1984, when he signed with William Morris, he had been working as a writer for almost a decade. But it had been a frugal existence supplemented by his business involvement with FPS and other consulting gigs. Still, he had enough confidence in his skills to approach Simpson, and he understood how he could be of value to the studios. Notes he made shortly after his trip to Los Angeles in May, however, offer a reminder that he was quite new to the business of screenwriting. He scribbled a list of questions such as, "How long should I be expected to take?" He wondered about the number of projects a studio would have in development at one time, and what percentage his agent would deduct from his earnings. Always protective of his time, Skaaren worried how "available" he would need to be to "these guys." Finally, he wrote, "WHO OWNS a screenplay which I write for someone else?"[12] This question would prove increasingly complicated, and the answer would change with each project, an industry reality that Skaaren would never quite make peace with.

He plunged into rewrites on *Captive Hearts*, which was first written by Sharon and Paul Boorstin and inspired by Sharon's 1978 article for *New West* magazine about a dance at a private all-girls Pasadena high school attended by boys from a nearby county probation camp. The Boorstins' script had been rewritten by Bill Phillips a year or so earlier. Phillips, who had had success in adapting Stephen King's novel *Christine* for the screen, also had a background in writing for television. Steel told Skaaren to improve the dialogue, highlight the romance, and "make a classic, not a kids [sic] picture," steering him toward *Romeo and Juliet* in terms of timeless themes.[13] Skaaren's rewrite process, shaped by Mark Saha's writing advice a decade earlier on *Spooks*, typically began with a detailed, multipage biographical sketch for each character. He would then make an outline of the script's dramatic beats, often charting the highs and lows on graph paper to visualize the story's pacing and balance. From there Skaaren would construct a chronological scene list, which would describe each scene's action in detail. As time went on, Skaaren would insist on having those in charge of each project sign off on the outline before he even began to rewrite the script itself. He viewed it as a way to exert some measure of control over what typically was a chaotic situation. He could then use the outline as a touchstone for everyone involved if he felt that the project was drifting off course because of too much input from multiple and often conflicting sources. What he didn't necessarily consider was that in Hollywood the writer rarely, if ever, had any control.

By August, Skaaren had completed a first-draft rewrite of *Captive Hearts*, less than a month after first receiving Bill Phillips's original script. "Good news—they liked it. Bad news—too long," he wrote of the response from Steel and producer Gary Nardino.[14] Head of television for Paramount, Nardino had recently set up his own production company within the studio. Skaaren collaborated well with Steel and Nardino, and he spent the remainder of the year working on *Captive Hearts* and auditioning for other projects. In October, for instance, he flew to Los Angeles to meet with producers Paula Weinstein and Doug Wick about writing an original screenplay set during the Spanish Civil War for Warner Bros. Wick had worked with New York–based director Alan Pakula on *Starting Over* (1979) before moving to Los Angeles. Weinstein also had roots in New York, where she had first worked in politics. "It's very hard to write anything historical and make it about now. Warren already was able to go into a historical period, into a lot of facts, and find something relevant and dramatic to say about two humans from different cultures," recalls Wick. "At the same time, it had a real sense of 'movie movie.' There was a theatrical world, there was action in it, it was engaging. This was clearly a fresh and original voice."[15]

In December 1984 Skaaren paused to take stock of what he called "a surprising year of rebirth." He often used the Christmas and New Year's holidays as a time to reflect in his journal and to catch up on correspondence with old friends like Jerry Hall. "I said I wanted to make my living from writing in 1982," Skaaren wrote, "and now I am doing it." By the end of 1984, having worked fewer than six months as an agented screenwriter, Skaaren already had earned in excess of $28,000, most of which was payment for his work on *Captive Hearts*.[16] He admitted that he was tempted to "sell other interests," such as his stake in FPS in Dallas, and focus solely on screenwriting. "But I am still a bit uncertain as to the 'why' of my recent screenwriting good fortune," Skaaren mused. "I guess I don't trust the judgement of those who are so excited and who pay me so well now—if they embrace me this quickly—will they turn away as quickly? Yes."[17]

By February 1985 Skaaren had done a rewrite and a polish on *Captive Hearts*. Although his experiences as head of the Texas Film Commission had prepared him well for the politics of Hollywood, he would have to learn another set of mostly unspoken rules as a script doctor. By the spring of 1985, relative newcomer Duncan Gibbins had been assigned to helm the film. The British-born Gibbins had directed several music videos for hit songs by the Eurythmics, Wham!, and Bananarama. *Captive Hearts* would be his first feature credit. Gibbins and Skaaren got along well, but his was yet another voice in a mix that already included Steel, Nardino, and lower-level executives at Paramount. Skaaren navigated the situation with aplomb, and his work continued to please those involved. "You have done an excellent job in addressing many of our concerns expressed in our last meeting," Nardino wrote in a memo to Skaaren in early March. Steel was more direct: "Well you did it, you old fuck!" she congratulated him by phone in her typical salty style. "I'm out there taking all the credit for making this a go, but you really did it." Skaaren laughed and responded, "Take it all—I'm in Texas. I don't care at all."[18] Skaaren continued to trim scenes for length and tighten dialogue, with a brief break in early March to honor a two-week-long writer's strike by the Writers Guild of America, of which he was now a member. Among other issues, the strike concerned writers' earnings from the fast-growing videocassette market.[19]

By late summer *Captive Hearts* had gone into production, and Warren and Helen made a short trip to British Columbia during filming so that he could be on hand for last-minute rewrites. As was typical of most writers' contracts, Skaaren received a credit bonus once Gibbins began principal photography. Mike Simpson negotiated a healthy rate for his new client: Skaaren's bonus on his first project amounted to an additional $30,000, nearly one and a half times his annual salary while at the film commission a decade earlier.[20] Several months prior to receiving the bonus, Skaaren had expressed his astonishment over such sums, writing, "I am overwhelmed at ease of getting money in this business."[21]

By November, with the film's production drawing to a close, Paramount submitted *Captive Hearts*' tentative writing credits to the Writers Guild of America. Paramount proposed giving Skaaren shared screenplay credit with Bill Phillips.[22] Along with the tentative credits, Paramount included a chronological list that detailed the project's history of authorship. *Captive Hearts*' list began with Sharon Boorstin's original *New West* article, published in July 1978, followed by a first draft and a revision by Boorstin and her husband, Paul, of a script based on the article. Writer Beverly Sawyer delivered a revision in 1979 (conceivably of the Boorstins' draft) before Bill Phillips began his involvement with the project, in 1983. Phillips is credited as the writer on five separate drafts before Skaaren took over, in August 1984. Like Phillips, Skaaren submitted a total of five screenplay drafts, according to Paramount's records.[23] Submission of the tentative credits and supporting materials was one of the first steps in preparing any studio film's official credits and was thus a common practice in Hollywood. Equally common, especially during this era of development, when the tendency of studios was to hire multiple writers for a single project, was that the assigning of specific story and writing credit on such projects often led to objections from one or more of the writers involved. Even a single objection would trigger an arbitration, the closed-door process of mediation conducted by at least three veteran Guild writers. Their job is to assess the studio's proposed credit against the materials submitted (typically, all of the treatments, outlines, screenplay drafts, and other written material associated with the shooting script as well as each writer's official Statement of Contribution). The writers who volunteer to be mediators remain anonymous to those writers affected by the arbitration decision. This process was overseen by the Guild, and most arbitrations rarely favored anyone but the first writer or team of writers.

In the case of *Captive Hearts*, Paul and Sharon Boorstin, the original writers who had been credited only with the story in Paramount's tentative list, challenged the assignation of credit.[24] The Boorstins believed that their initial work on the project amounted to more than just a "story by" nod, a credit one Guild writer once described as "tantamount to the verdict 'Your screenplay must have stunk.'"[25] The Boorstins also wanted screenplay credit, generally perceived as more valuable in the industry. The WGA informed Skaaren and the other writers that they each had twenty-four hours to submit a letter (which served as the Statement of Contribution) and any supporting materials to make a claim for a particular credit. This twenty-four-hour turnaround also was common practice according to Guild guidelines and (theoretically) kept the arbitration process moving forward and film release dates on track. The arbiters themselves generally had a matter of weeks to review all of the written materials, and the entire process—from notifying the writers about the arbitration to delivering a verdict on the credits—generally took less than a month. Skaaren submitted a letter proposing the writing credit to be "Screenplay by Bill Phillips, Warren Skaaren, and Paul and Sharon Boorstin."[26]

Shortly after New Year's, Skaaren received word from the WGA that the arbiters had reached a decision. *Captive Hearts*' writing credits would be listed as "Screenplay by Bill Phillips and Warren Skaaren and Paul & Sharon Boorstin," with an additional credit line of "Based on a story by Sharon Boorstin."[27] (The use of the word *and* between Phillips and Skaaren denotes that they wrote separately, while the ampersand between the Boorstins' names indicates their writing as a team.) Although Phillips's name was listed first despite Skaaren's having been the final writer on the project, Skaaren was satisfied with the final credit and the Guild's decision.

Skaaren would continue to be involved with *Captive Hearts* up until its release, in the spring of 1986, when it eventually came out as *Fire with Fire*. "It was a small movie," remembers Mike Simpson. "It had a fair amount of business. No barn burner, but it wasn't embarrassing, either."[28] It would be Skaaren's first official credit as a script doctor, and it led to his next project, which would be life-changing.

"What a difference a few days makes," Skaaren wrote in his journal in early May 1985. "Dawn Steel called. Problem with a script called *Top Gun*."[29] By the spring of 1985, Steel had been promoted to president of production at Paramount. When confronted with script difficulties on *Top Gun*, a big-budget action movie weeks away from a scheduled start date, Steel suggested to the film's producers that they meet with Skaaren to discuss a possible rewrite. The brainchild of producing partners Jerry Bruckheimer and Don Simpson, *Top Gun* was inspired by a 1983 magazine profile about the elite Navy fighter pilot school in Miramar, California. Bruckheimer and Simpson, who had a producing deal with Paramount and were enjoying back-to-back hits with *Flashdance* (1983) and *Beverly Hills Cop* (1984), developed the project with the actor Tom Cruise in mind for the title role of Lieutenant Pete "Maverick" Mitchell. Cruise agreed to consider the project as long as he could be involved in the screenplay's development, a request that he had the power to make thanks to his lead role in the successful 1983 comedy *Risky Business*. But as Cruise explained to *Premiere* magazine, in the beginning of its development *Top Gun* was far from the commercial hit it would become. "I liked it, but it needed a lot of work," said Cruise of the initial script, written by Jim Cash and Jack Epps Jr. "I was worried."[30] In fact, when Skaaren finally agreed to work on the screenplay, in late April 1985, the film was slated to go into production in mid-June and Cruise was so unhappy with his character and the overall story that he was on the verge of leaving the project.[31]

While Skaaren was an unknown entity to the heavyweight producers, Steel knew from working with him on *Fire with Fire* that he was a professional with a knack for characterization, which would appeal to any actor, but especially a rising star like Cruise needing to be enticed to remain on the project. Skaaren's ability to turn around a revision in record time would also help to keep the project's filming schedule from getting pushed too far into the future. Initially Skaaren turned down the project due to his other writing commitments, but when Simpson and Bruckheimer "came back with some fairly impressive numbers" and promised to work out an arrangement with the other studios to release Skaaren temporarily from his contracts, Skaaren agreed to work on *Top Gun*.[32]

The producers' journey with the project had begun two years earlier, when Bruckheimer discovered Ehud Yonay's article "Top Guns" in a copy of *California* magazine. "I came across this visual that struck my eye right away of this helmet with a visor down, and a plane reflected in the visor," said Bruckheimer, who was a former advertising executive.[33] Together the producing partners pitched Paramount on an action movie about a rebellious "hotshot pilot" trying to excel among the other elite Navy pilots at Miramar's "Top Gun" school. The studio's executives, namely Michael Eisner and Jeffrey Katzenberg, agreed to finance the film. Initially the producers offered the project to five screenwriters, but the writing team of Jim Cash and Jack Epps Jr. were the only ones able to accommodate the project's proposed timetable. By 1983, Cash and Epps had been working together for eight years and had sold five screenplays, none of which had been produced. Still, they were known in the business as solid writers, with Cash specializing in dialogue and Epps handling structure. They collaborated long-distance: Epps lived in Los Angeles, and Cash, a part-time film professor, worked from his home in Lansing, Michigan. Epps did research for the first draft of *Top Gun* (initially titled *Top Guns*) by interviewing forty Navy pilots and accompanying them on training missions in F-5F fighter planes.[34]

Together Cash and Epps wrote the draft in six months, delivering a 120-page screenplay to Bruckheimer and Simpson in May 1984. Both the producers and Paramount president Michael Eisner agreed that Maverick, the role intended for Tom Cruise, needed to be more sympathetic. Bruckheimer, who as a producer tended to ride herd on budget, thought some of the script's scenarios would be too costly. Simpson and Bruckheimer also objected to Maverick's love interest—a gymnastics teacher—as being an unrealistic choice for an elite fighter pilot. Members of the U.S. Navy, whom Simpson and Bruckheimer approached in order to secure permission to use naval aircraft and aircraft carriers in the film, also objected to this character as not being someone who driven Navy fighter pilots would feel was "on their level."[35]

Cash and Epps delivered a second draft of the screenplay two months later. "Jim Cash, in particular, was enamored of the female character," said Simpson of their revised draft, which still included the gymnastics teacher love interest. "We wanted this girl to be independent and contemporary and unique. [Cash] didn't agree with our assessment."[36] While Cash and Epps had written the girlfriend as an ambitious, award-winning athlete whose tough nature appealed to Maverick, their lives on the page seemed worlds apart and potentially incompatible.

The producers enlisted another writer for the project. Chip Proser was a screenwriter with a couple of credits who had known the producers for a while. He also had a background in aviation. He revised the original draft into a leaner screenplay (now titled *Top Gun*) in late February 1985 that the producers felt showed promise. Indeed, Proser's command of aerial jargon ("He's on your six, coming hard. Four hundred, losing airspeed!") resulted in more believable and dramatic exchanges than in Cash and Epps's drafts. Proser delivered another version a few weeks later, which introduced a new, more compelling love interest named Charlotte (Charlie), who was loosely based on real-life Navy consultant Christine Fox. The part, which eventually would be played by Kelly McGillis, was an improvement from the Cash and Epps drafts in terms of ambition, but it still needed work to flesh out Charlie's motivation and eventual attraction to Maverick. Proser further revised the script into late April. By this time Cruise had committed to the project with the understanding that he would have a hand in script development, and production was tentatively scheduled to begin that summer.

Skaaren first discussed the project with Simpson and Bruckheimer by phone on April 24, 1985. Early on, Skaaren had made it very clear to his agent that he would live and work in Austin and commute to Los Angeles when necessary. It was an unusual arrangement, especially for a relatively new screenwriter, but Skaaren made certain that the situation was honored as part of his "deal" memo, or contractual agreement, on each project. When pressed about this during one of his initial phone calls with the producers, Skaaren explained, "I have an environment here that's set up for me to get my work done. It involves a certain kind of place."[37] Skaaren valued the distance between Austin and Los Angeles, between him and the "noise" of the industry, which he believed was a tremendous distraction. Although Don Simpson would gripe about the long-distance "relationship" in later years, he and Bruckheimer honored it, as would others who wanted to work with the writer. Simpson would also come to understand that this strategy was one of the secrets to Skaaren's success. "Warren goes home and writes. It's very unusual. Most writers are hanging out or reading magazines. They write an hour a day. Warren listens, speaks, absorbs, then he gets on a plane [back to Austin] and writes," said Simpson after working with Skaaren on multiple projects.[38]

By the time Skaaren spoke with Simpson and Bruckheimer about the script, he had read Proser's latest draft and made copious notes. He also created a detailed intensity chart that delineated, on graph paper and using a different-colored pencil for each character, each one's story arc. Skaaren favored this kind of visual so that he could see on paper particular gaps, or holes, in the characters' development. "We'd really like to pick your brain here," began Bruckheimer, who also admitted that the partners were very "hands on" with the development of each of their projects. One of the biggest problems with the script, according to Skaaren, was that it didn't fully explain what drove the character of Maverick. "In the very beginning, I think we have to see him slightly crippled by that," Skaaren told the producers. "There's just too many good things happening to this guy." He also had issues with the love interest as written, describing her as too "flat—like the other tech types with tits."[39]

Bruckheimer and Simpson warmed to Skaaren's assessment. When he proposed making Charlie, Maverick's love interest, "as ballsy" as Maverick and even a bit aggressive in pursuing him for technical information that would boost her own career, Bruckheimer responded, "That's exactly what we want, Warren." Simpson, who envisioned the role of Charlie as "mid-80s modern, realistic," and similar to that of Faye Dunaway's character in *The Thomas Crown Affair*, was also enthusiastic. He would later explain that they had had trouble wooing actresses for the project because of Charlie's characterization in Proser's drafts of the screenplay. The forty-five-minute conversation ended with the revelation that Skaaren was not the only writer they were consulting for a rewrite. They were impressed enough, however, to send him the Cash and Epps draft, which they considered a better version structurally ("except for the girl") than Chip Proser's later drafts. Said Simpson of Proser's somewhat darker view of the story, "He saw Kafka, and this ain't Kafka."[40]

The following day, after Skaaren had read Cash and Epps's version of *Top Gun*, he had another phone conversation with the producers. Again they responded favorably to Skaaren's ideas for how to improve the screenplay and flesh out particular characters. They mentioned that he would need to talk with the director, Tony Scott, and the film's star, Tom Cruise, to hear their input as well. "He *sees* motifs, and that's unusual for an actor," said Simpson of Cruise. Eager to move forward with the project, which Bruckheimer revealed was only six weeks from shooting, Simpson told Skaaren, "This is where we sit. I'm going to on the phone say this without speaking to my partner . . . we want you to do this, quite simply. You're our choice."[41]

On April 30, after reading Skaaren's first scene outline, the producers convened with him by telephone. Bruckheimer's comments reflected his primary concern about the budget, which was about $13 million. "Anything that you don't have to rewrite, it makes it easier with the Pentagon," he told Skaaren, reminding him of the need to have the government's screenplay approval in order to use their planes and carriers in the film. Official cooperation would help the producers save money on production design and also keep the project moving toward the start date, tentatively set for mid-June. Bruckheimer was also sensitive to aspects of the story that would reflect negatively on Maverick's character and thus on Cruise's star persona. "We don't want to make a film about killing," he cautioned, noting that Maverick's motivation had to move beyond wanting to avenge his father's death in Vietnam, hinted at in Proser's drafts. He steered Skaaren away from a scene in which Maverick argues with his best friend because "it makes him unsympathetic."[42]

Skaaren suggested he maintain the script's original story structure and work on tightening dialogue, which seemed to satisfy Bruckheimer and Simpson. Within twenty-four hours they were back on the phone discussing Skaaren's second outline. Director Tony Scott also joined the conversation, as did Cruise, briefly. Scott in particular urged Skaaren to retain specific action sequences, such as a volleyball match between the bare-chested pilots that existed in the Proser draft, which Scott felt was a good scene because of its "physicality."[43] For a director, such scenes were infinitely more interesting and challenging to block and shoot than shots involving two characters talking. This scene also had the potential to be one of the film's more titillating moments, with its emphasis on the sculpted bodies of some of the industry's hottest young actors, like Cruise and Val Kilmer, who would be cast as Maverick's rival, Iceman. This graphic aspect also appealed to Scott, a former director of commercials known for their slick, sexy images.

The men finally came to a consensus about what scenes should appear in the outline, and Skaaren proceeded to work on the first draft. Although his contract stipulated that he had three weeks to write and deliver a first draft and a polish, Skaaren completed the draft within five days. He wrote for approximately thirteen hours each day and tried to offset the physical and mental exhaustion by getting massages and eating macrobiotic meals carefully prepared by Helen. He also visited a saltwater flotation tank, an occasional relaxation practice he had begun in the late 1970s. On the evening of the fourth day, when Skaaren was on the verge of finishing the draft, he received a phone call from Tony Scott and Tom Cruise, who wanted to offer their input. "The dynamic of the psychology here is something you should understand," Don Simpson had explained in an earlier call, referring to the relationship among the producers, director, and star. Simpson reiterated that he and Bruckheimer had told Cruise, in particular, that he could "have a shot" at the script.[44] With that in mind, Skaaren felt "trapped" into having the conversation with Scott and Cruise, which lasted two and a half hours.

At one point during the call Scott suggested to Skaaren that he had been led down "the wrong track" by Simpson and Bruckheimer in terms of story structure. "Above all, this love story has got to work. We've got to redesign the action to accommodate that rather than vice versa," said Scott. He also discussed how the film was going to be photographed: "It's gonna be like *Rocky* in the air—lots of cuts."[45] Reflected Skaaren a few weeks later, "It was a disaster because the director is a very confused communicator, so that I got confused just trying to understand what he said let alone to evaluate it and make decisions about how I wanted to incorporate his ideas into the script."[46] Skaaren thought Cruise's comments and suggestions, which focused primarily on fleshing out Maverick's character and his relationship with Charlie, were more helpful. Of one particularly emotional scene between the characters, Cruise said, "It's not hitting the core of who Maverick is. When I read the scene, I feel like, she can't know his pain." Pushed by Skaaren to articulate what Charlie "gives" to Maverick in the scene, Cruise said, "She's got to let him go in this scene for him to realize that he's loved."[47] Writing about the experience later, Skaaren mused, "I could tell that he and I would get along very well and I would be able to utilize a lot of his ideas in the screenplay."[48] Scott and Cruise's distracting phone call, and their feedback, which somewhat contradicted the notes he had received from Simpson and Bruckheimer, gave Skaaren an introduction to the delicate politics of script-doctoring a blockbuster movie.

Skaaren finished the draft a day later. He had pushed himself to complete the draft quickly to "take maximum advantage of this particular moment," a moment that he and his agent knew could make or break his screenwriting career. Still, the experience had taken a toll. Toward the end, Skaaren was wearing a patch over his left eye to compensate for its sudden inability to focus. His hands, which had become calloused from round-the-clock typing, were bandaged in bubble wrap.[49] Later, while reflecting on the grueling experience, Skaaren reminded himself to "always take two full weeks minimum to rewrite to first draft."[50]

Bruckheimer was the first to offer congratulations. "Excellent job. Excellent. I mean even Tony [Scott], who we thought wasn't going to like this because he doesn't have the kind of heart that we want this picture to have, loved it," he told Skaaren in a May 8 phone call. In particular, Bruckheimer liked the changes Skaaren had made to the character of Charlie, fleshing out her backstory and making her more of a professional, goal-oriented love interest. Skaaren, who had briefly majored in chemical engineering at Rice University, had met many young women training for careers in aeronautics at NASA and used this as inspiration for Charlie's background and motivation.[51] Simpson was equally happy with the draft, praising Skaaren's changes to Maverick's "through-line" and the supporting characters of rival Iceman and Goose, Maverick's best friend and flying partner (played by Anthony Edwards). Simpson also commented on Scott's approval of the draft, revealing that he was initially against Skaaren as a writer based on his outline for *Top Gun*, but that after reading Skaaren's first draft screenplay, he called Simpson and apologized.[52] Although the producers complimented Skaaren's work generously, their not-so-subtle asides about Tony Scott are typical of the kinds of power plays that tend to dominate such creative interactions in Hollywood. Cruise, out of town to fulfill a family obligation, had yet to read the script, but the producers were anxious to move forward. They asked Skaaren to fly to Los Angeles the following day. It would be the first time that Skaaren would meet the four principals in person.

They assembled in Simpson's office on the Paramount lot for an afternoon meeting that lasted nearly six hours. Skaaren took stock of the group dynamics, noting that the "natural political rivalries" that had grown among the men, some of whom had been developing the project for two years, had taken a toll and that the group "had lost perspective on their film. I found myself in the unusual position, therefore, of actually informing the owners of the film what the film was now about," said Skaaren of the experience. His political skills were honed in part from years as head of the Texas Film Commission, where he dealt with notoriously difficult personalities, such as filmmaker Sam Peckinpah and actor Steve McQueen; he could hold his own in many types of situations.

But his role had changed. Now he was a screenwriter and script doctor, positions traditionally low on the Hollywood food chain. The meeting wore on, and Skaaren could tell that Simpson and Bruckheimer, planning to attend an Eddie Murphy concert that evening, were anxious to come to a close. Sensing that Cruise's ideas for rewriting the script were being brushed aside by the producers, Skaaren stepped into the mix. He told Cruise that they could work on the script later. Cruise bristled, accusing Bruckheimer and Simpson of putting pressure on them to wrap up the meeting. Skaaren later chastised himself for trying to take over the dynamics of the meeting. "I must moderate that executive tendency," he noted. "I don't have to be all things in those meetings. Just the writer."[53]

Skaaren returned to Austin and began to work on the polish. Among other changes, Simpson and Bruckheimer had directed him to return to the Cash and Epps version to incorporate a few scene details and lines of dialogue from the screenwriters' earlier draft, like the immensely quotable "I have a need for speed" line spoken by Maverick. The revised draft, shorter by five pages, also included a new finale in which Charlie, Maverick's love interest, is reunited with the pilot as he returns to Miramar to take up a position as an instructor. The scene was leaner than in previous drafts, and it now gave Charlie, assigned to transport and brief the new instructor, a plausible reason to be back at the school, which offered stronger closure to the film's love story than in earlier drafts by the other writers.

While Skaaren was waiting for feedback about the polish, he received a $150,000 check from Paramount as per his contract. That amount represented $50,000 for signing the contract, another $50,000 for delivering a completed rewrite, $25,000 for beginning the polish, and another $25,000 for delivering a completed polish. Additionally, Skaaren's deal memo stipulated that he would receive $175,000 if he were to receive sole screenplay credit; or, if Skaaren's credit was shared with either Chip Proser or Jim Cash and Jack Epps, he would receive $100,000.[54] All told, he could receive as much as $325,000. (This contract would be amended two months later to reflect Skaaren's ongoing involvement with the project as it began principal photography.) During this time he also was interviewed by *Variety* columnist Army Archerd. Set up, quite possibly, by Don Simpson to heighten publicity about the project as it inched closer to production, the interview recapped Skaaren's whirlwind Hollywood screenwriting career and his involvement in *Top Gun*. When Archerd asked what kind of credit he was going to receive on the project, Skaaren answered, somewhat naively, "I have no idea, no idea." In addition to the high-profile publicity for the writer, the mention in Archerd's column served as a matter of public record that the project was now viable and that Skaaren was its current screenwriter.[55]

As Skaaren worked on fine-tuning the script, the producers and director auditioned actors and actresses for the various supporting roles. Demi Moore read for the role of Charlie, as did model-turned-actress Julianne Phillips (newly married to musician Bruce Springsteen). The part eventually went to Kelly McGillis, who had costarred a year earlier in Paramount's surprise hit *Witness*. Simpson brought Skaaren up to date on the casting decisions in a May 17 phone call in which the producer also discussed the next set of revisions based on his reading of the earlier polish. By this time Skaaren and Simpson had established a rapport, and Simpson would occasionally let down his guard with Skaaren during their time on *Top Gun*, revealing his struggles with overeating and a troubled childhood. Simpson liked to talk about himself, and Skaaren was a good listener. If Skaaren witnessed Simpson's drug use over the years, he never mentioned it, although he would acknowledge it obliquely in conversations about the downsides of the business in general. He did, however, become familiar with Simpson's drinking. During more than one late-afternoon conference call, Simpson could be heard slurring his words.[56] Skaaren recognized Simpson's powerful stature within the Hollywood ranks, a position based on his successes as a top production executive at Paramount in the late 1970s and early 1980s as well as his more recent box-office hits as an independent producer. He was grateful for Simpson's ability to speak for the studio, which meant one fewer layer of "principals" that Skaaren had to deal with while working on the screenplay.

The Paramount executives involved with *Top Gun* included David Kirkpatrick and Michael Roberts. Kirkpatrick, according to Simpson, was once the producer's own "protégé," and his script notes reflected training under Simpson, who credited himself, improbably, for starting Paramount's "tradition" of executives offering notes on early drafts of the screenplay. Having been in France attending the Cannes Film Festival when Skaaren delivered the polish, the studio executives had just made their notes available in a May 16 memo to the producers. The executives thought that Maverick's Achilles' heel needed clarifying and that Iceman's character arc remained too flat. Bruckheimer and director Scott thought that the volleyball scene also read "flat." This scene clearly was becoming pivotal to the film. Skaaren saw it as a sequence that could help to build the tension in the following, more intimate scene between Charlie and Maverick. The producers and Scott saw the volleyball scene as both an important plot point and a marketing tool. It offered an intense bit of action that would heighten tension among the pilots even as it showcased the film's buff male actors. Toward the end of one phone conversation, Don Simpson tried to motivate Skaaren as he prepared to tackle the next revision. The hyperbolic producer complimented Skaaren on the improvements he had made to Maverick and Charlie's love story, exclaiming, "You're building *Casablanca!*"[57]

Skaaren worked to revise the screenplay further, incorporating script notes from separate conversations with Bruckheimer and Scott two days later. Scott considered the Iceman character crucial to the script and wanted to see the conflict between him and Maverick amplified in the next draft. "There's no real adversarial role" in the film, Scott argued, other than Maverick's conflict with himself, and he wanted Skaaren to "focus the conflict" between these two characters. Scott in particular seemed impressed by Val Kilmer, who would play the role, and clearly wanted to showcase the actor in the film. He warned, however, that he didn't want the character (and thus Kilmer) to become "the Darth Vader of the piece." Bruckheimer also suggested that the audience "has to feel a little more depth" to the character of Iceman, who came off as too much of a villain in Skaaren's most recent revision.[58] They also rehashed the volleyball scene, which Scott described as "almost violent," like "a fistfight over a volleyball net."[59]

Skaaren addressed these and other issues in the polish draft that he delivered the following day, on May 20. Approximately ten days later, Skaaren turned in another revision that further trimmed scenes and dialogue to tighten the action and shorten the overall length of the film. Chief among these changes was the addition of a fairly explicit love scene between the romantic leads, where Maverick and Charlie, who was wearing only Maverick's button-down shirt, tumble into bed after a heated argument. This kind of graphic scene had been kept out of earlier drafts in deference to the Navy but also because of Cruise's reservations about Maverick's seeming like more of an "asshole" by having sex with Charlie early in their relationship. Revisions to dialogue between Maverick and Charlie, who reunite in the film's final scene, switched lines between the characters and had Charlie coyly repeating lines that a brash Maverick had spoken in one of their earliest encounters. It was a change that reflected a tendency toward formula on the part of the producers, who once told Skaaren, "We like to make pictures where you set up something in the first act and pay it off in the second and third."[60]

On June 17 Skaaren received a tentative shooting schedule for *Top Gun*, set to begin production on June 26. He was in Los Angeles two days later for rehearsals, which included Cruise, McGillis, Kilmer, Anthony Edwards (Goose), Meg Ryan (Carol, Goose's wife), Tom Skerritt (Viper), and a number of other actors playing smaller supporting roles. Skaaren sat in the background, making an audio recording of the table read and occasionally tapping on a portable typewriter as he made line changes to the script.[61] The actors seemed fairly relaxed as they read through the screenplay. When Cruise and Edwards played the scene in which Maverick tries to pick up Charlie in the Officer's Club by singing the Righteous Brothers smash hit "You've Lost That Lovin' Feelin'" with Goose, the entire room joined in for a good-natured rendition of the chorus. Skaaren had added the bit in one of his earliest drafts as a way to establish Maverick and Goose's close friendship as well as Maverick's initial cockiness. Unsure of the words to the song while writing the scene, Skaaren had called an Austin record store and asked a reluctant salesclerk to recite the lyrics over the phone.[62]

Simpson sent Skaaren a memo the next day with additional changes made after Skaaren departed for Austin, including one request from Cruise that illustrates the star's desire to control audience reaction to his character: "Tom would like to insert a short beat after the first fuck scene that communicates it was more than just a sexual moment. . . . Again, a short succinct scene that communicates the growth of their relationship."[63] Skaaren sent the producers fifty-nine pages of revisions the following day and continued to revise as needed once the film went into production on June 26. He revised another sixty or so pages throughout the film's principal photography, which lasted approximately forty-two days, and into the additional weeks set aside for aerial photography and the film's simulated battle scenes between the Navy pilots and their Russian counterparts. The filming of these scenes was carefully monitored for accuracy in action and dialogue by naval consultants, such as Admiral Pete Pettigrew. Skaaren also visited the set at least three times, bringing Helen to San Diego over the July 4th holiday weekend to watch filming at Miramar and to be on call for script revisions. Back in Austin he would review dailies, or each day's footage, on videotape, at one point accompanying a revised draft of an additional love scene with a memorandum that read, "Cruise MUST CONTROL THE 100,000 watt smile. We must never see it at more than 25 watts in this scene."[64] During this time Skaaren also was in touch with producer Doug Wick, with whom he was writing an original screenplay about the Spanish Civil War for Columbia Pictures. "Warren would talk about seeing dailies, that [Simpson and Bruckheimer] wanted him to see and comment on dailies, which is very unusual," says Wick of Skaaren's enhanced role on *Top Gun*. "That's an incredibly high compliment."[65]

In mid-August, toward the end of principal photography and while Skaaren was still submitting script revisions to the set, the screenwriter received a letter from Steve Kotlowitz, Paramount Pictures' legal counsel, notifying him that the company had submitted tentative writing credits to the Writers Guild of America on August 8.[66] Typically, writing credits are determined after principal photography has been completed, but in the case of *Top Gun* the studio was eager to have the WGA establish "separation of rights" in anticipation of preparing a novelization of the film for publication around the time of the film's release. Separated Rights are a group of rights granted by the WGA to the writer or writers of original material, such as a screenplay. In this instance, according to the WGA's *Screen Credits Manual*, the studio or company "must give the writer(s) with Separated Rights the opportunity to negotiate with publishers for rights and/or services." Once the studio determines which writer(s) are entitled to separated rights, the WGA then has to hold an "earlier preliminary credit determination" to figure out which writer receives the "qualifying" credit.[67] The studio's proposed credit gave sole story and writing credit ("Written by" as opposed to "Screenplay by," which is typically given to a writer who did not write the original story) to the script's initial writers, Jim Cash and Jack Epps Jr.

Skaaren was dumbfounded to be left out of the proposed credit. The letter from Paramount offered no further information. According to Guild rules, Skaaren had ten days from receipt of the letter to file a protest. (Cash and Epps and writer Chip Proser received the same letter from Paramount.) On August 26 agent Mike Simpson notified the studio that Skaaren was indeed protesting the credit and would be requesting shared screenplay and story credit with Cash and Epps.[68] Two days later, Skaaren flew to Los Angeles to assist with further on-set revisions of the script. That same day, Skaaren and the other screenwriters who had worked on the project received official notification from the WGA that because Skaaren was protesting the proposed writing credit, the Guild would be conducting an arbitration into the matter. In the letter, Grace Reiner, acting as screen credits administrator and arbitration

secretary, urged each writer to submit a statement to the WGA Arbitration Committee discussing his "writing contribution as it remains in the
final script and setting forth what you feel the credits should be." According to Guild rules, each writer had twenty-four hours to deliver his
statement in writing.[69]

For Skaaren, the prospect of not receiving at least shared writing
credit on *Top Gun* was unthinkable. His experience with this particular
arbitration would become a defining moment in his nascent screenwriting and script-doctoring career. But for more seasoned writers like Cash,
Epps, and Proser, the arbitration experience had become part of the job,
a necessary evil brought on in part by the development trend embraced
by the major studios of the time. Development, or "scriptwriting by consensus," was especially valued at Paramount, where Bruckheimer and
Simpson had their production deal.[70] Executive Jeffrey Katzenberg, who
had worked his way up to the position of president of production at Paramount by the early 1980s, not only encouraged but also enforced the belief that movies written by committee would become high-concept hits
like *An Officer and a Gentleman* and *Beverly Hills Cop*. Katzenberg also
expanded the role of the studio executive in the screenplay development
process. According to one published report, for instance, Paramount al-
located nearly $14 million for development in 1985, the year that *Top Gun*
went into production.[71] Dawn Steel took over for Katzenberg as president of production when he left for Disney in 1984. And as Steel told one
reporter at the time, "Development is the lifeblood of this studio."[72]

Screenwriting by committee often involves numerous individuals
weighing in on a screenplay, which usually leads to a number of rewrites
and, in many cases, a number of different writers hired to bring a particular type of expertise (story structure, dialogue, characterization, etc.) to
"fix" a problematic script. "Credit arbitrations are becoming more complex and more time-consuming because of this [rewriting] trend," observed Leonard Chassman, then–executive director of the WGA, in 1981.
"We've had films with twelve, thirteen, and fourteen writers on them."[73]
Throughout the years, various film industry entities have been responsible for assigning screen credit. The Screen Writers Guild, established in
1920, handled the allocation of screen credits until 1927, when the Academy of Motion Picture Arts and Sciences was formed. The Academy established one branch for writers, and this group assumed the responsibility of determining screen credits until 1941. At that time, after years
of behind-the-scenes drama and disunity among members of the Screen
Writers Guild, the Guild first negotiated a Minimum Basic Agreement

(MBA) with producers to further define the control of credit.[74] According to this agreement, the "signatory production company" (typically, a studio) is responsible for determining initial credit and must notify the writer(s) and the WGA once it reviews all relevant materials and decides how to allocate credit. Then, if the proposed credit is disputed, the writers have the option to resolve the dispute among themselves. Together they must come to unanimous agreement about the credit and how it should be stated, and that decision must adhere to the guidelines stipulated in Schedule A of the MBA.[75]

For whatever reason, the various *Top Gun* screenwriters did not discuss among themselves whether to share credit, something that Skaaren would vow to do on future projects. Instead, they all submitted written statements to the WGA Arbitration Committee, making the case for why their names should be on the film's final credits. This committee was composed of three Guild members selected by the WGA who remained anonymous to each other and to those involved in the credits dispute. (According to Guild rules, screenwriters involved in arbitration are given an alphabetized list of potential arbiters. They are allowed to strike "a reasonable number" of names from the list if they decide, for instance, that an individual might have a conflict of interest. Skaaren did not exercise his right to do this largely because, as a new writer, he did not know personally most of the Guild members listed.)[76] As with any credit determination, the Arbitration Committee was given at least a few weeks to sort through the written material, which included all of the treatments, outlines, and screenplay drafts and any original material (newspaper or magazine articles, books, etc.) that may have inspired the screenplay, as well as the writers' written statements about their contribution. Within the allotted twenty-four hours, Skaaren focused on writing a persuasive Statement of Contribution while, ironically, doing rewrites on the set of *Top Gun*.

The nine-page statement Skaaren sent to the committee members was a painstakingly detailed outline of his contributions and changes to the *Top Gun* screenplay. "After several sturdy attempts by other writers the producers of TOPGUN told me the scripts did not work," Skaaren began, laying out the various problems Simpson, Bruckheimer, and the other principals had noted in initial conversations with him. "They challenged me to change the screenplay and story from an airplane stunt movie about reckless hot shots to a story about a smart, attractive, complex individual, Pete Mitchell, who engages in adult professional and personal relationships, with adult conflicts," continued Skaaren. Aware of the Guild's policy, stated in its *Screen Credits Manual,* that changes to minor details like character names did not count toward a writer's significant contribution, Skaaren observed at the outset, "I did not engage in across-the-board attempts to change names. But I did fundamentally change every one of the main characters. I also wrote many new scenes."

This was not necessarily self-serving blather on Skaaren's part. His changes to the characters of Maverick (Cruise), Iceman (Kilmer), and Goose (Edwards), for instance, honed and heightened *Top Gun*'s drama. Skaaren's script revisions were subtle but substantial in terms of how they influenced character dynamics during key sequences. For instance, the enhanced presence of Carol (Meg Ryan) as Goose's wife ultimately softened Maverick's hard edges. On one hand, while Proser introduced the character (sans dialogue), it was Skaaren who drafted a poignant exchange between her and Maverick after Goose's death that made Maverick more dimensional and less of the "asshole" that had appeared in earlier drafts. This type of change, ultimately, had kept Cruise from leaving the project. On the other hand, the overall story that Skaaren had finessed was essentially the same, structurally, as Cash and Epps's initial draft. And without Proser's command of the technical aspects of aerial combat, the action sequences wouldn't ring true on the screen. Still, Skaaren wrote, "I invented new characters with backstory, motivation, interpersonal bonding and conflict. I moved the story from a wide-shot aerial movie to a fully drawn dramatic film, close-up on the characters."[77] This paragraph preceded an itemized list that, for Skaaren, illustrated how involved he had been not just in the revising of the screenplay but also in the actual production of the finished film. He mentioned attending *Top Gun*'s rehearsals, watching dailies, meeting with Navy personnel regarding rewrites to the action sequences, and reviewing the rough cut on an editing bench. His involvement throughout, he argued, affected scenes to be reshot.

The remaining six pages of Skaaren's statement articulated relationships, scenes, and characterizations "unique or new to my version" to distinguish his contributions further. It was Skaaren's knack for creating and fleshing out three-dimensional characters, in fact, that would come to define his style as a screenwriter and script doctor. As he wrote of the film's love story, "I completely invented and designed the love story which we actually filmed. It is that love story which attracted a major actress (Kelly McGillis)." Not only did the relationship between Charlie and Maverick interest McGillis, but certainly the fundamental changes Skaaren made to her character helped to convince the actress that her

role would serve the narrative beyond the love story itself. Indeed, producer Don Simpson said as much to Skaaren in a May phone call during
the casting process.[78]

In mid-October, with the WGA's preliminary credit determination
still undecided, Skaaren and agent Mike Simpson scheduled a conference call with Grace Reiner, who acted as the screen credits administrator and the arbitration secretary for the WGA. Reiner had worked for
the WGA's West Coast branch since 1983, when she first clerked in the legal department while still in law school. She became screen credits administrator after graduation, in 1984.[79] Although Reiner was intimately
involved with the Guild's arbitration proceedings and was the only individual with knowledge of the arbiters' identities and access to the writers' Statements of Contribution, she did not have a say in the decision
made by the arbiters. And while it is unclear what exactly precipitated
the phone call, it is likely that Skaaren requested it as a way to understand
the arbitration process more fully and to make his case as completely as
he could. Reiner was obliging throughout, but the anonymous nature of
the arbitration process meant that she could not provide Skaaren with
specific answers to some of his questions. For instance, when Skaaren
asked if the other writers had stricken any names from the list of potential arbiters, Reiner replied that she was not at liberty to reveal any content from the other writers' statements.[80]

At one point during the conversation Reiner attempted to put the
arbitration process in context. "There is a very strong bias for the first
writer of anything," she said, explaining that since the late 1930s the
Screen Credits Committee had felt the need to "protect" the first writer
"because they're the ones who came up with the first ideas and put it on
paper. They're often the ones who get most screwed at the same time because they'll get fired, someone else will be brought on . . . and they'll
suddenly lose their credit."[81] Reiner also explained the 50 percent rule,
which stipulates that a subsequent writer must contribute at least 50 percent of the final shooting script to receive writing credit on a script written from an original idea (as opposed to a contribution of 33 percent for
a script written from source material, such as a book). When Skaaren
asked if a first-time arbiter would be counseled to determine this percentage using a particular formula, or "thumbnail," Reiner replied,
"There is no thumbnail. It's entirely within the judgment of the arbiter." She continued to elaborate on the process: "It's not just dialogue and
it's not just motivation, it's the addition of characterization—the major
characters and motivations and internal dialogues and structure and

dramatic intent—all of it added together, with dialogue probably being lowest on the list."

Skaaren believed that he had met this rule based on his rewriting of the *Top Gun* screenplay, but he was still frustrated by the capricious nature of the WGA Arbitration Committee's decision. "My forté is character, and that's not a percentage quantifiable issue," he told Reiner. "But none of it is percentage quantifiable," Reiner calmly replied.

"There are literally hundreds of thousands of dollars that have evaporated for me," Skaaren continued, referring to the money he could lose from residuals resulting from sales of the film to videocassette, DVD, and cable and foreign television as well as potential future writing jobs if his name were not officially on the film. "I think we've got a hit film, that every moment of it has got my hand on it. The idea that it's gone is very difficult for me to reconcile with a fair and just proceeding. But I also understand it's very difficult to set up a proceeding that is universally just."

Reiner was sympathetic. "Believe me, I understand," she told Skaaren toward the end of the conversation. "It happens a lot," she added, referring to the more than 150 such cases per year that the WGA was arbitrating at that time.

While Skaaren's reaching out to Reiner was not a breach of Guild rules (Reiner did not reveal the identities of the arbiters or any content from the other writers' statements), it was a rather bold step for a relatively new screenwriter. For Skaaren, however, who was used to being in charge from his days at the film commission and as chairman of FPS, it was simply a matter of exerting his control. A few days later, on October 14, Reiner sent a letter to Paramount's Steve Kotlowitz on behalf of the WGA. The arbiters had made their determination, and they had awarded the Separated Rights to *Top Gun*'s first writers, declaring the film "Written by Jim Cash & Jack Epps, Jr." This designation allowed the studio to move forward on the movie's novelization, but the film's final writing credits would remain undetermined until the conclusion of principal photography. As disappointed as Skaaren must have been to be left out of the Separated Rights credit (and any profits from the novelization), he wasted no time in developing a plan to ensure a credit of some kind on the film. He considered making a case for an executive producer nod if the writing designation fell through as a way to document his involvement on the film and to recoup any financial losses.[82] Within a week, Paramount submitted another letter to the WGA announcing the completion of principal photography and proposing the final writing credit (as opposed to Separation of Rights) as "Screenplay by Warren Skaaren and Jim Cash & Jack Epps, Jr." and "Story by Jim Cash and Jack Epps, Jr."[83] This proposed credit seemed both to acknowledge Cash and Epps's essential role in the project's early stages and Skaaren's key involvement before and during production. Skaaren may have been relatively new to Hollywood, but he had powerful allies. In an October 28 letter to Paramount's Dawn Steel, Skaaren thanked her for staying in touch and revealed how he was feeling about the situation. "Please do not attribute any disappointment in my voice to you. I am just so proud of *Top Gun* and the teamwork we all shared that I am having a hell of a lot of trouble accepting the outrageous possibility that my name could be completely stricken from the credits."[84]

Days later Skaaren and the other *Top Gun* writers received a letter from the WGA's Reiner, explaining that because Cash and Epps were protesting the studio's proposed credit, an arbitration would take place. Although the writing team's protest was never articulated to Skaaren—and he never had contact with them—it's likely that Cash and Epps were objecting to a shared credit and to having Skaaren's name appear first. Once again the studio submitted a list of written materials to substantiate its proposed credit, this time with an additional five items (four sets of revisions and a final shooting script, all attributed to Skaaren). Simultaneously, Skaaren received a letter from Paramount senior vice president Ralph Kamen regarding his "services" as an associate producer. Kamen's letter outlined many of the tasks Skaaren already had completed, such as watching and analyzing screen tests, weighing in on technical issues like lighting tests, and watching dailies throughout production. The letter also included ongoing and future activities, such as "assisting the director in evaluating various cuts of the film; and related post-production functions."[85] Skaaren was not the first writer to receive a consolation producer credit from a studio. But Paramount's ongoing willingness to stay on top of the situation and "take care" of Skaaren was not, by any means, typical industry behavior.

Skaaren's second Statement of Contribution retained much from his earlier submission. By this point, however, he was a bit savvier about which areas to highlight, and he began the document by quoting from the WGA's *Screen Credits Manual* regarding what a second writer must contribute to receive a writing credit. Skaaren wrote that he believed that the committee, after examining the final shooting script, would agree that his contributions met the criteria "to support a credit that should read: 'Screenplay by Warren Skaaren, Jim Cash, and Jack Epps, Jr.'"[86] He proceeded to outline his contributions over the previous six months, which included six outlines and treatments, five drafts, and thirteen sets of page revisions ranging from eight to fifty-nine pages per revision.[87]

Skaaren also highlighted what he considered his "single most significant contribution": the "creation" of a realistic love story between Maverick and Charlie. "Their story takes up 33 pages of the 100 page final shooting script, or 33%. It packs about 60% of the emotional power of the film however."[88] He re-emphasized the significance of this contribution later in the statement, quoting a passage from the Guild's *Screen Credits Manual*:

> As per the WGA Manual's statement on page 8, that "there have been instances where a change in one portion of the script is so significant that the entire screenplay is affected by it and credit is awarded . . ."
> I believe that the RELATIONSHIP-LOVE STORY, between Maverick and Charlie, as well as THE CHESS GAME MODEL, are both significant enough to qualify me for shared credit.[89]

"Chess game model" was the phrase Skaaren used to explain to the producers, director, and actors how the love story unfolded strategically between Maverick and Charlie. Indeed, it was Skaaren's idea to include a first date between the characters that established tremendous sexual tension purely through dialogue.

Throughout the rest of November Skaaren was on call as *Top Gun*'s aerial sequences were shot, and in some cases reshot, in California. He revised the film's opening action sequence and Maverick's final encounter with a Russian fighter plane midmonth. On November 25 the WGA's Reiner notified all of the film's writers that the WGA Arbitration Committee had reached its final decision. *Top Gun*'s writing credits would read "Written by Jim Cash and Jack Epps, Jr.," giving the original team of writers full credit for the story and screenplay. Skaaren ultimately received a credit as associate producer. Mike Simpson, Skaaren's agent, had sent a letter to his client a few days prior to the WGA's notification. "The guild may choose to unjustly suppress your screen credit, but this town knows that you made two movies *happen*," he reminded Skaaren of *Top Gun* and *Fire with Fire*, which was released at the same time. "It's infinitely more important for the long run than the credit or the money."[90]

Mike Simpson was right. Despite how a film's credits might read, those working within the industry understood that the credits told only part of the production story, if that. Skaaren's reputation as a fast, talented writer for hire with a facility for characterization was made by his involvement with *Top Gun*. Around this time, director Martin Brest approached Skaaren with a screenplay for a drama about two brothers, one a yuppie con man and the other an institutionalized savant. Tom Cruise and Dustin Hoffman already were attached to the project. Skaaren loved the idea of working with Cruise again, and he considered Hoffman and Brest tops in their fields. "I know the material. I have had a Raymond in my family," Skaaren confided about one of the characters in a letter to Brest; he could have been referring to several relatives in either his or Helen's family. "I felt the heat and I felt the singular brain stretch of such a collaboration," he wrote, but he ultimately admitted that he had too many other commitments. "I'm disappointed that we aren't doing this picture together. But I shall never forget that you wanted me on that team," he told Brest of the script for *Rain Man*.[91]

In various interviews given at the time and in later years, Skaaren would remain diplomatic about the loss of the screenwriting credit on *Top Gun* and often explained the complexity of the film's arbitration without emotion. "The rule [crediting the first screenwriter] was supposed to protect writers from having their material usurped by the studios, but sometimes that means the person who did the final script doesn't receive credit," Skaaren told a journalist for the *Post-Bulletin*, a newspaper in his hometown of Rochester, Minnesota.[92] Years later, Don Simpson said of the situation, "I believe Warren got screwed when he didn't get shared credit."[93]

For Jim Cash and Jack Epps Jr., the WGA's decision to award sole screenplay credit to the writing team marked the first time that their names appeared in a film's credits despite their having written and sold five screenplays.[94] Chip Proser, who, like Skaaren, did not receive a writing credit on the film, publicly disparaged Skaaren's scene in which Maverick and Goose serenade Charlie by singing a Righteous Brothers tune.[95] He later admitted to leaving the project angry with the producers and the studio.[96]

In late January 1986, Skaaren attended an advance screening of *Top Gun* held for New York publicists and distributors and noted that they responded favorably to the film. "The women loved the volleyball sequence and all the male flesh," he recalled. Simultaneously, news came that the Space Shuttle *Challenger* had exploded during liftoff.[97] Three days later Skaaren traveled to Dallas for a test screening. Director Tony Scott, producers Jerry Bruckheimer and Don Simpson, and Paramount executives Ned Tanen and Dawn Steel flew in for the event. The executives worried that the audience might take issue with the air combat sequences given the recent *Challenger* tragedy, and they were worried that this would affect the screening's "numbers," or feedback score. The group huddled outside the theater, listening to the audience and waiting for the numbers. "Don and Jerry came across the room with the sheet and it was 83% excellent, 78% recommend," Skaaren recalled. "The numbers were astounding."[98] Still, the producers and director continued to tinker with the final cut of the film, inserting an additional love scene between Maverick and Charlie written by Skaaren in mid-March.

Top Gun's world premiere was held on May 12 at the Loews Astor Plaza on Broadway and 44th Street in New York City. The film opened theatrically on May 16 and quickly became a box-office favorite with audiences. *Variety* dubbed it the "reigning summer hit," with earnings of more than $43 million in its first twenty-four days.[99] The critics were less enthralled. Rex Reed, writing for the *New York Observer*, called it a "moronic" script that "telegraphs every emotion and every event before they happen."[100] Pauline Kael described the film as a "shiny homoerotic commercial" and took the producers and director to task for the film's glossy look and vacuous story. "Selling is what they think moviemaking is about. The result is a new 'art' form: the self-referential commercial," wrote Kael.[101] Vincent Canby tapped in to the film's contradictory mix of formulaic story and visceral action: "*Top Gun* is a truly absurd movie, yet I enjoyed it almost as much as the 8-year-old boy within me had anticipated after seeing the film's trailer last winter."[102] Perhaps the best indicator that *Top Gun* had entered into the cultural consciousness was *MAD* magazine's parody of the film on its December cover that year. The satirical publication also spoofed the film, dubbed *Top Gunk*, in a five-page comic strip featuring a main character named "Maniac."[103] But the negative reviews didn't seem to hurt the film. *Top Gun* became the year's highest-earning film, with a domestic gross of $82 million, which catapulted Paramount Pictures to the top studio spot for the first time in years.[104] The film also set records as a home video rental in 1987, with sales of 2.5 million units within a week of its initial VHS release.[105]

Skaaren received $62,500 as per his contract for being the last writer on *Top Gun*. The WGA's credit arbitration decision meant that he would not be entitled to any residuals or other payments as a writer, including the $150,000 bonus Paramount Pictures had agreed to pay if he were to receive a shared screenplay credit. Skaaren's role as an associate producer gave him one percentage point of the film's net profits, which was equal to approximately $5,000 for every $1 million gross earned by the film.[106] As an associate producer, he also received $50,000 for his consulting services on the film during postproduction.[107] Between February 1987 and August 1990, a few months before Skaaren's death, he had earned more than $330,000 solely from his profit participation in the film, nearly triple what he would have earned if he had received a writing credit instead.[108]

As Mike Simpson predicted, Skaaren's association with the film earned him numerous offers for more writing work. Several months after Top Gun's release in 1986, Skaaren would be rewriting Larry Ferguson's script for Beverly Hills Cop II for Simpson and Bruckheimer. Skaaren would become more familiar with the arbitration process over time, which helped him to become savvier about, and somewhat less invested in, the results. Still, his disappointing experience with the Guild over Top Gun had left its mark. Writing to his client after the WGA announced its Top Gun credit determination in November 1985, Mike Simpson appealed to Skaaren's deep interest in Eastern philosophy (as well as his ego) in an effort to assuage his frustration: "Your talent runs deeper than any of us yet know. Don't be discouraged by the turn of events. . . . Like all good samurais we simply turn the enemy's attack to our advantage. We learn and grow stronger."[109]

FIVE

Hollywood Gothic

I liked Warren right away, because he was so original. His ideas were strange, but his mind was very organized.

TIM BURTON

Passersby on the grounds of the Capitol building in downtown Austin may have looked twice at the unlikely pair mugging for photos in the spring of 1986. Skaaren, who had recently celebrated his fortieth birthday, was squiring around a twenty-seven-year-old filmmaker named Tim Burton, whose first success had come a year earlier with a relatively small, offbeat comedy called *Pee-wee's Big Adventure*. Made for around $6 million, the film grossed $45 million in the United States alone upon its release. Burton had grown up in Burbank, California, and attended the California Institute of the Arts, founded by Walt Disney. The cartoonist's namesake studio hired a twenty-one-year-old Burton to work as an animator. Burton's baggy clothes and shaggy hair, which journalists frequently described as "unkempt," contrasted sharply with Skaaren's business-casual style and overall tailored appearance. They stood shoulder to shoulder for one jokey photo, a beaming Skaaren in his short-sleeved polo and a deadpan Burton in a loose black shirt, re-creating Grant Wood's "American Gothic" painting.

For Burton, the photograph would come to symbolize their relationship, which in spite of their differences was founded on a kind of kinship. Despite his California roots and early start in the business, Burton often felt like an outsider in Hollywood. Skaaren, relatively new to the business and based in Austin, could relate, even if his outward demeanor conveyed confidence and collegiality to those in power in Hollywood, who perceived him as "the rock of Gibraltar," according to Burton.[1] The filmmaker also felt that he himself got along well with writers in particular. "Most of my friends are writers, because I identify with what they go through. In terms of the artistic pain, they're in a bad place in Hollywood. I can relate to them. I feel closer to them," he once said.[2] Burton also had a "distant" relationship with his parents, much as Skaaren did with Pearl and Morris. "It was like this acknowledgment of each other and, with the knowledge of that, this kind of [understanding] to just let it go," said Burton shortly after Skaaren's death.[3]

Skaaren and Burton did share an agent, and Mike Simpson thought that the two creatives might be able to help one another. Burton had been struggling to find a follow-up project after *Pee-wee*. Then he received Michael McDowell's screenplay about a deceased husband and wife who enlist the help of another ghost, Beetlejuice, to help them take back their New England home from the new yuppie owners who have moved in. McDowell was a horror novelist who began writing for television in the early 1980s. He had written the screenplay in early 1985, based on a story by him and fellow writer Larry Wilson. By the spring of 1986, Burton was attached and the project had found a home at Warner Bros. via the music- and film-oriented Geffen Company. After three drafts by McDowell, someone—the studio, Burton, perhaps even McDowell—had thought it was time to move on. Although Burton believed on one level that the studios put too much emphasis on development ("I don't know why there's so much second-guessing in the movie business"), he also could see the benefit of multiple writers. "Sometimes you need a fresh perspective, and bringing in new writers is like going to a doctor for a second opinion," said Burton of the rewrite process.[4]

Skaaren had first heard about the project in early March 1986. Jerry Bruckheimer and Don Simpson were still tinkering with *Top Gun*, but Skaaren's work on the film was essentially done. Skaaren liked the ideas expressed in McDowell's script, and although he didn't know it at the time, he and McDowell shared a deep interest in death. McDowell was an avid collector of death-related memorabilia, from ads for burial gowns and pins that could hold a lock of a deceased loved one's hair to dozens of postcards that Victorian-era parents made from photographs of their dead children.[5] One of Skaaren's favorite books was Ernest Becker's *The Denial of Death*, which won the Pulitzer Prize in 1974 for its exploration of humankind's struggle to come to terms with its own mortality. Prior to working together in Austin, Skaaren "met" Burton over the phone and discussed changes to McDowell's script. At one point, Burton described

to Skaaren how he envisioned the main character, a kind of trickster figure named Beetlejuice. "Make character real so it can go out to the edge,"
Skaaren jotted down during that first conversation.[6]

Two days later Skaaren chatted with Eric Eisner, who was president of the Geffen Company. Founded in 1980 by David Geffen, who had
roots in music and film production, the Geffen Company would be producing Burton's latest project, and Warner Bros. would be handling distribution. Eisner gave Skaaren notes on McDowell's drafts, telling him
that Geffen wanted the tone of the story to fall somewhere between "Al-
bert Brooks and *It's a Wonderful Life.*"[7]

Skaaren spent the next week sketching out how he would approach
McDowell's existing drafts based on his early conversations with Burton and Eisner. While Skaaren drafted an outline, Mike Simpson was negotiating the terms of his deal for what was supposed to be a relatively
short period of work. Within three weeks, Skaaren would provide a rewrite and polish of the *Beetlejuice* script. In return, he would be paid just
over $175,000, a bump up from his initial fee for *Top Gun*. On March 11,
Skaaren sent an outline and memo to Eisner, Burton, and Mark Canton, who was an executive vice president at Warner Bros. Skaaren's outline included nine steps that he thought would solidify the structure
of McDowell's last draft and address issues raised by Burton and Eisner the previous week. The first step in the outline—"Select and invent
a stronger, more simple story line"—reveals the kind of clear-minded,
no-nonsense approach that Skaaren offered as a script doctor. This was
part of his value in Hollywood, as a script doctor is often brought on
to a project during times of chaos and extreme panic, when the principals typically have lost focus. Producer Doug Wick was working with
Skaaren during this same time on the period romance *Lillie and Beck*
and on *Flawless*, a comedy for Jane Fonda. "Warren was smart enough to
understand the difference between what they meant and what they were
saying, and then he was a very talented guy, so he could come up with
real solutions," says Wick.[8]

When Mike Simpson first mentioned Skaaren to Burton as a possible writer on *Beetlejuice*, he steered Burton toward Skaaren's work on the
soon-to-be-released *Top Gun*. "I didn't even go by *Top Gun* because that's
not my kind of thing," recalled Burton, who instead relied on how he felt
about Skaaren during their initial meetings. At first he may have worried
about Skaaren's capacity to tease out the story's darkness and twisted humor, particularly in the "trickster" character of Beetlejuice, but he soon
realized after spending time with Skaaren in Austin that they shared an

appreciation for the strange and bizarre. "When I met Warren, he had the reputation of being the voice of reason, Mr. Logical, [but] was completely one of the weirdest people I'd ever met."[9]

Skaaren made sure to include Burton's charge to expand and sharpen the script's humor in his original outline. "Extend the humor in each gag, including a setup and an afterlaugh" and "Twist the language a bit" were two of the outline's nine points. A memorandum accompanied the document and reads like the pitch it was: "I salute The Geffen Company and the previous writers for having created a fascinating and one-of-a-kind story. I hope to have the opportunity to help you bring it to the screen," Skaaren wrote.[10]

By the end of the month, Skaaren was out in Los Angeles meeting with Burton and Eisner. He fine-tuned his outline based on additional feedback from the pair, paying particular attention to Burton's desire to shorten the script and declutter it of characters and plotlines. Burton appreciated Skaaren's presence on the project and what he represented to "management" figures like Eisner, especially during meetings. "Warren was looked upon as a therapist in a way to a lot of insane people in Hollywood," said Burton. "He'd make somebody like me look like there was some sort of anchor involved."[11]

Skaaren returned to Austin in early April and began working on a first draft of the rewrite. He consulted Becker's *The Denial of Death* for inspiration. "Death concentrates the mind," Skaaren observed, jotting down ideas for *Beetlejuice*'s deceased husband and wife, such as having them work on projects they never had time for while they were alive (like completing a model kit). In McDowell's draft, the family who moved into the deceased couple's home had two daughters, Cathy and Lydia. Per Burton's instructions to pare and simplify the story, Skaaren reconfigured the family as having only one daughter, Lydia, who began as a ten-year-old and eventually became a teenager in later drafts. As much as the deceased couple, Adam and Barbara, would become the audience's "heroes," to quote Eisner, Skaaren conceived of Lydia as also having a significant role in cultivating audience identification. "Lydia should have some questions about death, which are really questions about life," wrote Skaaren in his earliest notes.[12]

A few days before his contracted deadline, Skaaren delivered a first draft to Burton, who gave Skaaren feedback that filled two notebook pages. Burton liked the first half of the script but noted that "things go off" in the second half. Characters seemed less well developed, especially Beetlejuice, and the tone became almost too dark. Things didn't "get bigger or more buoyant," noted Burton of the script's second half.[13] Skaaren spent another week and a half trying to address Burton's concerns, particularly about tone and making Beetlejuice, whom the audience first sees in the graveyard of Adam's miniature model town, into more of a performer.[14]

On May 16, Skaaren was in Los Angeles to meet with Burton and Eisner about the first draft. A few days earlier, Burton had sent a two-page memo to Eisner outlining his priorities for *Beetlejuice*. While the script was important, he was most interested in locking down a start date of early August for the film's production. Burton hadn't been in production since shooting *Pee-wee's Big Adventure*, and he was eager to get behind the camera again. Burton's memo seemed to imply that he hoped executives at both Geffen and Warner Bros. would do what they could to speed the rewrite process so as not to delay production. Burton wanted a workable script so that he could begin budgeting for locations and special effects, of which there would be many. He was also eager to begin storyboarding, the previsualization process in which he would graphically illustrate the scenes that would occur in the film. "This (along with the script) is my most important phase," Burton wrote to Eisner. "I work out most of my bugs in this process, and I would like to start immediately."[15] He also indicated that he considered script revisions "an ongoing process. It will be worked on throughout, simultaneously with all the previous points" such as location scouting and budgeting.[16]

During Skaaren's May 16 meeting in Los Angeles and in follow-up conversations with Burton throughout the month, a number of story issues became clearer. Streamlining the script in terms of length and action was still a top priority. "People don't like ghost stuff and rules," Skaaren noted of the first draft, which expanded on the idea from McDowell's original script that Adam and Barbara get stuck in a kind of afterlife limbo after their deaths in a car accident. Eisner, Burton, and others who were reading the script also took issue with the ending, which had the sensitive Lydia remaining with the nurturing, deceased couple in the afterlife in lieu of staying on earth with her self-absorbed, superficial parents. Lydia's characterization also was problematic, according to the notes Skaaren received. "Too Madonna-ish," he was told, referring to the pop singer who was at the height of her popularity.[17]

As *Top Gun* began its domination at the box office that summer, Skaaren hunkered down for several months of rewrites on *Beetlejuice*. In addition to ongoing notes from Burton and Eisner, Skaaren heard from new Geffen hire David Bombyk, formerly an independent producer, as well as company founder David Geffen. The executives in particular expressed their concern about the character of Beetlejuice, wanting to know "who he is and what he represents" in the story. Bombyk suggested, for instance, that the out-of-control, slightly malevolent trickster could function as the Id to Adam and Barbara's Superego. The character of Lydia remained a concern as well. The executives wanted to change her from a young adolescent to an older teenager (presumably to appeal to the top demographic at the box office), and they feared her characterization lacked definition. "Poetic melancholy or a punkish type? Make her consistent in look and language," Bombyk told Skaaren.[18] While Burton meditated on the push to turn Lydia into a teenager, Skaaren struggled to stay focused on the revisions, faxing pages of new material to Geffen Company executives every few days.

In early July, Warner Bros. executives Lisa Henson and Mark Canton, vice president of worldwide motion picture production, met with Geffen's Eisner, Bombyk, and other "suits" to discuss progress on *Beetlejuice*. Notes from their meeting indicate misgivings about the story's clarity and focus and questions about Beetlejuice himself. "Is he the devil or an agent of the devil?" wondered one executive. Warner Bros. and Geffen again emphasized wanting Lydia to be written as a fourteen-year-old. Their overarching concern was expressed toward the end of the two-page interoffice memo: "The thrust of the story (the ghosts wanting to keep their house and the daughter they always wanted, and Lydia finding the parents that she had always wanted) becomes lost amidst the special effects and confusion. The humanity of the story must always prevail."[19] Burton, for one, felt the frustration he often experienced during studio meetings. "They say their normal things—'The third act needs work,' or 'It's too dark'—they have a list of ten things in the Studio Executive List of Comments. None of it has any bearing on how the fucking thing turns out!"[20]

Around this time Skaaren also touched base with *Beetlejuice*'s first screenwriter, Michael McDowell. Originally Skaaren drafted a lengthy letter to McDowell, explaining that he wanted to make contact to avoid a messy credit arbitration in the future. "My approach to this comes entirely from my experiences. They are two. One horrible. And one good," wrote Skaaren, referring to *Top Gun* and *Fire with Fire*, respectively.[21] Although it is unclear whether he sent the letter, he and McDowell, who lived in New England, did speak on the phone in mid-July. McDowell and Skaaren chatted easily about the project, and they were in agreement about sharing credit for the screenplay. McDowell revealed, however, that a Warner Bros. executive had told him that while they supported that decision, it would cost the studio an additional $50,000 in fees and, presumably, residuals, to split the credit between the writers. "He said repeatedly that I should share credit, and I would. He does not want this thing to go to arbitration," recalled Skaaren in notes he kept about the phone call.[22] During the conversation Skaaren told McDowell that on *Fire with Fire*, the shared credit helped the writers avoid an arbitration. "We all got credit, all got some money, and I think we added a lot to the strength of the creative class in Hollywood," Skaaren explained somewhat loftily. He described the more recent experience on *Top Gun* as "dehumanizing" and "upsetting." Clearly Skaaren was trying to avoid a similar situation on *Beetlejuice*, and he ended his phone call with McDowell confident that they were in agreement even if the studio was trying to create a divide between the two screenwriters.

Skaaren spent the remainder of July and August rewriting the script, sending a shorter, snappier second draft to Burton and the others. Coming in at 114 pages, the second draft addressed the problem of length by losing fifteen minutes of scenes and dialogue. It clarified Beetlejuice's "otherworldly" capabilities in a funny new introductory scene with Barbara and Adam, and Lydia's discovery of a ghost-oriented "handbook" seemed to alleviate concerns about making clear the rules and regulations that governed the afterlife.

Work on the project slowed as the summer drew to a close. Skaaren took some time to enjoy his growing wealth, perhaps heeding the advice he had once received from Tom Cruise to invest in real estate and other tangible assets. In late July he purchased a 1984 Mercedes 280 SL convertible for around $30,000. Skaaren, who stood more than six feet tall, looked almost comical crammed into the driver's seat of the compact two-door sports car, but the relatively frugal Norwegian loved the car and drove it every chance he got. While Burton worked on the *Beetlejuice* budget and storyboarded the existing draft, Skaaren turned his attention to a couple of other projects that had been percolating in the background. Earlier that summer, Skaaren had expressed concerns about protecting his time to agent Mike Simpson. Simpson addressed this in a memorandum to Geffen, reminding Bombyk and others that Skaaren's original agreement called for only a few weeks of work, thus necessitating an accounting for the writer's additional time on the project, which Simpson estimated was worth around $37,500.[23]

By the fall of 1986, *Lillie and Beck*, the Spanish Civil War project that Skaaren had been working on with writer-producer Doug Wick, had fallen victim to a management shakeup at Warner Bros. The project had been in development since the spring of 1985, with Paula Weinstein attached as a producer, but once Weinstein's boyfriend, executive Mark Rosenberg, was out at Warner Bros., it became clear that getting the period romance greenlit by a new string of executives would be an uphill battle. Wick knew Jane Fonda, and he and Skaaren had approached the Oscar-winning actress a year earlier about writing a script for her.[24] Fonda was enjoying a string of critical and commercial successes that included *On Golden Pond* (1981), *Agnes of God* (1985), and *The Morning After* (1986) in addition to her lucrative series of fitness books and workout videos. She was interested in doing a comedy after so many dramas, and in February 1986 an item appeared in Army Archerd's column in *Variety* announcing a project with Wick and Skaaren as writer-producers along with Lois Bonfiglio, an executive at Fonda's production company, Fonda Films.[25]

Although Skaaren's collaboration with Wick had begun before the release of *Top Gun* in May 1986, he had already grasped what the Simpson-Bruckheimer blockbuster could do for his career. In notes made sometime between 1985 and 1986, Skaaren observed that he needed to "consolidate the gains of *Top Gun*" by establishing himself as a writer and a producer. Skaaren also genuinely liked the Harvard-educated Wick, who was sharp and smart about the business but did not take it or himself too seriously. Once *Lillie and Beck* fell through, he saw the Fonda project as an opportunity to expand into production and continue working with Wick.[26]

After several meetings with Fonda, Skaaren and Wick began to tease out a story about Tracey, a jilted, well-to-do Connecticut housewife, and her new pal, Reno, whose street smarts and own dire straits inspire an unlikely alliance set within the wholesale diamond industry. As the story developed, Fonda approached Whoopi Goldberg about playing Reno. Goldberg also was enjoying recent success in Hollywood, having received a Golden Globe win and an Oscar nod for her stirring portrayal of Celie Johnson in *The Color Purple*. Goldberg wanted to work with Fonda and liked the idea of a female buddy movie. By mid-1986, she became loosely attached to the project, now called *Flawless*. "We came up with a story that, in a funny way, preceded *The First Wives Club* [1996]. Warren was ahead of it," says Wick of Skaaren's ability to tap into ideas that often came to fruition years later, such as the similarities between one of his earliest efforts, *Spooks*, and the release a decade afterwards of *Ghostbusters*.[27]

By mid-November 1986, *Flawless* had found a home at Columbia Pictures. Coincidentally, Columbia had hired a new chairman three months earlier, appointing independent British producer David Puttnam as head of production. Skaaren knew Puttnam, who had been on his short list for producing *Of East and West*. Although Puttnam had passed on that project, he had been generous in his praise of Skaaren's spec script about the Gurkha soldiers. *Variety* announced the *Flawless* deal, noting that Skaaren would be writing and producing with Wick and Bonfiglio.[28] Skaaren had been enjoying the break from *Beetlejuice* and the chance to work with Wick, but he was less enamored of Bonfiglio, who was also president of Fonda Films. When negotiations about his and Wick's level of involvement got mired in Columbia's bureaucracy, Skaaren suspected that Bonfiglio was needlessly complicating matters. In assessing the situation, he made a detailed list of what he perceived to be Bonfiglio's "patterns" of behavior and privately questioned her ability to produce. He resolved that he and Wick should "act like professionals and demand to be treated as professionals" as far as Columbia was concerned. He also decided that the best way to deal with what he saw as aggression from Bonfiglio was to "reassure Lois that she is ravishing and worthwhile and a needed part of the process."[29]

"I always thought of Warren as kind of a bastion of dignity in a sometimes crazy Hollywood world," recalls Wick. "He was calm, gentlemanly, and sometimes a little bit taken aback by some of the more vulgar sides of Hollywood." Once, they were in a pitch meeting with a movie star and the star's senior development executive, described by Wick as someone whom "Warren was tolerating but [who] was clearly very disinterested in their input":

> Warren was sitting in a chair across from the star, and the senior development executive got up to go to the bathroom. As they walked by Warren, just by coincidence he was sitting in such a way that their ass was about a quarter inch from his face, and as they walked out of the room they accidentally farted in his face. No one in the room said anything; I was trying really hard not to laugh. Obviously I spoke to him about it afterwards. He was just kind of calmly discussing it afterward, and it was just sort of indelible for me. Somehow it was almost a cartoon of Warren in Hollywood.[30]

Skaaren may have been gentlemanly, but he was not afraid to speak his mind in those types of meetings. This, says Wick, made him all the more

valuable as a rewriter. "It's a very special skill. Warren was sort of natu-
rally nonconfrontational, but he had a very strong point of view, so he
was able to listen to different people and understand their concerns."[31]
Skaaren also received a rather unusual offer around this time, one that
seemed to underscore his value to the film industry. Warner Bros. invited Skaaren to take an advisory position at the studio, created solely
for him, beginning in January 1987. The position as special assistant to
the president, which he could accept on a three-month trial basis, would
pay around $30,000 per month. While it's unclear whether Skaaren seri-
ously considered the offer, it most likely would have required a move to
Los Angeles, something that Skaaren resisted throughout his brief career
in Hollywood.[32]

After a couple of days in Los Angeles to meet with Wick, Skaaren
began working on a second draft of *Flawless*, enlivening the scenes between Tracey and Reno but trimming the script's length overall. He
also was back in contact with Tim Burton, who was moving ahead with
production on *Beetlejuice*. With that film scheduled to begin shooting
in mid-February 1987, Skaaren was focused on enhancing some of the
screenplay's key scenes, such as Beetlejuice's "demise" at the end of the
movie.

Reinvigorated by a mountain vacation in his beloved Santa Fe,
Skaaren resumed work on the *Flawless* revision after Christmas while
staying in touch with Burton about *Beetlejuice*, whose latest script revision was being timed and broken down into individual shots for the
start of production. In January, new Columbia chairman David Puttnam
weighed in on *Flawless*, suggesting a number of relatively minor changes
to the last act and wondering if *Gems* might not be a better title. "I think
you have accomplished a tremendous step forward with this new draft,"
Puttnam wrote encouragingly to Skaaren.[33] Puttnam's support mattered
little, however, when on January 30 Disney's Touchstone Pictures released *Outrageous Fortune*, a female buddy film costarring Bette Midler
and *Cheers* star Shelley Long. The comedy grossed more than $52 million
at the box office and effectively cooled Fonda's interest in *Flawless*. "It
was amazing how similar they were," agent Mike Simpson recalled of the
scripts for the Fonda project and *Outrageous Fortune*. "Jane Fonda saw
that movie and read that script and said, 'I'm out.'"[34]

All told, Skaaren had earned roughly $235,000 for his involvement
on *Flawless*.[35] If he was disappointed about Fonda's decision, he didn't
have much time to dwell on it. *Beetlejuice* was just weeks away from going into production, and Skaaren was faxing pages of revisions on an

almost daily basis to Tim Burton. Although Skaaren and Doug Wick would not have the opportunity to partner on another project after *Flawless*, the two stayed in touch. When Wick and his wife, Lucy Fisher's, first daughter was born in the summer of 1989, shortly after the release of *Batman*, Skaaren wrote a sweet letter to the infant, jokingly promising her a future job in Texas.[36]

Between February and May 1987, Burton was in production on *Beetlejuice* for approximately sixty days. Most of the film was shot on a Los Angeles soundstage, while exteriors and several scenes were filmed on location in East Corinth, Vermont. Skaaren was in Los Angeles for some of the shoot, particularly in the early weeks, when Burton asked him to work with the actors Catherine O'Hara and Jeffrey Jones, who had been cast as Lydia's self-absorbed parents. Skaaren was comfortable running lines with actors, which he had done on *Top Gun* when he sat in on rehearsals. O'Hara was a SCTV regular who had transitioned into film. Jones had played mostly dramatic roles prior to appearing in Rodney Dangerfield's *Easy Money* (1983), which showcased his comedic timing and led to a series of memorable appearances in films like *Ferris Bueller's Day Off* (1986) prior to *Beetlejuice*. Both expressed to Skaaren their discomfort with the "sense of non-reality" in the screenplay. "Kathy [*sic*] said her character was written as if witnessed from the outside. She wants more motivation and inside stuff . . . she wants more little things to play with, business," Skaaren noted of their meeting.[37] Three days later, Skaaren turned in twelve pages of script revisions that focused on the introduction of O'Hara's and Jones's characters, Delia and Charles Dietz, and seemed to address some of the actors' concerns.

Shortly after Skaaren's death, Burton joked about Skaaren's ability to write lines that only he could interpret. "My first meetings with Warren, he'd write this stuff, and there'd be a couple of things, and I was like, 'I don't understand it,' and then Warren would read it to me, and I'd go, 'Oh, I understand it now.'" An editor friend of Burton's, who had worked with Skaaren on an earlier project (most likely *Top Gun*), told the filmmaker that Skaaren made himself "invaluable" because no one else knew how to say his lines. Burton called it "a bizarre gift" that Skaaren could read his own dialogue so convincingly even though he wasn't even a "good actor."[38]

Production on the film continued through mid-May. According to press reports that appeared after the film opened in the spring of 1988, both Skaaren and first writer Michael McDowell were "retained" throughout the two months of production, and the two worked "in harmony" on the revisions.[39] Although Skaaren's notes don't necessarily reveal the extent of this collaboration, his relationship with McDowell as suggested through their correspondence did seem cordial and collaborative. By the end of August, WGA screen credits administrator Grace Reiner informed Warner Bros. that the Guild had assessed the story materials and proposed credit submitted by the studio. *Beetlejuice*'s final credits would read, "Story by Michael McDowell & Larry Wilson, Screenplay by Michael McDowell and Warren Skaaren."[40] It is unclear whether Skaaren's impulse to reach out to McDowell a year earlier made any difference in the final outcome, but it certainly gave Skaaren a sense of control over a situation in which he had once been badly burned.

Control was becoming more important to Skaaren by the late summer of 1987 in part because he seemed to be losing his bearings in his personal life. He was experiencing more tension in his relationship with Helen, who he felt had become increasingly dismissive of his career as a Hollywood rewrite man. In response, Skaaren had retreated into his work, which could keep him busy morning to night if he let it. The opportunity to purchase a new home also presented itself that summer. A year or so earlier, the Skaarens had become interested in a newly built property nestled on a secluded cul-de-sac with room for only a handful of other houses. It was called Wren Valley Cove. The discreet area appealed to Skaaren's sense of privacy, as did the fact that the lot itself backed up to the Wild Basin Wilderness Preserve, the same natural area that Skaaren's documentary *Breakaway* had benefited at its premiere screening a decade earlier. The real-estate deal had grown complicated, however, due to a lien on the house, described as an "elegant Italian villa" with four bedrooms and five and a half baths. Skaaren very much wanted the upscale property, which boasted details such as massive solid mahogany double doors in the entryway, wood-beamed ceilings, and handmade ironwork handrails and accents that reminded him of his father's craftsmanship as a welder. He asked a friend familiar with the practice to consult the *I Ching*, and he was advised that the situation represented "youthful folly" and that "something entangled" suggested that he was not being given all of the necessary information.[41] Reluctantly, Skaaren had pulled out of the deal.

But in July 1987, the property's builder contacted Skaaren with the news that the lien had been settled and the property was once again available. The house, situated on 1.3 acres but still only minutes from downtown Austin, was priced just under $790,000. Skaaren told friends at the time that he needed a place where he would feel comfortable hosting Hollywood types like Michael Douglas, with whom he had begun working on a sequel to *Jewel of the Nile* (1985) and who would occasionally come to Austin in lieu of Skaaren's flying back and forth to New York, where Douglas lived. Still, noted Skaaren intimate Amon Burton, the Skaarens' then-home in the same part of town, which had more than 2,000 square feet and a converted garage office for Skaaren, had plenty of room to accommodate overnight guests. Douglas had already stayed at the more modest property, as had Tim Burton and others. The Wren Valley property clearly represented something to Skaaren, perhaps a sign that he had arrived as a screenwriter, and he was determined to buy it.

Around this time, Skaaren jotted down a rather jarring observation: "A thought—could this chest mole discharge be from the computer screen?"[42] For the previous several months, perhaps longer, Skaaren had been aware of a lesion growing on his chest. He had confided only in Helen, whose antipathy toward Western medicine paralleled the attitude embraced by Skaaren's mother, Pearl, throughout his childhood. By August, however, Skaaren could no longer ignore the mole, which had grown large and discolored and whose bloody discharge had begun to seep through his button-down shirts. Finally he reached out to good friend and psychiatrist Bob Rynearson. "He opened his shirt up and here was this fungating melanoma. It didn't fit with the typical melanoma in terms of its color, but it looked malignant," he recalls. "Okay," a concerned Rynearson told Skaaren, "you've got to see a surgeon."[43]

On September 4, 1987, Skaaren met with Dr. Robert Fox, a local dermatopathologist, who examined the mole and did a biopsy. The diagnosis was spindle cell melanoma, and Dr. Fox advised Skaaren to have the mole and its surrounding area removed immediately and tested to see if the melanoma had spread. One of three types of skin cancer, melanoma can move quickly to other parts of the body. It is also the most deadly form of skin cancer. Five days later, plastic surgeon Dr. Jim Fox (no relation to Robert) performed surgery on Skaaren to remove the cancerous growth. As Dr. Fox anesthetized the area around the mole, Skaaren focused on jazz pianist Bill Evans's album *You Must Believe in Spring*, which he had requested be played during the surgery. The meditative album's tracks explored themes of loss and death. "The experience was not bad," Skaaren wrote of his surgery. "Dr. Fox was relaxed and funny. [The music] was truly beautiful."[44]

Skaaren appreciated the gravity of his diagnosis enough to schedule and undergo the surgery. Years later, he confided to a friend that he retreated inward after the operation and spent much of those first few days crying.[45] But as someone with a keen interest in macrobiotics, he wanted to learn about treating his cancer through holistic means. On the day Skaaren received the diagnosis from Dr. Robert Fox, he also called his friend Blake Gould, who had trained in holistic medicine in Japan for two years. Everything that Gould shared with Skaaren about macrobiotics' healing potential sounded promising. "Cancer is a symptom of excess, so avoid overeating. Cancer is a blood quality disease. Clean it up," Skaaren wrote after talking with Gould.[46] He reminded himself to chew his food slowly and mindfully, as many as 100–200 times per bite, and to avoid eating at least three hours before bedtime. A day prior to his surgery in Austin, Skaaren had made a call to the HolliBalance Well-Being Center in Boston, and he seems to have spent time at the center in the week or two following his surgery. Skaaren was choosing to pursue alternative means of healing despite being cautioned by his doctors and Rynearson that metastasis was likely and aggressive measures might be necessary. Ten days after Skaaren's surgery, Rynearson called his friend and offered to share the research he had gathered about the latest medical treatments being used to fight cancer. Skaaren thanked his friend but told him "I wanted to slow this whole medical process down. Wait a couple of weeks, strengthen myself."[47]

After the surgery, Skaaren had assured his wife that the doctor had given him a clean bill of health, but according to friends in whom he confided later, that wasn't the case. "It's my understanding now that the physician at that time really gave him all of the information about the prognosis, that early diagnosis is the key to a cure," said friend Diane Haug, who had hospice experience. "He essentially isolated himself for two to three weeks and just dove into his fear, his terror, went back and re-explored all of the threads of his life that might have contributed to the disease, just marshaled all of the inner resources he knew how to access in the spirit of really healing himself," she said of what Skaaren had told her about that period.[48] At the time of his diagnosis, however, Skaaren spoke to very few intimates about the situation. So successful was he at compartmentalizing his life that even Amon Burton and Skaaren's new assistant, Linda Vance, knew nothing of his illness.

Vance had been a history professor at Texas A&M University before moving to Austin in the early 1980s. Prior to assisting Skaaren, Vance had conducted research for an Austin-based professor who was working on a project for public television. When that project ended, she decided that she would seek out a research position in the entertainment field, if possible. Vance sent letters of introduction to several of Austin's top writers, including Skaaren. For a time she heard nothing back from him, but then not long after the release of *Top Gun*, he called her. Feeling overwhelmed by the day-to-day management of his fast-rising career, Skaaren hired Vance, who started in the fall of 1986.[49]

Tall and blonde with strong features, Vance clearly was intelligent, as evidenced by her first career as a history professor. She was also thoughtful, efficient, and discreet. She and Skaaren shared a similar sense of humor, and she quickly became a part of his working life. And yet, Skaaren was able to keep the mole, his diagnosis, and his subsequent surgery from Vance, who met with him almost every day and spoke with him by telephone as many as seven times a day. "How did he do it and I didn't know? It's a big question mark," Vance said later.[50] Looking back at the calendar she kept during that time, however, she noted a two- to three-week period in September 1987 where she recorded that Skaaren was on a trip in New England. It was during these weeks, she later realized, that he probably had had the surgery and then traveled to Boston to explore holistic treatment of his cancer.

"Seek balance, and you'll get better," Skaaren wrote after another consultation with Gould in mid-September.[51] Despite his various writing projects, Skaaren attempted to devote a significant portion of his time that fall to finding balance in his personal life. Vance recalls how Skaaren began to speak openly and frequently about macrobiotics, saying, "You know, people have been healed of cancer with this lifestyle." Vance, who tended to eat a relatively clean, mostly vegetarian diet anyway, began to join him occasionally for lunch at the East West Center, a local nonprofit dedicated to alternative health. "I think that was probably the time when he had put all of his marbles into the macrobiotics to heal him," Vance said.[52]

While Gould counseled Skaaren on living a cleaner lifestyle, other figures, such as therapist Dan Jones and members of a men's group, helped Skaaren to examine and shore up his inner life. He embraced the process of visualization, for instance, to revisit and confront past experiences and traumas. He intensified his lifelong habit of keeping a journal, recording his feelings, frustrations, and dreams on an almost daily basis. He wrote about feeling like a failure because of his relationship issues, particularly with Helen, despite his incredible career success. He was angry and alone, and he felt misunderstood and isolated. "Here is what is up for me to deal with," wrote a seemingly resigned Skaaren shortly before Thanksgiving in 1987, noting that he needed to confront his relationship issues with both genders, but especially with women. "Mother told me scary stories of the world to keep me close to her, to shore up her world view, to make me rescue her. I then set off to be with women in rescue situations."[53]

One visualization that Skaaren performed repeatedly during the fall of 1987 was something that he referred to as a "treasure map." In one scenario, Skaaren envisioned himself three years in the future, at home, confident and cured. He called it "The Ideal Scene": "A doctor calls and discovers what I already know. I am cancer-free, clean, balanced, vibrantly healthy and radiantly happy. I cry and thank the earth."[54] In an undated letter he wrote to his wife around this time, Skaaren drew parallels between the dysfunctional relationships in his life and his cancer. "Now I have seen a disease process in me which I know is related to my alienation—I'm not willing to die to maintain this house of denial."[55] Skaaren seemed committed to his recovery from cancer, but on his terms. His doctors, therapists, and macrobiotic counselors, all at separate times, had strongly encouraged Skaaren to take time off. He dutifully recorded their advice in his journals, telling himself, "Don't work so hard. Give myself time to enjoy my life." He was keen to carve out more time to be outdoors, and he wanted to devote himself to the "spiritual quest" that his cancer diagnosis had inspired. "Shift time from doing-ness to BEING ness," he wrote.[56]

Meanwhile, Skaaren's colleagues in Hollywood knew nothing of his illness or even that Skaaren had taken time off from his screenwriting duties. Even his agent, Mike Simpson, did not know what had transpired that September. Skaaren communicated through faxes and by phone when necessary, and as luck would have it, projects like *Beetlejuice* were moving forward on their own steam or were in a temporary lull. For a while, at least, it seemed as if Skaaren might be able to heed the advice to take it easy. But by January 1988, Geffen and Warner Bros. were test-marketing *Beetlejuice*, and Skaaren was called upon, along with Michael McDowell, to write additional scenes. Exit polls at special screenings showed that teenaged viewers loved Michael Keaton's performance as the titular character. The new scenes introduced Beetlejuice earlier in the film and included him in the closing credits. Interest in the film among this younger demographic also prompted Warner Bros. to move up the film's original release date, from late April to March 30, to take advantage of the Easter break.[57] Anticipation in the press was building as well. *Starlog*, a science-fiction magazine, plugged the film's upcoming release in its February issue, noting that "Burton directs from a screenplay by horror master Michael McDowell and legendary Hollywood rewrite man Warren Skaaren." Although Skaaren's name had occasionally appeared in Army Archerd's *Variety* column and in other trade papers, this was probably the first time he was described as something of a veteran writer.[58]

On March 7, just weeks before *Beetlejuice*'s opening weekend, approximately 9,000 members of the Writers Guild of America went on strike. The striking writers represented 96 percent of the Guild's film and television writers, and Skaaren was among them. Unlike the two-week work stoppage three years earlier, this strike seemed to surprise both sides, who until the very last minute had been negotiating such issues as residuals for hour-long television series and increased creative rights for writers that would give them a voice in the selection of actors and even directors for some projects. The contentious strike would last through August 7, a record twenty-two weeks.[59]

Inadvertently the strike would give Skaaren the time off that he had been counseled to take. He continued to pursue his spiritual healing through therapy appointments, journaling, and regular meetings of a men's group. He also kept busy with research for original scripts that he hoped to write, such as a possible adaptation of John Lee's self-help book *The Flying Boy: Healing the Wounded Man*, which dealt with Lee's struggle to free himself from dysfunctional and addictive relationships. There was also renewed interest in Skaaren's spec script *Of East and West*. British editor Garth Craven, who hoped to break into directing, was in touch with Skaaren that March about purchasing an option to direct the historical epic. Unlike some industry writers (and script doctors in particular), Skaaren's financial situation was quite comfortable by this point, even with the recent purchase of, and move into, his and Helen's spacious new home on Wren Valley Cove, so he didn't seem too bothered by the potential loss of income the ongoing strike represented. Skaaren also received good news from a friend in mid-March. Traveling in Oklahoma, the friend had consulted a psychic on Skaaren's behalf. "He said they had gotten 94% of cancer and it was okay," he noted in his journal.[60]

Beetlejuice's spectacular opening at the end of March brought more good news. The decision by Warner Bros. to release the film on a holiday weekend paid off. In less than a week of play, *Beetlejuice* grossed $8 million on 1,000 screens around the country, earning the number-one spot at the box office.[61] Twenty days later, the film remained in the top position, with more than $40.3 million in domestic grosses.[62] Skaaren's contract gave him a healthy 2.5% of the film's net profits, although he wouldn't see any of that money for at least a year due to the film's high production costs, which Warner Bros. estimated at more than $16 million.[63]

Skaaren flew to Los Angeles to attend the film's official premiere at the historic Grauman's Chinese Theatre on May 15. Skaaren photographed the theater's marquee and saved his oversized premiere ticket, which prominently displayed his and McDowell's writing credits. Skaaren was enjoying *Beetlejuice*'s box-office success and carefully kept track of the film's grosses as well as its critical reception. Pauline Kael gave the film one of its best reviews, lavishing praise on Keaton for his performance as Beetlejuice to the point that, she wrote, she wished he had been onscreen more often. "Still, the best of W. C. Fields was often half gummed up, and that doesn't seem to matter fifty-five years later. With crazy comedy, you settle for the spurts of inspiration, and 'Beetlejuice' has them," she wrote in her *New Yorker* review.[64] Critics seemed to fall into two camps about the film. One group, like Kael and Rita Kempley of the *Washington Post*, appreciated the film's wacky elements and was willing to go along for the ride. The other group, which included reviewers like Roger Ebert, wanted less of what Burton called a "weird kind of funny."[65] Ebert responded instead to Barbara and Adam, the deceased couple played by Geena Davis and Alec Baldwin, and wished for more screen time with them. "I would have been more interested if the screenplay had preserved their sweet romanticism and cut back on the slapstick," wrote Ebert in the *New York Post*.[66] Skaaren's early rewrites of the script did just that with the couple, but these tender opening scenes were later cut in favor of appealing to the teen viewers who clamored for more Keaton.

Skaaren expressed his frustration with some of the reviews (and their authors) to agent Mike Simpson, faxing a copy of Janet Maslin's negative *New York Times* review in which she described what would become a very popular scene of the characters "breaking into the 'Banana Boat' song for no reason." Skaaren underlined *for no reason* and scribbled, "This woman is a cretin."[67] More than a few of the critical assessments of the film tended to fault the script, such as Austin critic Kevin Phinney's review in the local paper. Under the headline "INVENTIVE IDEAS FRITTERED AWAY IN *BEETLEJUICE*," Phinney found the film too loose and unstructured and its wackiness unappealing despite its potential for humor and novelty. "There's enough creative waste in this movie to make two or three good ones," he wrote.[68] Even *Beetlejuice*'s distributor seemed to dismiss the story to some extent. In an unusually candid admission from the studio, Sandy Reisenbach, president of world-wide advertising and publicity at Warner Bros., told one journalist, "We sold the concept of the movie's tone, not the unwieldy story."[69]

Burton seemed to take the negative reviews in stride. He sounded almost gleeful in a *Rolling Stone* interview a few months after the film's release, while it was still among the top hits at the box office. "These bland newscasters, they have to show a clip—and I don't care what anybody says, it makes me wanna see the movie," said Burton. "It's like [you're] watching some hallucination, like somebody putting something else behind them that they don't know about. It was like the feeling I got when I saw Andy Warhol on *The Love Boat*."[70] If there was any doubt that *Beetlejuice* and its success had made an impact on the popular culture of the time, the satirical *Cracked* magazine clarified the situation. "Warren, you're parody-able," wrote Warner Bros. executive Bonni Lee on the copy she sent to Skaaren, featuring a *Beetlejuice*-inspired cover with a character dubbed "Spittlejuice."[71]

As the writers' strike continued into the summer, Skaaren took advantage of the downtime to pursue a growing interest in songwriting. Earlier that year, Skaaren had been seated next to George Harrison on a flight to Los Angeles, and he struck up an occasional correspondence with the former Beatle in which they discussed music, books, and their outdoor hobbies. Skaaren had always dabbled in music and kept a keyboard, a guitar, and other assorted instruments in his office. In the wake of the ongoing strike, however, he began to pursue songwriting in earnest. He and Ed Rynearson, the musically inclined son of Skaaren's psychologist friend Bob, partnered on a number of compositions. Skaaren seemed especially interested in pursuing writing for the music business, and he worked his industry contracts to arrange meetings with the appropriate agents. He also consulted with his own agent about the possibility of adding a clause to future screenwriting contracts that would give him some say in the project's soundtrack development.

Skaaren's activities during the 1988 writers' strike suggest that he was interested in leveraging his success as a script doctor. Four years in to what even he was hesitant to call a career, given the finicky nature of the film business and, perhaps, his own ambivalence about making so much money "fixing" screenplays, Skaaren seemed to be taking stock of his creative life. Expanding into a producer's role and having a say in a project's musical development were two areas of potential interest for him. He was also eager to nurture his spiritual growth while being aware that the intense and occasionally shallow nature of his work might make this difficult. "I have been avoiding my true power," Skaaren wrote, somewhat cryptically, during this time. "I can love the world and make a change in the hearts of people. I've always been able to do it. But for years I've avoided it. I've come close to misusing my gift. Thank god I've got another chance."[72] His parents' fiftieth wedding anniversary that summer, which Morris and Pearl were celebrating with a family party in Rochester, gave Skaaren the opportunity to practice some of the healthier behaviors he had been exploring through therapy. Skaaren and Helen attended the party in late June. At the time, they were experiencing renewed tension within their own marriage over what Warren described as the "seemingly huge differences between them," which encompassed everything, in his view, from the way they handled angry feelings to their travel and eating preferences. He was hopeful, he wrote to Helen before the trip, that they could support one another during their time in Rochester, "and then we can have a happy 50th anniversary in the year 2019!" During the anniversary party, Skaaren spoke warmly about his parents' relationship despite his conflicted feelings about their dynamic and the way he thought it shaped how he himself approached relationships. Privately, he viewed the event as a "celebration of my independence from them."[73]

Beetlejuice continued to dominate the box office that summer, eventually grossing more than $70 million in the United States alone. By the fall, the film had begun its overseas run, screening in the United Kingdom and Australia and earning just under $1 million and $500,000, respectively, during its opening weekends in each location. Other international cities continued to open the film into 1989. So popular was the film, in fact, that Geffen and Warner Bros. partnered on a line of toys and other merchandise that included action figures, trading cards, and stickers. Plans were in the works before the end of 1988 to produce an animated television series, which premiered in the fall of 1989. Although Skaaren wasn't involved in the writing of the television program, he would play a key role in the development of a *Beetlejuice* sequel two years later.

In the months following *Beetlejuice*'s 1988 premiere, Skaaren enjoyed tracking the film's success. It would eventually become the top-grossing movie of the year. By the fall of 1989, Skaaren had made nearly $100,000 in residuals from the film, but what he seemed most satisfied with was the lack of drama surrounding the film's screenwriting-credit arbitration. It certainly helped that Skaaren received what he considered to be the appropriate shared credit, unlike his arbitration experience on

Top Gun two years earlier when his name was left off the writing credits. But for Skaaren, who believed in the power of karma and wanted to be thought of as not just a top Hollywood script doctor but also a valued colleague, he was especially pleased that on *Beetlejuice* he shared credit with Michael McDowell, who had been one of the project's original writers. The two writers had maintained a cordial relationship, even as they both were retained by Burton and the studio to work on the film virtually right up until its release.[74] "Someday the energy will come back around," Skaaren wrote to McDowell in the summer of 1986. "Either from me or from you or from Tim or the studio. But what goes around comes around."[75]

SIX

One Hit After Another

Warren is a professional. He's an exceedingly well-adjusted,
even-tempered human. There's no attitude or hidden agenda.
That makes him extremely productive.

PRODUCER DON SIMPSON

L inda Vance's telephone rang late one night in the fall of 1986.
A few weeks earlier Warren Skaaren had called Vance in
response to a letter she had sent offering her services as a re-
searcher and an assistant. Skaaren had essentially interviewed her over
the phone. She thought the conversation had gone well, but weeks went
by and she hadn't heard from him. Then she received his late-night
phone call.

"Can you be at my office by 10 A.M. tomorrow?" Skaaren asked.

When Vance arrived at the converted garage behind his and Helen's
ranch-style house the next morning, Skaaren pointed to a thick document lying on his desk. He needed it formatted onto a floppy disk so that
it was compatible with his new Macintosh Plus.

"Can you do it?" Skaaren asked.[1]

The document was an early draft of *Beverly Hills Cop II*, which
Skaaren had brought back to Austin after meeting with Jerry Bruckheimer and Don Simpson in Los Angeles. The *Top Gun* producers were
barely a month out from production on the sequel to the original *Beverly
Hills Cop*, a fish-out-of-water action movie that starred Eddie Murphy
as Detroit cop Axel Foley. Released in December 1984, *Cop* had made
back its $14 million production budget on its opening weekend and
would eventually gross $350 million worldwide.[2] The film also secured

the twenty-two-year-old Murphy's successful transition from stand-up comedian and *Saturday Night Live* cast member to certified movie star. Martin Brest had directed the film and, according to Hollywood lore, was so ambivalent about the project that he flipped a coin to decide whether or not to be involved. He was more decisive about turning down *Cop II*, so Bruckheimer and Simpson reteamed with *Top Gun* director Tony Scott, whose sleek, glossy aesthetic was more in line with the producers' high-concept storytelling. In print, at least, Simpson and Bruckheimer declined to call the follow-up a sequel. "This is more like a series, like Indiana Jones or James Bond," Simpson told one interviewer once the film had gone into production, comparing Axel Foley to two well-known (and profitable) franchise characters. "Eddie goes to different places and has different adventures."[3]

The screenplay for *Cop II* already had had an interesting journey when the team approached Skaaren in 1986. Unbeknownst to him at the time, fellow Austin writer Bud Shrake had done a first pass with his *Sports Illustrated* colleague Dan Jenkins a year earlier. Next came writer Larry Ferguson, who had most recently scripted the action film *Highlander* (1986). Dennis Klein was working on a revision when Simpson and Bruckheimer reached out to Skaaren in early October. Klein, who would work in tandem with Skaaren but on separate parts of the script, was a veteran teleplay writer and former staff writer for Francis Ford Coppola's Zoetrope Studios. Given the culture of development in 1980s Hollywood, the producers and the studio felt reassured by hiring multiple writers for a project, particularly one as high-concept as an action sequel. To Simpson in particular, it just made good business sense. "We had 10 screenwriters on *Top Gun* and 11 on *Beverly Hills Cop II*," Simpson boasted in an article about why he and Bruckheimer pulled out of a bidding war to adapt Scott Turow's bestseller *Presumed Innocent* shortly before *Cop II* opened in 1987. A "good" producer, said Simpson, should spend at least $1.5 million on screenwriters for an adaptation like Turow's.[4]

As with *Top Gun*, Simpson and Bruckheimer contacted Skaaren at a particularly crucial point in *Cop II*'s development. Weeks away from a start date, the producers had a star dissatisfied with the script for an expensive sequel that had the potential to be another blockbuster as long as Murphy didn't walk. They trusted that Skaaren could salvage the script's flimsy structure and pump up Foley's characterization. They also knew Skaaren could work quickly. The deal was a good one: Skaaren would be paid approximately $300,000 for what was supposed to be two weeks of work and would receive 2.5 percent of the film's net profits. Despite some residual bitterness regarding his credit arbitration experience on *Top Gun*, Skaaren generally enjoyed working with Simpson and Bruckheimer and thought that he could leverage his *Top Gun* credit to greater advantage on his deal for *Cop II*.

At that time, in the fall of 1986, he was working on *Flawless* for Jane Fonda but on a break from *Beetlejuice*, so he had room in his schedule for a two-week pass on the *Cop II* screenplay. But by then Skaaren knew enough to realize that the two-week window proposed by Simpson and Bruckheimer probably would run longer, particularly with a demanding star like Murphy. Still, Skaaren was game. And while Skaaren's involvement with the project would indeed prove profitable—*Cop II* would become 1987's top-grossing feature—the ensuing screen-credit arbitration would make his *Top Gun* experience pale in comparison. The battle over screenwriting credit on *Cop II* would pit Skaaren against some of the other writers, including his Austin friend Bud Shrake, and it would eventually devolve into a lawsuit described as one of the most "prominent legal challenges" in screen-credit arbitration history.[5] Although Skaaren prevailed in the end, the case itself would outlast even him, continuing on appeal for months after his death.

Back in early October 1986, however, Skaaren's main concern was having a formatted copy of the current *Beverly Hills Cop II* draft on his home computer. Vance's first week as Skaaren's assistant was a flurry of tasks that included everything from picking up his dry cleaning and handling his banking to faxing Skaaren's notes on the 100-plus-page *Cop II* script sheet by sheet to Simpson and Bruckheimer's office in Los Angeles. At the end of her first two weeks on the job, Vance took advantage of a lull in the activity to sit down with her new employer. "I'm Linda Vance," she said, poking fun at the intense pace of her new position. "My name's Warren Skaaren," he replied with a smile. "It was that wild in the first week and a half that I worked for him," said Vance in the year following his death. "From there on, it was just one hit after another."[6]

Writers Daniel Petrie Jr. and Danilo Bach had received an Academy Award nomination for *Beverly Hills Cop*'s screenplay and story, respectively. It is unclear whether or not they worked on a follow-up, but within approximately eight months of *Cop*'s 1984 release, Simpson and Bruckheimer had hired Bud Shrake and his colleague Dan Jenkins to draft the sequel. Shrake and Jenkins wrote a script in which Foley returns to Beverly Hills and goes undercover to investigate suspicious activity at a warehouse. They submitted the script in late December 1985. Titled *Bev-*

erly Hills Security Guard, the follow-up reportedly didn't appeal to Murphy. Simpson and Bruckheimer soon became consumed with *Top Gun*, and Shrake and Jenkins had other projects in the works, which effectively ended their involvement in the *Cop* sequel.[7]

According to executives at Paramount Pictures, which released the film, Murphy and his manager, Robert Wachs, pitched a story idea for the sequel to producer David Kirkpatrick on February 24, 1986.[8] By August, press reports about the film were still describing it as Murphy going undercover as a security guard in Beverly Hills to investigate the theft of a military weapon.[9] From May to September of that year, however, writer Larry Ferguson worked on multiple drafts of the screenplay based on the idea credited to Murphy and Wachs, in which Axel Foley returns to Beverly Hills to try to solve a series of crimes that have nearly killed his good friend Chief Bogomil, lead investigator on the case. While Ferguson's drafts gave structure to the initial idea, the pacing was slow and the characterizations weak in spots. Ferguson's female characters, in particular, were crude caricatures. "Her huge gowangas hang over shimmering candlelight," was how Ferguson described one female character in the script.[10]

By late September, Simpson and Bruckheimer had stopped returning Ferguson's phone calls.[11] At that point, they had moved on to veteran writer Dennis Klein. Beginning in the early 1970s, Klein had written episodes for various television comedies, such as *The Odd Couple* and *All in the Family*, and was head writer on the series *Mary Hartman, Mary Hartman*. Simpson and Bruckheimer charged Klein with punching up the script's comedic scenes and consolidating the story so that Axel's return to Beverly Hills happened earlier in the script. Murphy, a seasoned stand-up performer, was known to go "off book" and improvise his own very funny lines during production, particularly while making features. It seems likely that the push to tighten the screenplay was coming more from the studio than from the producers. Between the release of the first *Cop* and the start of production on the sequel, Paramount had undergone a changing of the guard, with Frank Mancuso replacing Barry Diller as chairman of the studio. Simpson and Bruckheimer, however, had worked with Murphy before and most likely were less concerned about the comedic elements of Axel's dialogue being sharpened prior to shooting than they were about the overall structure of the story and being able to pin down locations and a shooting schedule (and thus a budget) based on a revised script.

Skaaren approached the *Cop II* script as he did every rewrite. He first made a flow chart of the existing draft's major scenes so that he could have a visual sense of the story's pacing and development. He made note of weak transitions and potential plot problems as he added new scenes during the rewrite process. He also looked for one-dimensional characterizations, as he had been charged with adding more humanity to Murphy's Foley. After reading yet another crude physical description of a female character in Ferguson's draft, Skaaren scribbled in the margin, "No real women. No softness."[12]

Within a week of coming on to the project, Skaaren sent Bruckheimer and Simpson an outline for the film's opening that immediately established Foley's tight relationship with his Beverly Hills friend and mentor, Chief Bogomil, and facilitated Axel's arrival in Beverly Hills. Using eight beats, or separate scenes, Skaaren set up the pair's long-standing friendship, introduced a threat to that relationship by having Bogomil shot while investigating a case, and created a need for Foley to leave Detroit and return to Beverly Hills.[13] As Skaaren would later explain in his statement to the WGA Arbitration Committee members, one of his "challenges" on the project was to "solve the main motivational engine of all sequels: Why would Axel Foley and the Beverly Hills Cops reconvene?"[14] The new opening addressed this, and the team in Los Angeles gave Skaaren the green light to flesh out the opening and revise the existing draft.

As Linda Vance recalled, the periods during which Skaaren was working on any screenplay were intense, but films like *Cop II*, a project in crisis and headed into production, were especially stressful. It would not be unusual for Skaaren to receive phone calls from Los Angeles every three hours during the workday. Between October 8 and October 17, when Skaaren submitted his first draft, he immersed himself in the existing screenplay, originally written by Ferguson, and focused on designing a strong "detective" story around the original idea of a series of crimes associated with the alphabet. It was also his responsibility, ultimately, to create deeper characters whose motivations were more clearly defined, to ease the story through its transitions from scene to scene, and to "increase the warmth, the comedy, and the suspense" of the existing draft.[15] In the memo that accompanied his first draft, Skaaren noted, "In five days I have only laid out the story beats. I have not attempted to re-fashion the characters. Nor have I addressed length. That's next. Goodnight, muthers!"[16] On Saturday, October 18, Skaaren held a conference call with producers Simpson and Bruckheimer. They liked some of Skaaren's changes and additions, such as an early scene in which Foley in Detroit and Bogomil in Beverly Hills have a friendly telephone chat about an upcoming fishing trip, which established their ongoing friendship. They also liked Skaaren's suggestion to introduce a new character, Jan, Bogomil's twenty-something daughter, who would interact with Foley once her father was shot and emphasize Foley's close relationship to the family. Simpson later expressed qualms, however, about Jan's agency in the third act and its potential effect on Murphy's star turn, telling Skaaren, "Her activeness takes away from Foley."[17] Director Tony Scott also chimed in on the first draft, angling for more action and, specifically, suggesting that a scene be shot on location at the Playboy Mansion. (The scene, in which Hugh Hefner makes a cameo appearance and Playboy bunnies compete in a friendly volleyball game, was similar in its cheesecake tone to the volleyball scene in *Top Gun*, which featured Tom Cruise, Val Kilmer, and other shirtless young actors. It had been Scott's idea as well.)

Time was of the essence, and Skaaren had a second version of the script drafted within three days. He finished a third draft later that same week, making the bulk of his changes to the development of the script's second act. By November 5, production had begun. A second-unit camera crew filmed exteriors in Detroit, but the majority of the *Cop* sequel was shot throughout Los Angeles on location at sites such as the Max Factor Museum on North Highland Avenue, which stood in for a jewelry store where one of the earliest alphabet crimes takes place. The *Cop II* shoot lasted approximately three and a half months, and Skaaren was on call to revise existing scenes and write new ones throughout filming. Two days before the end of the year, in fact, Skaaren was faxing pages that compressed the film's opening scenes into one.[18] This continued even into postproduction, with changes being made to scenes as late as March 1987, two months prior to the film's Memorial Day weekend release.

After a New Year's trip with Helen to Santa Fe, Skaaren returned to Austin in January 1987 ready to tackle a full plate of projects that included *Cop II*, the ongoing *Flawless* project with writer-producer Doug Wick for Jane Fonda, and Tim Burton's *Beetlejuice*, which would begin shooting in mid-February. The new year also presented Skaaren with the opportunity to do original work. In mid-January, Skaaren met the actor Michael Douglas, who was interested in developing a follow-up to the adventure-romance films *Romancing the Stone* (1984) and *The Jewel of the Nile* (1985), in which Douglas costarred with Kathleen Turner. The critical and financial success of the pair's *Romancing the Stone*, which had introduced audiences to Douglas as a washed-up explorer and Turner as a lonely romance novelist, led immediately to *Jewel,* in which the pair continue their adventures as a couple struggling to adjust to a relatively low-key married life until the next adventure comes along.

Douglas was a successful producer (beginning with *One Flew Over the Cuckoo's Nest* in 1975) and a shrewd businessman in addition to being a second-generation Hollywood movie star (the son of actor Kirk Douglas), and Skaaren was eager to meet with him. As was his way, Skaaren prepared extensively for their first meeting. He devoted hours to watching the earlier films on videotape in addition to other similarly successful action-adventure films of the time, such as *Indiana Jones and the Temple of Doom* (1984). Then he analyzed the scripts, breaking them down into their major sequences.[19] Skaaren also prepared an outline that sketched out his work habits ("Left brain/right brain. Do character outlines. Do basic beats") and ideal interpersonal dynamics ("Collaborator. With a FEW good men. Have fun. Good spirit. No games.").[20] His and Douglas's first meeting took place over two days in late January, with Douglas stopping in Austin en route from Los Angeles. Their discussion was easy and wide-ranging, covering each other's personal and professional backgrounds as well as Douglas's goals for the project. The film, which would eventually be called *Crimson Eagle,* was to be shot on location in Asia and would center on Jack (Douglas) and Joan's (Turner) efforts to expose a black-market rare-animal ring run by the Chinese mob.

Skaaren's agent Mike Simpson began working out the details of his client's deal even before that first meeting in Austin. At the time Douglas had a production deal with 20th Century-Fox, and that studio would be financing Skaaren's work on *Crimson Eagle.* Skaaren would receive $500,000 for all writing services up until the start of principal photography, which was tentatively scheduled for 1988, the following year. Bonuses for sole writing credit and a proposed 5 percent of the film's net profits were also on the table. The writing schedule allowed Skaaren sixteen weeks to deliver the first draft of the screenplay, eight weeks to complete the revisions, and another month to finish any additional revisions.[21]

Two weeks after meeting Michael Douglas, Skaaren flew to New York. On February 2 he met Kathleen Turner at her manager David Guc's office, where they discussed the *Crimson Eagle* story. Turner was straightforward about Joan, her character, and what she envisioned for Joan and Jack's relationship in the film. While Skaaren's introduction and subsequent conversation with Turner went well, he and Douglas seemed truly to have developed a rapport and to enjoy each other's company. They met the following day at Douglas's Upper West Side apartment on the corner of 75th Street. Skaaren took pages of notes during their conversation, jotting down script-related questions that veered from the inane ("How many words can a parrot say in a row?") to more substantive matters. Skaaren returned to Austin and within a week had written a six-page outline for the *Crimson Eagle* screenplay. Set in New York and Hong Kong, the story quickly establishes the marital conflicts between Jack and Joan as well as the theft from a New York zoo of a pair of exotic eagles and a rare and valuable eaglestone. Within Eastern cultures the eaglestone, a hollow geode, was thought to be a source of virility and offer protection during childbirth. It could be found in the nests of eagles and had tremendous value on the black market. The theft intrigues Jack, and he encourages a rather reluctant Joan to make it the subject of her next novel. Together the couple embark on an adventurous trip to Hong Kong to find the missing crimson eagles and recover the valuable stone, fixing their frayed marriage in the process.[22]

Skaaren shared the outline with both Douglas and Turner, and two weeks later he faxed Douglas five pages of a rough first draft.[23] That same month, he and Douglas met in Los Angeles to discuss another potential project. Douglas was interested in reviving the 1960s television series *Mission: Impossible*, either as a television reboot or as a feature film, and he had asked Skaaren to come on board as a producer and writer. While in L.A., they met to discuss the idea with veteran producer Leonard Goldberg, who had a long track record of successful television projects, including *Charlie's Angels*, *Fantasy Island*, and *Hart to Hart*.[24]

Also in February, Skaaren momentarily turned his attention back to *Beetlejuice*, which was about to begin shooting, and to *Beverly Hills Cop II*, which was in postproduction. He also received word around this time that Paramount Pictures had submitted tentative writing credits for *Cop II* to the Writers Guild of America, a step that was typical for studios preparing a film for an upcoming release. The credits read "Written by Larry Ferguson and Warren Skaaren," giving the writers shared credit for the story and screenplay. The accompanying list of participating writers included Bud Shrake, Dan Jenkins, Larry Ferguson, David Giler, Dennis Klein, and Skaaren. On March 3, the studio and the writers received a notice from the WGA that Ferguson had protested the shared credit, an action that automatically triggered an arbitration, according to Guild rules. By now Skaaren was all too familiar with the process. He and the other writers had the option to submit a statement that detailed their contributions to the screenplay. Only the three anonymous arbiters chosen from the Guild's membership were permitted to read the statements. They were not made available to the other writers whose credit was at stake.

Skaaren submitted a nineteen-page statement that documented his contributions to *Cop II*'s shooting script and the drafts leading up to it. In addition to original dramatic construction (new scenes, new relationships, etc.) and original characterization (new characters and the scenes their presence facilitated), Skaaren drew the arbiters' attention to the original dialogue that he had contributed. "It is a mathematical consequence of my having written so many new scenes (fifty-one new scenes) that I originated a large percentage of dialogue. Also, due to the nature of comedy writing, I RE-WROTE a good portion of the remaining dialogue in the film. Examples are throughout the script and too numerous to detail," he wrote, possibly in response to a claim by Ferguson that Skaaren's work concerned mostly dialogue as opposed to more substantial changes to the story itself.[25] According to Guild rules, dialogue is low on the list of elements to be considered in determining screenplay credit because it is an area that can be easily altered by subsequent writers, or "fixers," but may contribute no "substantive change" to the overall script.[26]

Skaaren was also occupied during this time with preparations for a ten-day trip to Asia. As part of the *Crimson Eagle* project, Skaaren had agreed to undertake a research trip to Hong Kong and nearby islands. As with *Flawless*, Skaaren's role on *Crimson Eagle* seemed to include some producing duties, and the Hong Kong trip functioned not just as research for the screenplay but also as a location scout. He referenced his notes from a January phone conversation with Linda Vance's uncle James Polk for deep background on the city's drug and black-market activities as well as those of the rest of China, which by 1987 was cultivating a more prominent role in the U.S. heroin trade. Polk had done customs work for the Office of Strategic Services (the OSS was the precursor to the CIA) during World War II and had been stationed in Hong Kong for a part of his postwar career. A few weeks before Skaaren's late March departure, Douglas flew into Austin for another script meeting. Still working from his six-page outline, Skaaren and Douglas tossed around ideas in the Skaarens' modest living room. "He wants Jack looser, more raucous," Skaaren scribbled on one page, referring to one of Douglas's suggestions. "Think about Crocodile Dundee," he added in the margin.[27]

The itinerary of Skaaren's overseas trip was designed in part to expose him to Hong Kong's occasionally sordid nightlife in order to write convincing villains for this third film in the *Romancing the Stone* series.

In the weeks leading up to his departure, Skaaren received, as did the other *Cop II* writers, a list of written materials submitted by the studio to the WGA detailing each writer's contributions. Skaaren was surprised to note that the studio was crediting some of his revisions in the final shooting script to the film's producers. He faxed a letter to the WGA's Grace Reiner, screen credits administrator, alerting her to the mistake and providing materials to substantiate his claim. He left Austin on March 23 uncertain of how the *Cop II* situation would play out.[28]

Skaaren landed in Hong Kong on March 25. He met his driver, John Lam, and they made their way to The Regent, an upscale hotel on Salisbury Road in Kowloon's business and tourist district. Popular hostess clubs like Club Volvo, Red Lips, and Bottoms Up, which catered to well-off businessmen and offered escorts as well as karaoke, were close by. Kowloon was also home to the Walled City, a densely packed area measuring approximately six and a half acres whose population had increased dramatically after World War II. Two months earlier, in January 1987, the Hong Kong government had announced plans to demolish the enclave, which had once been a Chinese military fort. At the time of Skaaren's visit, the population of the Walled City was approximately 33,000. "Perfect flight with rice and shitake on board. Room with a view," Skaaren telegrammed to Helen upon his arrival.[29]

Within the first few days of his arrival, Skaaren established a routine of waking up and walking around the city for a couple of hours before meeting up with his local guide, a quiet but friendly man named David Huang. Skaaren meandered along the narrow city streets that were crowded with fruit and vegetable markets, storefront butchers, and small manufacturing operations that produced metalwork and other materials. As he would do throughout the trip, he spoke into a tape recorder, observing the many small houses they passed and generally taking note of the everyday customs and traditions being practiced in the region.

On Friday, March 27, guide David Huang arranged for Skaaren to meet with Gregory Noo, who was the chief detective in charge of a special forces unit for the Hong Kong police. Over dinner Noo explained to Skaaren that his area of expertise was to "run" the group of informers (gang members, prisoners, etc.) whom the police relied on for information about the drug trade, black-market activities, and other illegal goings-on. After dinner the group went to Apollo 18, a popular club, where Noo filled in Skaaren on the animal and reptile smuggling trade. Skaaren would later use details from their conversation to flesh out smuggling scenes in the *Crimson Eagle* script. He took note of the club scene in general, paying particular attention to the guests singing karaoke, a popular pastime. Skaaren would eventually write a scene in which a heavily made-up and costumed Joan (Turner) charms the smugglers by singing at the club.[30]

The following day Skaaren and his guide spent the morning on Herb Street. The narrow thoroughfare was bordered on each side by hundreds of herb shops and stalls. Aggressive proprietors cajoled and made deals with customers. Large bins and baskets of dried herbs sat next to containers holding horses' bladder stones, tigers' penises, and dried lizards on lollipop sticks. That same day Skaaren and Huang visited the cacophonous Bird Street, another crowded space that had potential as a *Crimson Eagle* location, particularly for a dynamic chase sequence. But given that the film's plot turned on the disappearance of the valuable crimson eagles, Skaaren was most interested in the goods for sale on Bird Street. Sellers had all types of birds, from beautiful parakeets and adorable baby ducks to rare eagles and the more exotic Chinese *hwamei*, or painted eyebrow bird.[31]

On Monday, March 30, Skaaren traveled with his driver, John Lam, from Hong Kong to mainland China. Lam knew some plot details about the *Crimson Eagle* project and offered to take Skaaren across the border to see trappers, sellers, and other elements of the illegal animal trade. They traveled two hours to the border and made their way by car up a steep and rutted mountain road. The animal market was set up on the outskirts of a village, hidden away behind market stalls selling fresh produce and dried herbs. Round wire cages set low to the ground contained a variety of snakes, such as cobras, rattlers, and black mountain snakes. Another stall sold dog meat and displayed a number of dead chow dogs, their hair singed off. Much to his surprise, Skaaren's "sophisticated" driver purchased eight snake bladders, which he then had cleaned and "purified" with rice wine. Lam told Skaaren that the snake bile was believed to guard against poor eyesight and also was thought to bring men virility. Lam drank half a glass and passed it to Skaaren, who finished the strong concoction to be polite, much to the delight of the villagers who had gathered to watch. The experience of witnessing so much "primitive cruelty" depressed Skaaren, but he struck a more manly tone in the telegram he sent to Michael Douglas: "Been on trail of animal smugglers. Yesterday in mountains of people's republic. I found them. Eagles and all. Be back US Friday."[32]

Several days after his return to Austin, Skaaren wrote a letter to guide David Huang in Kowloon, thanking him and his wife, Ann, for their hospitality and help during his stay in Hong Kong. He had almost rebounded from his jet lag, and he was busy organizing research notes and dozens of photographs to bring along when he next met with Douglas. Skaaren ended his letter to Huang with a postscript: "It appears that I WILL get the screenplay credit on Beverly Hills Cop II—What luck!"[33]

That situation was about to change, however. During Skaaren's overseas trip, Paramount had submitted to the WGA a revised notice of tentative writing credits that read, "Story by Eddie Murphy & Robert D. Wachs, Screenplay by Larry Ferguson and Warren Skaaren." Skaaren had been surprised to learn that Paramount claimed Murphy and Wachs were "inadvertently omitted from the original notice" of writing credits. As evidence of their contribution, the studio had submitted a memorandum from executive David Kirkpatrick, dated February 24, 1986, outlining the *Cop II* story idea as pitched by Murphy and Wachs. The memo included a handwritten statement by Wachs, Murphy's manager, dated March 23, 1987, that read in part, "I confirm that this is an accurate presentation of the story conceptualized by Eddie Murphy and me."[34] Shortly after his return from Hong Kong, Skaaren wrote a letter to the WGA's Reiner suggesting that "since all the writers (and their associates) have now become thoroughly familiar with the elements of the final screenplay, I urge that your office use special scrutiny on any new alleged material, outlines, memos, etc."[35] Although he didn't say as much, clearly Skaaren was questioning the authenticity in particular of the Kirkpatrick memo that supported the studio's giving story credit to Murphy and Wachs.

Larry Ferguson took the matter one step further. He contacted the WGA and requested that the organization's Policy Review Board examine the situation. Ferguson's claim, submitted through a lawyer, stated that "there was a misinterpretation, misapplication and/or violation of Guild Policy" in two distinct ways.[36] Ferguson took issue with the fact that Murphy and Wachs, as production executives on the project, were unable according to the terms outlined in the WGA's *Screen Credits Manual* to receive any kind of writing credit while also serving as producers. While this was technically true, the matter became less clear because the pair was being awarded story credit and were not claiming screenplay authorship per se. Ferguson's second point referred directly to Skaaren's credit, which Ferguson disputed based on the 33 percent rule stipulating that for a writer to share writing credit his or her contributions must equal or exceed 33 percent of the entire screenplay. Skaaren may have agreed with Ferguson's protest over Murphy's and Wachs's story credit, but he was furious that Ferguson was challenging his co-screenwriting credit. This second matter, however, did not concern the WGA. When a writer makes an appeal to the Policy Review Board, the board (made up of the chair or vice-chair and any two other members of the Screen Credits Committee) has only one concern: "to determine whether or not, in the course of the credit determination, there has been any serious deviation from the policy of the Guild or the procedure as set forth" in the *Screen Credits Manual*.[37] Unlike a screenwriting-credit arbitration, the policy review process is a matter that is handled internally among Guild staff. The screenwriters involved are not allowed to submit Statements of Contribution or the like. In the case of *Cop II*, Ferguson, Skaaren, and the others affected by the determination of the writing credits would have to wait to hear the board's final determination.

On April 28, the WGA sent a letter to the studio and all of the individuals involved in the *Cop II* writing arbitration notifying them that the Policy Review Board had found "no evidence of misinterpretation, misapplication or violation of Guild policy." As far as the WGA was concerned, the matter was closed, and *Cop II*'s official writing credits would read: "Screenplay by Larry Ferguson and Warren Skaaren, Story by Eddie Murphy and Robert D. Wachs."[38] Mike Simpson immediately contacted Paramount to verify that Skaaren's deal memo did in fact entitle his client, as final writer on the film, to 2.5 percent of the film's net profits now that the credits issue had been decided.[39]

Skaaren turned his attention back to the *Crimson Eagle* project. Two weeks earlier he and Helen had spent the long Easter weekend in New York at the invitation of Michael Douglas.[40] Together Skaaren and Douglas pored over the notes and photographs from the Hong Kong trip, and they also made a location scout to Manhattan's Chinatown neighborhood. Skaaren was a firm believer in the integrity of a film's three-act structure, and he preferred to chart his projects' plotlines prior to writing a first draft. Before flying to New York, he had constructed a detailed flow chart for *Crimson Eagle* that included potential locations for each act. From this he created a thirteen-page outline, which he modified and revised while meeting with Douglas. Skaaren continued to fine-tune the outline after he and Helen returned to Austin, and by early May, Susan

Braudy and Robert Singer, executives at Douglas's production company, had weighed in on the project's main "beats." They suggested a third-act revision that imbued the story with more tension. They thought that the character Joan Wilder took a backseat to Jack and needed to be shown doing more on her own. (Skaaren disagreed.) "As it stands now, it falls a little flat for us that Joan and Jack just take this project because we see they need a common goal . . . something to bring them together. It's just not a fresh or compelling enough problem for them," the readers wrote of the outline in general.[41]

Skaaren would need to address these points as he wrote the first draft, which he would work on throughout May and into June. His attention was diverted somewhat, however, by the impending release of *Beverly Hills Cop II*, which was scheduled to open on May 20. The film's world premiere would take place a day earlier at Mann's Chinese Theatre on Hollywood Boulevard. Prior to flying to Los Angeles for the event, Skaaren sent a letter to director Tony Scott, thanking him for the opportunity to work on the film. "Someday I'm sure you'll tell me of all the serpentine moves that went into my being hired on Cop II. Someday. I'll know who paid for what and why and when. Someday. Or not," Skaaren joked.[42] Perhaps Skaaren felt the need to reach out to Scott given the thorny situation surrounding the film's screen-credit arbitration. But no matter what he thought of *Cop II* in its final form, Skaaren was grateful for the work and for receiving shared screenplay credit, which he had been denied on *Top Gun*, the last Simpson and Bruckheimer project on which he and Scott had worked together.

Buzz had been building about *Cop II*, so much so that Paramount moved up its release, originally scheduled for Memorial Day weekend. Gearing up for the opening, Simpson and Bruckheimer returned to the concept of promoting *Cop II* not as a sequel but as a franchise. In a profile that ran in *Premiere* magazine, Bruckheimer described the "series" as similar to Peter Sellers's *Pink Panther* movies. "It's a continuation of the adventures of Axel Foley," said Bruckheimer, insisting that the character, like Sellers's Inspector Clouseau, was already established. "They know exactly who they are, and so does the audience. All we have to do is embellish them, make them funnier, elevate the series."[43]

Within days of *Beverly Hills Cop II*'s opening on May 20, *Variety* had christened Paramount and its star, Eddie Murphy, "The Golden Pair." The film opened in the number-one spot in more than 2,300 theaters in North America and earned approximately $26.3 million. *Cop II* did "booming" business over the long Memorial Day weekend, bringing its total box office to more than $33 million and nearly tying the holiday weekend record set by *Indiana Jones and the Temple of Doom* in 1984. By the end of its first week, *Cop II* had made more than $40 million at the box office.[44] The film was well on its way to blockbuster status.

The reviews, however, were mixed. Writing in the *New York Times*, Janet Maslin praised the film's energy and action but noted that "lively as it is, *Beverly Hills Cop II* can't help but suffer from the lack of any originality at all. All of the key original actors . . . have returned this time, and the screenplay (by Larry Ferguson and Warren Skaaren) works hard to give them more to do." She also took issue with the film's depiction of its female characters, something that Skaaren had struggled to improve during rewrites. "The new film is more noticeably misogynist than its predecessor, and more intent on cheesecake, which is where the crowd of volleyball-playing bunnies come in," Maslin observed of the scene, filmed at the Playboy Mansion, that director Tony Scott had fought to include.[45] The *Washington Post*'s Hal Hinson made a similar point about the film's "misogynist" tendencies but singled out Chief Bogomil's daughter, a character created by Skaaren, as one of the few female characters who had some depth.[46] Roger Ebert took issue with Axel Foley as played by Murphy, whom he described as unlikable in the follow-up, and he lamented the "recycled" plot. "For what producers Don Simpson and Jerry Bruckheimer probably paid for the screenplay for this movie," wrote Ebert in the *Chicago Sun-Times*, "they should have been able to buy a new one."[47]

Skaaren collected and read the reviews, but he didn't seem much bothered by the negative comments. At his request, Vance organized a small celebratory dinner at a local restaurant for several of the Skaarens' closest friends. In the past, according to intimates, Skaaren had appeared not to want to draw attention to his growing success in Hollywood, but things seemed to shift with the release of *Cop II*. "I think that was the first one that got so much notoriety, locally, and he got credit, too. By that time, he was on the map in Austin," says Vance.[48]

At the end of May, agent Mike Simpson boarded a plane in Los Angeles, headed to Oklahoma. En route, he opened up a copy of *Variety*. "I saw the Paramount BHC II congratulatory ad and couldn't help but wonder why the writers of the screenplay weren't mentioned," Simpson wrote in a telegram he fired off to Simpson and Bruckheimer. "Warren Skaaren couldn't understand either, particularly since Cash and Epps were mentioned in similar 'Top Gun' ads." Simpson went on to say that while Skaaren had been disappointed in the *Top Gun* credit arbitration, he understood that it was a Guild decision. "This is not the case of BHC II," continued Simpson, who made sure that the telegram also went to Paramount chief executive Ned Tanen and head of production Gary Lucchesi. "I hope it has nothing to do with the meritless suit brought by the other credited writer. The official credit has been designated, and to shirk from affirming it could be inferred as lending credence to the complaint."[49] Simpson was referring to writer Larry Ferguson's recent lawsuit, filed in California Superior Court, seeking to have the WGA make a new credit determination for *Cop II* that would give Ferguson sole credit for the story and the screenplay. At the time it seemed unlikely that Ferguson's lawsuit would gain any traction, in part because the Guild's Minimum Basic Agreement for its members, which writers are required to sign upon beginning a project, stipulates that writers will "abide by the guild's determination of credits."[50]

This stipulation had recently been challenged, however, by author Gore Vidal, who filed a lawsuit against the Writers Guild of America West and author Steve Shagan in February of that year. The suit, which concerned the writing credit for the film *The Sicilian*, due to be released in June 1987, was thought to be unprecedented. The WGA had determined through arbitration that Shagan should receive sole credit for the screenplay. Vidal's suit claimed that essential documents had been left out of the story materials sent to the arbiters and that these documents would reveal that his contribution to the screenplay "was far greater than was represented."[51] In the suit over credit for *Beverly Hills Cop II*, Ferguson's attorneys were arguing along the same lines (Ferguson didn't believe that Skaaren had contributed the required 33 percent to receive shared credit), but they were also asking the court (rather than the Guild) to determine credit allocation according to WGA standards.[52]

After the initial hoopla over *Cop II*'s opening had died down, Skaaren turned back to the *Crimson Eagle* draft. The project was still very much in play, with Skaaren in contact with both Douglas and Turner, but its projected start date had been pushed from later that year to the spring of 1988 with the news that Turner was expecting her first child. Skaaren had written a first draft by July, which he shared with both actors. He also had secured representation in the Ferguson matter through the Los Angeles office of Jones, Day, Reavis & Pogue, and his attorney, Gary Feess, alerted him to new updates on the case. Ferguson had recently submitted to the court "declarations" by writers (and Guild members) Nicholas Meyer and Leslie Dixon, who had reviewed a portion of the materials submitted by Ferguson and had determined that Skaaren's contribution to the final script was, respectively, 5 percent and 15 percent. Meyer was on the Guild's board of directors although he was "on leave" in 1987. His written statement to the court seemed to take greater issue with Murphy's and Wachs's story credit, but he also noted that he believed Skaaren shouldn't receive shared screenplay credit based on his contributions.[53] Dixon's statement was more detailed. "I believe there are only four changes in story or plot structure from the Ferguson final draft screenplay to the first shooting script," she wrote.

> Of these four changes, the first two . . . were not created by Mr. Skaaren, leaving only two additions by Mr. Skaaren (i.e., Jan and the red mud plot clues). . . . Most of Mr. Skaaren's work consisted of cutting what Mr. Ferguson wrote. Simply put, the changes made in the Skaaren final draft screenplay are not significant, nor are they sufficient to contribute to 33 percent of the screenplay to Mr. Skaaren.[54]

Skaaren faxed a response to Feess, who had noted that another attorney on the case would seek to bar admission of these documents solicited by Ferguson and his attorney. "I was shocked to see the involvement of other writers in this matter. But not so shocked when I saw Mr. Meyer's name," Skaaren wrote. He explained that Meyer had recently lost the arbitration on Michael Douglas's upcoming release *Fatal Attraction*. In addition to threatening to sue the WGA, Meyer had resigned from his position as the Guild's board president and had circulated a letter alleging various "conspiracies" within the Guild. "He has been following the Ferguson matter very closely since hearsay has it that if Ferguson wins, Meyer will immediately file a similar suit against the WGA on *Fatal Attraction*."[55]

By 1987 in development-mad Hollywood, trouble was clearly brewing. As Gore Vidal told the *Los Angeles Times*, "As far as I know, no writer has ever sued the Writers Guild. I'm doing this for a principle. I don't need a screen credit or money or publicity. But it's my script and I like it and I want my name on it."[56] Ferguson, whose career was less established than Vidal's, may have been suing for more than just principle. What these cases and the subsequent 1988 writers strike reveal, however, is the escalating tension over authorship in Hollywood. The industry's trade publications followed both cases closely, reporting on the details of each suit as they unfolded.[57] Despite being enmeshed in the Ferguson case, Skaaren was able to perceive what Meyer's and Dixon's analyses of his *Cop II* writing contribution revealed about the assignation of credit in general. "Dixon says 15% and Meyer says 5%. That's an indication of how tough the real arbitration process is and why the [WGA] has such stringent rules for arbitration."[58]

Progress on Ferguson's suit would be delayed, however. Sometime that summer, Ferguson claimed to have suffered debilitating burns during a household accident that had prevented him from appearing in court. The delay gave two other writers on *Cop II*, Bud Shrake and Dan Jenkins, the opportunity to file an amended petition to challenge the validity of the WGA's arbitration awarding Ferguson and Skaaren cocredit and Murphy and Wachs shared story credit. That August, Skaaren and his wife moved into their new home on Wren Valley Cove. The following month, Skaaren finally sought medical attention for the oozing lesion on his chest. Doctors diagnosed the growth as malignant, and Skaaren secretly underwent surgery for its removal.

In late September, as Skaaren recovered and began to pursue a plan of treatment that eschewed traditional measures, such as chemotherapy and radiation, in favor of macrobiotics and talk therapy, he received word from his Los Angeles attorneys that Ferguson's lawyers were planning to depose him. Skaaren's memos and letters regarding this matter reveal a sense of fear, almost a franticness, about this possibility. His reaction may have had less to do with the deposition itself than with the fact that this might force him to address publicly, even on a limited level, his recent health scare. As Skaaren would reveal later, he believed that any admission of weakness or vulnerability would count against him in Hollywood. "If this gets out in L.A.," Skaaren thought at the time, "it will kill my career."[59]

In mid-October, Skaaren sent Michael Douglas a second draft of the *Crimson Eagle* screenplay. Douglas's latest film, the dark thriller *Fatal Attraction*, had opened in theaters a month earlier and was doing very well at the box office. "Congrats on having the second largest grossing movie of the year!" Skaaren wrote in an accompanying note. "You can imagine what it feels like to have the first!" he added, needling Douglas with the fact that *Cop II* remained in the number-one spot more than four months after its initial release.[60] Ironically, Douglas's success with *Fatal Attraction*, in which he played a darker, more dramatic role than in previous films, would ultimately convince him to move beyond the Jack Colton character in the script for *Crimson Eagle*. Consequently, that project never got made.

During this time Skaaren dove deeper into the various healing strategies that he had begun to explore a month earlier. He kept regular appointments with his therapist, sought psychological input from his men's group, and generally tried to "seek balance" in his increasingly complex and stressful life. At the end of October, Skaaren received positive news from his L.A. attorney regarding the *Cop II* arbitration case. Although the petition for a redetermination of writing credits filed by first writers Bud Shrake and Dan Jenkins was still being considered by the court, the judge had denied Ferguson's attempt to determine the identity of the three Guild members who had rendered the original credit decision back in the spring. Observed Feess in his letter to Skaaren, "That was a critical victory for the Writers Guild in this case."[61] Skaaren, who had also learned that the judge had rejected Ferguson's request to have him deposed, was relieved. He was hopeful that the case was finally coming to an end.

SEVEN

Batmania

You ever danced with the devil in the pale moonlight?

THE JOKER, *BATMAN* (LINE WRITTEN BY WARREN SKAAREN)

Warren Skaaren received a package from Warner Bros. in the final days of August 1988. A handwritten note accompanied a screenplay tucked inside a manila envelope. "Here is the new draft of *Batman*," it began. "We love the movie but we need you!" Signed "xx, LUCY," the note was from Lucy Fisher, executive vice president of production at the studio. Married to writer-producer Doug Wick, Fisher had first met Skaaren a few years earlier when he and Wick began working together on the unproduced screenplay *Lillie and Beck*.[1]

Fisher's note may have been a plea to get Skaaren to take the project. As he would later reveal in print, he turned down *Batman* four times before he agreed to work on the blockbuster. It wasn't until he received a call from a friend who was a studio executive, Skaaren told an interviewer, that he reconsidered. "You don't know you're an idiot, but Jack Nicholson is going to do this role and you and he are going to get along and you and he are going to create a character that will live forever. You ought to do this," is how Skaaren related the story after the release of *Batman*.[2]

Batman would prove to be the most complex rewrite experience of Skaaren's career, and it would also become the most rewarding creative project that he had worked on to date. Skaaren was used to writing screenplays by committee, but *Batman*'s "layers" of executives and producers ran deep given the film's outsized budget and overseas production. The film's budget would skyrocket during shooting, adding to the tension surrounding the project. Rumors about *Batman*'s troubled London set and outraged comic-book fan protests over the film's darker tone and eclectic cast also would keep the film in the news for months. *Batman* would achieve blockbuster status shortly after its May 1989 release, and its critical and financial success would catapult Skaaren into an elite group of script doctors who could command seven figures per project and gross points. This success would lead to more press and a more visible public profile, and it would also contribute to his separation from Helen in the summer of 1989. The intense nature of the project and its attendant stresses would also impact Skaaren's health, already compromised by his cancer diagnosis in the fall of 1987. He would later describe his role on *Batman* as "part scriptwriter, part referee/therapist," and as his agent Mike Simpson recalled, "He played that role importantly." In the months before his death, Skaaren confided to one friend that he had "paid a price" by working on the film.[3]

By late summer in 1988, Skaaren had plenty of reasons to say no to *Batman*, which would reunite him with director Tim Burton. One reason involved Tom Cruise. The actor had contacted Skaaren in January 1987 and asked him to meet over dinner. At a nondescript Chinese restaurant in the San Fernando Valley, Cruise told Skaaren about a film he was eager to make, an original project that was close to his heart. It involved car racing, a hobby that Cruise had been introduced to by Paul Newman, his costar in *The Color of Money* (1986). After writing a five-page treatment, Cruise asked Skaaren to work with him on the project. Skaaren liked Cruise and respected his story sense. They discussed Skaaren's role, which would include producing as well as writing the film. Skaaren began working on an outline, but within a month they both realized that their schedules would make collaboration difficult. Cruise was involved with two films, *Cocktail* (1988) and *Rain Man* (1988), and Skaaren had just begun working with Michael Douglas on *Crimson Eagle* and was still in the throes of *Cop II* rewrites. Skaaren sent his outline to Cruise, encouraging the star to go forward with the project on his own. Although Cruise had told Skaaren in 1987 that he wanted to do the project without Don Simpson and Jerry Bruckheimer, the producers became attached to the film, now called *Daytona*, by mid-1988. Around the time that Lucy Fisher reached out to Skaaren with *Batman*, Don Simpson got in touch about the script for *Daytona*, which by then was in development.[4]

Skaaren also was still involved in Larry Ferguson's ongoing suit concerning authorship of *Beverly Hills Cop II*. Despite the fact that the judge had in December 1987 upheld the Guild's original credit determination, Ferguson was considering an appeal. The case, along with Gore Vidal's suit against the Writers Guild of America over credit on *The Sicilian* (1988), was being closely followed in the trades. In January 1988, even the mainstream magazine *Premiere* did a story on the two cases and what it might mean for the industry if Ferguson and/or Vidal were success-ful in their suits against the Guild.[5] Once the twenty-two-week writers strike began, in early March, the lawsuits received even more coverage. They were seen as high-profile evidence of the increasing dissatisfaction felt by writers about their status in the film and television industries. The strike, which was supported by 96 percent of the Guild's writers, includ-ing Skaaren, concerned issues such as residuals for hour-long television series and increased creative rights for writers. It would become the lon-gest strike in WGA history, and trade papers would dub it "the blood-bath of 1988."[6] That same year, Skaaren began receiving checks equal to his 2.5 percentage points of *Cop II*'s net profits. A letter from Para-mount accompanied a check for $3,242.00, advising Skaaren that if Fer-guson appealed the judge's ruling, as he was expected to do, and as a result Skaaren lost his writing credit on the film, he would be required to pay back any earnings he had previously received.[7] Skaaren promptly cashed the check.

By September 1988, the stress of the ongoing Ferguson matter was beginning to wear on Skaaren. In July, Vidal had scored a victory on ap-peal in his case concerning credit on *The Sicilian*, making it more likely that Vidal could find out the identities of the Guild members who had served as arbiters on *The Sicilian* credit determination. "My blood chilled more than a little when I read of the Gore Vidal victory on appeals," Skaaren wrote to L.A. attorney Sara Staebell, who had taken over his case from Gary Feess. "Wasn't this the unthinkable outcome that every-one said was impossible? How good is this for Mr. Ferguson by prece-dent?"[8] (By August, the California Supreme Court had ordered that this decision be depublished, and Vidal never did find out the arbiters' iden-tities.) Skaaren had spent nearly $18,000 on legal fees, and while he was by no means in dire financial straits, he resented having to fund what he described as Ferguson's "litigatory terrorism."[9]

Later that month Ferguson's attorneys approached Skaaren's lawyers about a settlement involving either a portion of Skaaren's earnings from the film or a transfer of his 2.5 percentage points of the film's net grosses (which, Skaaren later discovered through court documents, Ferguson also had despite arguing that Skaaren received more points in his deal with Paramount). Skaaren wrote a lengthy letter to George Kirgo, president of the WGA, venting about the case and asking for guidance. He referenced his unsuccessful arbitration on *Top Gun*, writing, "You told me that the arbitration process is just like that—you win some, you lose some. But it is *fair*. So I wept bitterly but recovered, proud that the fellowship in the Writers Guild had forged a painful but fair self-government." Although Skaaren told his lawyers that he did not want to settle with Ferguson, he had heard that the WGA might be considering a settlement to end the matter. But as he wrote to Kirgo: "For God's sake don't look to me for cash. After Eddie Murphy took his gross off the top, Simpson–Bruckheimer took theirs, and Paramount 'processed' the rest, Mr. Ferguson and I MAY each get about 140K. After commissions and legal fees, what the hell is Ferguson after, my typewriter?"[10]

While the *Daytona* project and the Ferguson case were legitimate distractions, Skaaren may have resisted taking on the *Batman* rewrite simply because of the complicated nature of the project. Skaaren was used to dealing with input from multiple players, having worked on big-budget projects such as *Top Gun* and *Beverly Hills Cop II*. But *Batman* was in a class by itself. Not only would Skaaren's revisions have to satisfy director Tim Burton and producers Jon Peters and Peter Guber, he also would be receiving input from Warner Bros. cochairman and co-executive officer Terry Semel; Lucy Fisher, who was Semel's second-in-command on studio production; and Bob Kane, one of the original creators of the Batman comic-book character who had been hired as a consultant on the project. Given the character's franchise nature, *Batman*'s comic-book fans also would become another "voice" that would influence the script's development. Additionally, stars Michael Keaton (Bruce Wayne/Batman), Jack Nicholson (Jack Napier/the Joker), and Sean Young (Vicki Vale) would weigh in once production began in London that October. Young would break her arm during an action scene and be replaced by Kim Basinger, a last-minute switch that would increase on-set tensions and require Skaaren to rewrite the character and her lines during filming.

But Skaaren eventually did say yes to *Batman*, and Fisher called him on August 30 to brief him about the project's "political" background. She explained the film's history, that producer Peter Guber had purchased the rights around 1980 when he and Jon Peters had their film production company, Casablanca FilmWorks Ltd., at Polygram. They were known for "innovative marketing strategies" and "pioneering synergistic campaigns" on hits such as the remake of *A Star Is Born* (1976) and *Midnight*

Express (1978).[11] When they moved their production company to Warner Bros. in the early 1980s, the project came with them. In 1986, DC Comics released Frank Miller's *The Dark Knight Returns*, a graphic novel mini-series featuring a darker, more complex Batman than had been depicted in earlier DC publications. Pitched to a more adult audience as well as longtime comic-book fans, *The Dark Knight Returns* became a success and rejuvenated the project at Warner Bros. The studio turned to Sam Hamm, who had shared a writing credit with future writer-director Curtis Hanson on Walt Disney's *Never Cry Wolf* (1984) and was under a two-year contract at Warner Bros. Hamm's 1984 script *Pulitzer Prize* sold to Columbia, which led to his deal at Warner Bros. He also was a longtime fan of comic books, so he was familiar with the Batman franchise. Prior to Hamm, writers Tom Mankiewicz (son of director Joseph L.) and Julie Hickson had each worked on drafts and/or outlines for the project.[12]

Hamm's original draft, which he wrote in 1986, gave Batman a complex psychological profile and situated the story in a deeply troubled Gotham City. "Peters got Tim involved. Sam Hamm did draft, which got it alive," noted Skaaren during his phone call with Fisher.[13] Burton appreciated the screenplay's dark themes, and the success of *Beetlejuice* in 1988 convinced the studio to greenlight *Batman*. Meanwhile Hamm had drafted several versions of the script, but the project was sidelined in March 1988 by the writers strike. Once the strike ended, in August, the studio executives agreed to bring in Skaaren to try to salvage Hamm's screenplay, which was deemed "too dark" for a film that was expected to appeal to a range of viewers. Warner Bros. also felt that Hamm's script followed too closely the original Batman "mythology" crafted by Bob Kane and other writers beginning in the 1930s.[14]

From Fisher, Skaaren also learned that Jack Nicholson had script approval, but she assured Skaaren that he was a "good guy," meaning that Nicholson should be listened to but that his involvement wouldn't complicate script development too much. Fisher also shared her take on the other executives involved in the production. "Peters—wants to be one of the guys, has medium ideas. Lisa Henson is smart and knows story. Mark Canton is just nervous," noted Skaaren. He had worked with both Henson and Canton on *Beetlejuice*, and he felt comfortable with the executives, who oversaw worldwide film production for Warner Bros.

Despite *Beetlejuice*'s success, however, the studio was concerned that Burton had never made a film on the scale of *Batman*, whose production budget was rumored to be around $30 million, about $10 million above that of the average feature film at that time.[15] Peters and Guber "made sure he was surrounded by experienced individuals, highly skilled in their fields for this type of production," a group that included London-based art director Terry Ackland-Snow (*The Deep, Superman I* and *II*), set decorator Peter Young (*Superman I–IV*), and special-effects veteran Derek Meddings (*Superman I* and *II, The Spy Who Loved Me*).[16] With Skaaren's experience writing for stars and special effects on *Top Gun* and *Beverly Hills Cop II* in particular, he was a natural choice. He was also a known entity at Warner Bros., and executives like Canton valued his analytical approach and laser-like focus, not to mention his ability to instill a sense of calm over a production that some felt was veering out of control.

While Skaaren analyzed Hamm's draft and traded phone calls and faxes with Warner Bros. and Tim Burton, who was already in London, Mike Simpson negotiated Skaaren's deal. For six weeks of work on *Batman*, Skaaren would receive around $750,000, his highest fee to date. That amount would increase to around $1 million once his points and bonuses kicked in. For the first time in his career, Skaaren would be entitled to a portion of the film's grosses (1 percent of gross proceeds after an initial breakeven) in addition to 2.5 percent of the film's net profits. The deal also included provisions about Skaaren's being on set in London during the rehearsal period but noted that "he shall not be obligated to stay in London" beyond rehearsals—although Skaaren would feel intense pressure to do so once shooting began that November.[17]

Within hours of the screenplay's arrival, Skaaren was sequestered in his Austin office, analyzing the script's structure and making notes for a preliminary outline to share with Burton. Hamm's draft, Skaaren noted, had a "'crippled' structure; it had little 'credible character conflict'; and there was too much action and too little plot development."[18] In general, Skaaren thought the characters lacked goals and the story was without forward momentum and deadlines that would vary the pacing of the film. He noted a struggle in tone between humor and horror. He also observed that the film's protagonist, despite being a superhero, seemed a bit passive. Following one character's statement that he didn't like Bruce Wayne, Batman's alter ego, Skaaren scribbled, "Do we?"[19] During one of Skaaren's initial conversations with Burton about the project, the filmmaker revealed why he wanted to cast actor Michael Keaton, known mostly for his comedic roles in films like *Beetlejuice*, in the dual lead role of Bruce Wayne/Batman. Burton knew that the actor he chose would need to convey the character's tension as well as the "schizophrenia, the humor" also implicit in the Batman persona. The filmmaker had met with and considered Robert De Niro, Christopher Walken, and even Arnold Schwarzenegger. De Niro and Walken were wired enough, Burton told Skaaren, but Keaton seemed best able to handle the character's emotional complexity and dark humor.[20] The studio had yet to approve the choice, however.

On September 1, Skaaren flew to Los Angeles to take a series of meetings on *Batman*. While Burton looked over his initial structural outline in London, Skaaren met with producer Jon Peters and his associate, Michael Besman, as well as Warner Bros. executives Lisa Henson and Mark Canton. Terry Semel weighed in via speakerphone. With rehearsals less than six weeks away, the *Batman* contingent gave Skaaren a mix of broad thoughts about the direction of the script and very detailed notes about characters ("Batman's hobbies are computers and polo; hard to be with") and lines of dialogue (Semel indicated Skaaren should write a scene where the Joker says "festival schmestival"). In turn, Skaaren shared with the group what he saw as the script's main ideas, such as its portrayal of Gotham as "crime-riddled and on downslide," as well as the screenplay's problems, including its weak "foundation" and "imbalanced polarity between Joker and Batman." The dialogue lacks "gleam," he told the group, and everyone agreed with Skaaren that the script's third-act introduction of Dick Grayson (aka Robin) would need to be saved for the "next movie." Although Jack Nicholson's casting as the Joker was a done deal, other key roles were still being decided, according to the studio. Skaaren learned that Sean Young was a top choice to play photographer and love interest Vicki Vale and that Harvey Keitel also was under consideration, possibly for the role of Carl Grissom (which would eventually go to Jack Palance).

Later that day, Skaaren made the winding drive up to Jack Nicholson's longtime residence on Mulholland Drive, a California Modern–style house filled with French art. Nicholson told Skaaren that he liked his character through about the middle of Hamm's fourth draft, but he had problems with Jack Napier/the Joker's characterization, particularly in the third act. "He is planning to be really crazy, do and say completely unpredictable stuff. He doesn't fancy too much linear stuff in script," Skaaren noted after the meeting. "He doesn't think Jack should be a go-getter trying to off the boss," he added of the script's plans for Napier to edge out Carl Grissom. "He thinks Jack should be velvety and deadly." Nicholson revealed his love of philosophy, particularly the writings of Friedrich Nietzsche, and hinted that he'd like to see some lines worked into the rewrite. Nicholson, who at that point was collaborating with writer Robert Towne on the screenplay for *The Two Jakes*, a follow-up to *Chinatown* that he planned to direct, regaled Skaaren with his thoughts on everything from art to women. "He railed about how good [inventor Nikola] Tesla was, how he wanted to do that character. And his favorite subject. Eating pussy." Skaaren thought privately that Nicholson's voice was a bad match for the Joker, and he marveled that the fifty-one-year-old movie star famous for his sex appeal "hobbled" like an old man. "He may not be able to walk or talk, but Jack is always ready for pussy," Skaaren observed drily. The meeting was cordial enough, but Skaaren later told a friend that it took a while for them to click while working on *Batman*.[21]

Still, Skaaren was open to Nicholson's thoughts about the Joker, a character of comic-book origins arguably as iconic as Batman. Earlier that day Warner Bros. executives had given Skaaren very specific notes about the legendary superhero, cautioning the writer to make him "ferocious on action" as well as "silent" and "strong." "Batman should not be funny. Bruce should be Michael Keaton," they told Skaaren, by way of explaining how the duality of the character should be distinguished on screen.[22] But Skaaren received the most pointed comments about the character from its cocreator, Bob Kane. "As you must know—I am the creator of Batman as well as the 'project consultant' on the Batman movie," began Kane's letter, written on stationery adorned with a Batman logo. Kane, a comic-book artist, actually worked with writer Bill Finger in the late 1930s to create the Batman figure and subsequent series for DC Comics. At the suggestion of Lisa Henson, Kane wrote, he was forwarding his notes on Hamm's fourth draft so that Skaaren could consult them as he wrote.

Kane's letter was fairly high-handed, and he was not shy about sharing his suggestions with Skaaren. He noted that he had met with Nicholson a few days prior to discuss specific scenes concerning the Joker, citing Nicholson's support of his idea to enhance the "black comedy" of a particular scene and not-so-subtly conveying to Skaaren his position in the hierarchy of players on the project. Some of Kane's ideas would appear in the final script (having the Joker deface Leonardo da Vinci's *Mona Lisa* with crayon, for instance, instead of Hamm's original suggestion of violating a religious painting of Jesus Christ). Other ideas and observations revealed that Kane saw himself as a custodian of the Batman persona and legacy. "I have already commented on my distaste for Bruce wearing Vicki's black silk stocking over his head to camouflage his identity. See my critique for alternative and less stupid scenario to this scene," he wrote. In particular, Kane objected to lines by other characters that poked fun at Batman's costume or challenged his masculinity, such as a line in which the Joker says, "You fucking mouse in drag."[23]

While Skaaren disagreed with a few of Kane's ideas, generally he understood that it was his job as "the fixer" to juggle input from numerous and often conflicting sources. "I got a note from Bob Kane yesterday with some good ideas in it," Skaaren wrote in a fax to Burton. He cautioned Burton, however, about Kane's suggested scene change in which the Joker kills his rival crime bosses. "He claims Jack liked the idea. Who knows, but at any rate it is a bad idea! We *need* the Joker's hit list murders to escalate the energy in the film," Skaaren explained. "Be prepared if Jack, for some reason, brings it up, to quash it fast."[24] Regardless of whether Burton appreciated Skaaren's input, the fact that he offered it so directly suggests the comfort level Skaaren felt not only with Burton but also with his own role on the project.

With a promised first draft delivery date of September 15, Skaaren had two weeks from his first official meeting on the project to construct an outline and write a draft of the screenplay. Skaaren's outline focused the script's three-act structure, tweaking the setups in Hamm's draft to improve flow and clarify character goals and motivation. An early party scene at Bruce Wayne's estate added more chemistry between Wayne and Vicki Vale, for instance, while a new scene between Batman and the Joker increased the conflict between the two characters. Skaaren was quick to point out to Burton that the new scene "only requires dressing the front of the set differently. . . . I also think that this cuts our budget somewhat but am not sure."[25] Skaaren's experience with production management from both his film commission days and his time as chairman of FPS, which oversaw below-the-line production costs on the television series *Dallas*, increased his value on projects like *Batman*, where last-minute script changes so close to production could result in cost overages.

After getting Burton's approval from London, Skaaren faxed his outline revising the film's three-act structure to Warner Bros. on September 6. In a telephone conference the following day, producer Jon Peters and studio execs Terry Semel, Lisa Henson, and Mark Canton shared their thoughts. "Tim loves it," Canton assured Skaaren, having spoken with the director prior to the meeting. Henson had some minor issues with a few plot points, while Semel seemingly had the most questions and notes for Skaaren. Semel still had concerns about the appropriateness and tone of some of the scenes, particularly one in which the Joker hijacks Gotham's anniversary celebration. "Make sure we don't see mass genocide," Semel advised Skaaren about the writing of the scene. Producer Jon Peters, who wanted Skaaren to travel with him to London later in the month for the start of rehearsals, countered Semel's caution with Don Simpson–like hyperbole. "Genius," he told Skaaren over speakerphone. "As a matter of fact let's go with it. Forget if Terry Semel has a nit to pick, I'm going to use [the outline] as a prototype of how I want things to be on all pictures before going into production."[26]

With the studio's and Burton's blessing, Skaaren set to work on a first draft. Working from Hamm's fourth draft screenplay, he added new scenes, trimmed or deleted some existing ones, amplified the story's action and forward momentum, and enhanced key relationships, such as the budding attraction between Bruce Wayne and Vicki Vale. Skaaren took inspiration for the superhero's and his nemesis's character development from a collection of resources on loan from Jon Peters. He consulted *The World Encyclopedia of Comics*, for instance, for Batman's basic character traits and for background information on the Joker, a character originally created by Kane's assistant, Jerry Robinson. The description of the 1939 Batman as an "avenging vigilante" intrigued Skaaren, and he kept that in mind as he plotted the film's third act in particular. Similarly, Batman's depiction as a "pillar of righteousness" and some of the Joker's dialogue from the 1986 comic book *Shadow of the Batman* inspired Skaaren to create memorable lines, such as, "You ever danced with the devil in the pale moonlight?"[27] This line became a clue that linked Jack Napier to the killing of Bruce Wayne's parents, a subplot that Skaaren also invented for the film.

The draft Skaaren submitted to Warner Bros. on September 15 ran 140 pages. Skaaren intended this first pass to introduce his new story ideas without losing much from Hamm's last version.[28] Although it was longer than Hamm's draft by more than ten pages, Skaaren's version tightened existing scenes by omitting specific shots within sequences (what he considered excess dialogue between characters, etc.) and adding lines for greater humor and characterization. By the end of Skaaren's draft, Vicki Vale transformed into a more defined and independent character, but the script's third act remained heavily descriptive and overly long. Carol Bahoric, a story analyst at Warner Bros., compared Skaaren's draft to Hamm's at the request of Lisa Henson. Given that *Batman* was about to go into production, this step seems as much budget-driven as anything else, spotlighting as it does scenes that are new (and may require set changes, etc.) and others that have been cut. Bahoric observed that Vale's character had changed, adopting a more "aggressive" approach that Skaaren shaped in part by giving her some lines of dialogue that previously were spoken by her newspaper colleague Alexander Knox. The analyst noted a shift in tone to a darker Batman as well. The biggest change to the screenplay, Bahoric wrote, is that in Skaaren's draft Vale did not know that Bruce Wayne and Batman were one and the same.[29] Skaaren believed this was essential to establishing tension (romantic and otherwise) between the two characters and to raising the stakes of the overall story.

Two days later, Skaaren was in Los Angeles for a meeting with Semel, Peters, Henson, and Canton. Semel's chief concern was length, and he instructed Skaaren to cut at least ten pages to tighten the existing material and shorten the film to a more manageable running time overall. He also wanted a clearer distinction between the Bruce Wayne and Batman characters, instructing Skaaren to clarify their personalities in more detail. Among Peters's comments was the directive to invent a "better Batmobile gag to dazzle" the audience. Patched in by phone from London, Burton agreed with Semel that the draft was too long, so he suggested tightening scenes in the third act (a problem area since the project's inception). "Do a quick second draft," he told Skaaren, who was due to arrive on set with Peters less than two weeks later, on September 28.

Within a week, Skaaren had finished a 113-page second draft that he felt addressed both length and the creative and aesthetic concerns. "Let's all read this script with new eyes," he wrote in a memo to Burton and the other *Batman* executives: "I urge you to focus on the creative issues now, discuss them with Tim and based on those discussions, I'll do another draft next week which incorporates the results of those creative discussions. Then we'll start rehearsals on Oct. 3 with a mature script which is the right length and offers a good approximation of our creative goals, too."[30]

The memo's confident but collaborative tone was quintessential Skaaren. Combined with Skaaren's changes to the second draft, its effect on the frenzied production was almost balm-like. "We were thrilled to read this skillfully edited draft. We miss almost nothing that was cut," Peters and partner Peter Guber practically purred in a reply to Skaaren and Burton. "There are so many positive changes that we don't list them individually, but we want to specifically say how pleased we are with the new tag scene. It hit the right final notes," they wrote of Skaaren's work on the problematic finale.[31] The producing team had plenty of notes, of course, but everyone's focus was turning to London, where rehearsals were to begin the following week.

Skaaren touched down at Heathrow Airport on Friday, September 30. For the next eleven days he would be commuting approximately fifteen miles between the Athenaeum, a small luxury hotel in London's central Mayfair neighborhood, and Pinewood Studios, a legendary production facility that was home to the British film industry. Skaaren was no stranger to film sets, but *Batman* wasn't a typical project. Its budget was at least double that of *Beetlejuice*, Burton's last movie, and its special effects and comic book–inspired set design required teams of crew members in excess of 300 people. *Batman* sprawled across nine soundstages and utilized the majority of a ninety-five-acre back lot at Pinewood.[32] Skaaren was as fascinated with how a filmmaker ran such a large set as he was with the production differences between the United States and the United Kingdom. He also wanted to know more about Pinewood itself, which had once been a secluded, privately owned estate used for top-secret political meetings throughout the early part of the 1900s. Millionaire flour tycoon J. Arthur Rank transformed the property into a film studio in the mid-1930s, basing it on the unit production model of multiple soundstages and departments that Thomas Ince had made popular in Hollywood. At the time of Skaaren's visit in the fall of 1988, Pinewood was celebrating a profitable decade, thanks mostly to a succession of James Bond films that had used the studio's facilities.

Natural curiosity fueled Skaaren's interest in Pinewood and British production in general, but he also was taking notes because Hollywood producer Ray Stark (*The Way We Were*, *The Sunshine Boys*) had recently expressed interest in *Of East and West*, the original screenplay that had first launched Skaaren in Hollywood. He was still eager to bring the epic story about a friendship between a British officer and a Gurkha soldier to the screen. While touring *Batman*'s sets, Skaaren interviewed key crew members like Bob Ringwood, a costume designer who had worked his way up the ladder on movies such as *Excalibur* (1981) and *Dune* (1984). Skaaren particularly enjoyed talking with production designer Anton Furst, whose previous work included *Full Metal Jacket* (1987) with Stanley Kubrick. "Anton has a gleam in his eyes. Horizons are deep here," Skaaren observed of Furst's enthusiasm for the tonally dark and visually complex project. Furst later revealed that inspiration for the set, which incorporated elements of German Expressionism and had a vaguely industrial feel, had come from the Orson Welles–directed film *Chimes at*

Midnight (1965).[33] Having worked in the business since the mid-1970s, Furst understood studio politics. "Stakes are high," he told Skaaren, referring to the film's unprecedented $40 million budget and the fact that Warners hadn't had a hit since *Beetlejuice* and had nothing in the pipeline beyond *Batman*.[34]

Adding to the on-set stress was Tim Burton's health, which was being severely compromised by pneumonia-like symptoms. Still, he pushed on, bringing Skaaren in to watch makeup tests with Jack Nicholson, whose input was solicited in such a way as to "give JN the sense of creating his own makeup," Skaaren observed later. Burton also confided to Skaaren his fear that Peters and Guber, who were also in London and often on set, would take one look at the Joker's face and object to his makeup. Skaaren felt empathy for Burton, who essentially was carrying the film.[35]

Skaaren was feeling the stress as well. He was making daily changes to the script based on rehearsals and his meetings with the individual actors and key personnel. But he enjoyed the rehearsal process and working one-on-one with actors. Although Skaaren rarely, if ever, discussed directing, he clearly appreciated having some measure of control on a project beyond the role screenwriters and script doctors typically played in a production. When Robert Wuhl requested a character sketch for his role as reporter Alexander Knox, Skaaren told him that Knox was intrepid and inquisitive, "like Bernstein in Watergate."[36] Peters and executive Mark Canton went back and forth about how independent to make Vicki Vale, worrying that too much agency would dampen her romantic appeal.[37] Sean Young, cast to play Vale, pulled Skaaren aside as well, soliciting more character details from the writer as well as making the case to give "more power to Vicki" in the rewrites.[38]

But perhaps the biggest debate during rehearsals and into production concerned the character Bruce Wayne. Burton pushed for Wayne as a "lonely outsider," but Peters envisioned the moody character as more accessible and "heroic" to the audience. When Michael Keaton asked for a description of the character in an earlier meeting, Skaaren characterized Wayne as "never rude, never brash."[39] As with his attending rehearsals and being asked to comment on dailies for *Top Gun*, Skaaren's presence on the set during this stage of *Batman*'s production revealed how highly regarded he was by Burton and Warner Bros. alike.

Story conference meetings and table reads often took place in a library-like room on the Pinewood lot. Peters, Canton, Burton, Skaaren, and the cast sat around an immense conference table strewn with bottles of water and *Batman* paraphernalia from Warner Bros. Skaaren's cassette recorder, about the size of a hardcover book, was a familiar sight. He relied on these recordings while writing and rewriting, paying attention to comments from Burton and the producers that may have escaped his notes, and listening to the inflections and line readings of each actor so as to tailor changes and future dialogue. Of all the *Batman* cast members, Jack Nicholson proved the toughest nut to crack for Skaaren. He could tell that Nicholson wasn't entirely satisfied with the Joker, so he worked overtime to tweak lines and strike just the right mix of humor and edge. Prior to a table read on October 6, Skaaren sent Nicholson script pages featuring new lines of dialogue. "This rather bizarre document is a print-out of most of your lines as they appear in my fifth draft. . . . Some are unchanged but in others I have twisted in some Nietzsche. See if your tongue likes it," Skaaren wrote. Mixed in among Skaaren's papers is a copy of *The Portable Nietzsche*, a 1977 translation of the philosopher's four major works by noted scholar Walter Kaufmann. Nicholson gave the book to Skaaren during preproduction on *Batman*. A heavily notated section of the book ends with an essay titled "Toward a Psychology of the Artist": "If there is to be art, if there is to be any aesthetic doing and seeing, one physiological condition is indispensable: frenzy."[40] Just as Skaaren amplified the darker tones in Batman's characterization, he played up the Joker's menacing qualities so that they glimmered just beneath the surface of the character's clownish antics. This meeting of the minds was a turning point for Skaaren and the actor. "Nicholson is brilliant," he wrote to producer Ted Flicker after the trip. "He didn't get me at first, then one day he did and we had a great relationship."[41]

Skaaren flew back to the United States on the Concorde, eventually arriving in Austin on October 11. Meanwhile Burton and the cast and crew began production on the film, scheduled to shoot for three months, with completion of principal photography tentatively set for mid-January of the following year. Skaaren spent only a short time in Austin before he headed out again, this time for a research trip to the southeastern part of the United States for *Days of Thunder* (the eventual title of Tom Cruise's racing film). The project, which had originated with Cruise, was alive again now that longtime producers Don Simpson and Jerry Bruckheimer were on board. The story about a hotshot driver new to NASCAR was inspired by Cruise's experience driving in two NASCAR races with Rick Hendrick, who owned a successful car dealership in Charlotte and would go on to race in two Winston Cup series, in 1987 and 1988. Cruise also revealed to Simpson and Bruckheimer that he drew inspiration for the main character's challenges from his own experiences after *Top Gun*. "Once the success comes, after *Top Gun*, the kind of responsibility, what are you going to do with that kind of success?" Cruise explained to the producers in one of their earliest meetings about the project.[42] Although Cruise had expressly told Skaaren in early 1987 that he did not want to work with the *Top Gun* producers, they eventually signed on, most likely so that Cruise could get the picture made in a timely fashion while utilizing Paramount's resources.

Skaaren's assistant, Linda Vance, had spent a good deal of time researching the sport, the teams, and the drivers so that Skaaren could familiarize himself with the world of American auto racing. In the late fall of 1988, Cruise arranged an introduction between Hendrick and Skaaren, who traveled to North Carolina to meet the team owner and attend a number of races as part of his research. He took driving lessons from Hendrick and Geoff Bodine, a motorsport driver who had recently won the Daytona 500 and the International Race of Champions (known as IROC), a stock-car race.[43] Skaaren was not as passionate about racing as Cruise, but he understood the attraction to high-performance cars and the sport of racing itself. He returned from his November research trip energized to write one of the film's first race scenes. "I love the form of the race because with the pit crew, the announcer and the driver there's nothing I can't cover," he told Cruise in a conference call after his trip. Cruise cautioned him about getting too complex with the structure. Don't bury the character, he told Skaaren, suggesting he take inspiration from *An Officer and a Gentleman* (1982) as to how to balance expositional information and characterization.[44]

The team that had bonded three years earlier on *Top Gun*, however, did not jell as easily on *Days of Thunder*. For starters, Simpson had reservations about the project. According to Skaaren, the producer "detested" NASCAR. "He found it boring and bumpkin and was convinced the audience would too," Skaaren wrote in the statement he submitted to the Writers Guild in 1990 once the writing credits went to arbitration. Because of this, Simpson pushed for a more sophisticated angle to what he called "the Ferrari Story," suggesting that Cruise's character had loftier dreams than simply winning the Daytona 500. Cruise resisted Simpson's idea, and in general Skaaren witnessed a growing tension between the two men during his time on the project. Part of the problem, Skaaren thought, was that Cruise, now twenty-six, was three years older and three years into a career that had surpassed his role as Maverick in

Top Gun. "The Tom Cruise with whom I met to launch *Days of Thunder* in 1987 was *not* the same Tom Cruise we encountered after Oliver Stone and *Born on the Fourth of July*," Skaaren observed of the film that Cruise had just wrapped in the fall of 1988. By that time, wrote Skaaren, Cruise had become interested only in making "significant" films and in having greater artistic control over these projects. Simpson "bristled" at this perceived change in Cruise, and their differences of opinion eventually threatened the project.[45]

In November 1988, while Skaaren was in the middle of writing *Days of Thunder*, he received an early-morning call from a frantic Mark Canton in London. Less than a month into production on *Batman*, Sean Young had fallen off a horse while rehearsing a scene and broken her arm. She would have to be replaced. Tim Burton reportedly wanted to offer the part to Michelle Pfeiffer, but she and Michael Keaton had recently ended a relationship, and Keaton feared it would be "awkward" to work opposite one another.[46] Other actresses were considered, but ultimately Kim Basinger was brought on to the project. Canton wanted Skaaren to return to the set immediately to be on hand for revisions. Skaaren resisted Canton's pleas, not wanting to leave the *Days of Thunder* project just as he was getting into a rhythm on the screenplay.

Skaaren reached out to Young, with whom he had struck up a friendship. In Hollywood, gossip swirled that somehow Young's accident had been orchestrated due to her difficult reputation on set, but Skaaren had a different take on the actress, whose vulnerability seemed to bring out the caretaking instincts he often felt around women. He thought she was very bright and unwilling to kowtow to those (mostly men) in charge, which unnerved and angered them. "She was scared and rejected, but I thought I had built her a safe place in the picture," Skaaren confided to a producer friend.[47] "Kim Basinger is someone else's Vicki. I can't comment if she's good or bad. Would George Bush make a good Pee-wee Herman? I can't comment. I don't know," Skaaren wrote in a fax to Young. He advised her to find a therapist and experience the frustration and anger of the situation. "Get every poisonous drop of irony out of your system, forgive the horse and everyone else and don't look back."[48]

In the weeks leading up to Thanksgiving, Skaaren was on call for *Batman* rewrites, faxing or in some cases phoning in revisions of scenes between Bruce Wayne/Batman and Vicki Vale and tweaking lines for Basinger. A front-page story in the *Wall Street Journal* only compounded the pressure that was being felt in the top office suites at Warner Bros. and on the Pinewood Studios set. The article, titled "FANS OF BATMAN

FEAR THE JOKE IS ON THEM IN A HOLLYWOOD EPIC," chronicled comic-book fans' anger over the casting of Keaton as Batman, among other complaints about the in-progress film. According to the article, fans had booed Warner Bros. representatives when they appeared at a recent comics convention and brought a photograph of Michael Keaton, whom fans considered "too average Joe" for the commanding, dark character. A smaller faction of disgruntled fans protested Nicholson's casting as the Joker. Even Bob Kane's role as consultant was called into question, with fans unimpressed by Kane's promise that the film was sufficiently brooding and even melodramatic in parts.[49]

Skaaren was able to resist Canton's initial requests to return to London, but on Thanksgiving Day an agitated Jon Peters left him a phone message reiterating that he was needed on the *Batman* set. When Skaaren finally touched base with Peters, the writer once again emphasized that he was "under great pressure" to finish the Cruise project. Peters coaxed, cajoled, and finally hinted that Skaaren hadn't spent enough time in London during his first trip to prep the actors for shooting. By the end of the conversation, Skaaren had agreed to rewrite a scene, and that seemed to pacify the *Batman* producer to some degree. The following Monday, however, Skaaren sent a fax to his agent, recapping the phone conversation and expressing his concern that given the general chaos on the project, another writer might be brought on.[50]

Despite Skaaren's protests about needing to work on *Days of Thunder*, he did decide to return to *Batman*'s London set. In the March 1989 Statement of Contribution he sent to the Writers Guild, Skaaren indicated that one of the reasons he flew to England was that he had proposed a significant change to the problematic finale of the film, and that Warner Bros. had asked him to be on set to rehearse the sequence and write the scene. In addition to working with the actors, it was important, according to the studio, that Skaaren write the scene while keeping in mind the new sets that Peters had authorized and that were under construction. The thirty-eight-foot model for the scene's cathedral bell tower alone was rumored to have cost $100,000.[51]

Skaaren arrived on December 7 and stayed for a week. During those seven intense days, Skaaren was on set to write and revise scenes, working on areas that developed the relationship between Bruce Wayne/Batman and Vicki Vale and the finale with Batman, the Joker, and Vicki Vale in the bell tower. He also continued to tweak lines for Nicholson, trying out excerpts from a variety of poems about death, from Thomas Gray's "Elegy Written in a Church Courtyard" to Edgar Allan Poe's "The

Raven." Basinger was struggling to adapt to a character that Skaaren essentially had customized for Young, so he spent time reworking and rehearsing lines with her. "The audience experiences much of the movie through her eyes," he said by way of explaining Vale's importance in the film. "Her curiosity is her key characteristic. You must show it on your face."[52] At one point Skaaren found himself in the rather awkward position of counseling producer Jon Peters and Basinger, who had begun a not-so-secret affair during production. He met with the pair in Peters's suite at the St. James Club hotel, listening to their issues and offering advice about how they could better communicate with one another.[53]

By the time he returned to Austin, Skaaren was eager for a break. While in London he had taken a conference call with Cruise and the other *Days of Thunder* principals in between rewrites on *Batman*. He had also received new information from a representative of the Writers Guild regarding Larry Ferguson's *Cop II* civil lawsuit. Although it seemed likely that a judge was going to deny Ferguson's request to appeal the ruling and reopen the dispute over the film's writing credit, Ferguson, along with writers Bud Shrake and Dan Jenkins, was still pushing for more money from those who did receive screenwriting and story credit. Skaaren contacted the L.A. attorneys representing him in the case, estimating at the time that he would earn approximately $140,000 in profits on the film and reminding them that he and Ferguson had the same profit-sharing terms. By the end of 1988, when Skaaren spoke with his attorneys, he had earned approximately $50,000 since the film's 1987 release. His profit checks were getting smaller, too, which indicated that the earnings might be slowing down. "By the way, Murphy, as story credit holder, is likely to be getting much less than 2.5% of the net for that contribution, so where is all this money that [Ferguson] is looking to take from us?" Skaaren wrote in frustration.[54]

After a two-week trip to Santa Fe with Helen, Skaaren returned to Austin after the New Year and to his work on *Days of Thunder*. He had agreed to finish a first draft before the end of January 1989 and wanted to move forward on the project, which was in danger of becoming shelved due to the escalating tension between producer Don Simpson and star Tom Cruise. At Pinewood Studios, production on *Batman* limped through its final weeks. Shooting on the film's climax in the cathedral bell tower was fraught, mostly because of last-minute changes made to the sequence. British writer Charles McKeown was brought on set to polish the lines of Nicholson and others in this particular scene. "Tim Burton . . . was sick and exhausted by that time and wanted to have a writer around in case something was missed. I was 6,000 miles away. So McKeown was brought in," wrote Skaaren.[55] The three *Batman* principals were struggling to figure out their motivation in the scene, and Tim Burton later admitted to being terrified that he didn't fully understand the scene, either, in part because it had been Jon Peters's idea, carried out on the page by Skaaren, to add Vale to the final duel between Batman and the Joker. Said Burton of Peters's influence on the final scene, "Here was Jack Nicholson and Kim Basinger walking up this cathedral, and halfway up Jack turns around and says, 'Why am I walking up all these stairs? Where am I going?' And I had to tell him that I didn't know."[56]

Skaaren sent an eleven-page fax to Burton and the film's producers on January 10, 1989, that included revisions to a romantic scene between Bruce Wayne and Vicki Vale.[57] Production on *Batman* ended later that month, and Valerie Levett, story editor (West Coast) for Warner Bros., sent the film's tentative writing credits to the WGA on February 9. The Notice of Tentative Writing Credits from the studio read, "Story by Sam Hamm; Screenplay by Sam Hamm and Warren Skaaren." Two weeks later Sally Burmester, who served as the screen credits coordinator for the Guild, notified all of the *Batman* writers that the organization would be conducting an arbitration on the screen credits because a protest had been received from British writer McKeown. Skaaren's Statement of Contribution ran twenty-eight pages and included exhibits such as photographs of pages from the original *Batman* comic book that inspired certain plot points. Several pages of the statement noted new scenes that Skaaren added to and/or substituted in place of ones that had existed in Sam Hamm's final draft. He also delineated new characters and dialogue, although he knew that the WGA Arbitration Committee would consider changes to the dramatic structure of the screenplay to be the most heavily weighted in terms of deciding credit. He also admitted that he was uncertain as to who should receive story credit on the project, supplying a list of the story elements that he created and noting that "they speak for themselves and I'll defer entirely to your experience."[58]

For Skaaren, a lot was riding on this project in terms of authorship and money. If McKeown were to receive a credit, he would be considered a "subsequent" writer, thus nullifying the provision in Skaaren's deal memo that as final writer he would receive 2.5 percent of the net profits over and above his salary and bonuses. By now a veteran of several arbitrations, Skaaren had a friendly relationship with the Guild's screen credits administrative personnel, and he kept tabs on the process. When Warner Bros. inadvertently credited some of Skaaren's final dialogue revisions to McKeown, Skaaren was able to rectify the situation fairly quickly. Concerning the January addition of the intimate dinner between Bruce Wayne and Vicki Vale that also featured Alfred, Wayne's butler, Skaaren observed, "I rewrote that scene many times, because of acting problems between Michael Keaton and Kim Basinger. I could flood you with drafts of that scene which represent what's fundamentally in the final draft. I won't." Indeed, pages containing several versions of the scene fill up multiple folders in Skaaren's archive.[59]

On April 18, agent Mike Simpson had copies of an interoffice memo delivered by hand to William Morris agents around the globe. "Flash! Just got the word—Warren Skaaren received shared screenplay credit for his rewrite on BATMAN."[60] Clearly, Skaaren's stake in the Warner Bros. film was noteworthy. Trade and even mainstream press reports had dogged the project throughout 1988, noting its escalating budget, casting problems, comic-book fans' protests, and on-set chaos. But when the *Batman* trailer appeared in theaters on Christmas Day 1988, the tide of public opinion began to turn. The one-and-a-half-minute preview played up the film's mayhem, visual darkness, and best lines. Jon Peters had insisted that the trailer have no music, keeping with the minimal style he had encouraged production designer Anton Furst to pursue when creating the film's spare poster, which was unnervingly stark for a Hollywood blockbuster: an image of the Bat symbol and the movie's release date against a black background.[61] Audience members actually applauded the preview and the film's stars, Michael Keaton and Jack Nicholson, whose casting had originally sparked controversy. The trailer got fans buzzing, and Warner Bros., which had spent at least $40 million on the production alone, did everything in its power to maintain that excitement.

Stories by reporters and film reviewers who had been invited to Pinewood Studios during production began running as early as January 1989. *Newsweek*'s Jack Kroll included a few of Skaaren's lines in his two-page article about the production, using them to demonstrate the film's "tricky but deft attempt to fuse fantasy and reality, pastiche and put-on."[62] In the weeks leading up to the film's late June release, more than 300 specially licensed *Batman* products began flooding the market. One of Skaaren's favorites was Ralston's Batman-themed cereal, which featured sweetened corn–flavored pieces shaped like small bats and included a toy bank as a prize. ABC Television's primetime news program *20/20* featured a fifteen-minute segment about the film a week prior to its June 23 release, offering behind-the-scenes footage from the Pinewood sets and the studios where musician Danny Elfman had worked on the film's orchestral soundtrack two months earlier. "Will *Batman* go zonk or zowie?" asked Barbara Walters at the beginning of the *20/20* episode.[63] Warner Bros. executives were praying for the latter.

In mid-May, when Mike Simpson noticed that Warner Bros. was leaving Skaaren out of some of the film's initial prerelease hype, he made sure to contact John D'Artique, the studio's vice president of publicity, to remind him that his client had received shared screenplay credit on the film.[64] Sam Hamm's name kept popping up in many of the advance articles, and although Skaaren was mentioned as a cowriter, Hamm's occasionally arrogant quotes were the only ones included. In a lengthy *American Film* article about Hollywood's growing interest in pulp-based films over prestige pictures, Hamm implied that it was his refusal to work on the script during the 1988 writers strike that had caused Mark Canton and the other producers to seek out Skaaren's help once the strike ended in August. "I don't think it's the same take on the character," said Hamm in comparing his initial characterization to the final cut's portrayal of Batman.[65] Skaaren had done only a smattering of interviews for his previous credits, which made sense given his role as a rewriter—a position the industry tended to downplay when promoting its films. But *Batman* was different, and Mike Simpson knew this. He wanted to see his client recognized for his contributions to the potential blockbuster. And of course it could only reflect well on Simpson that two of his clients were attached to what everyone was hoping would be the biggest movie of the summer.

Skaaren was aware of the *Batman* hype, but he also was busy with *Days of Thunder*. He had written four drafts of the NASCAR-based screenplay since January, and he was set to fly to Italy with Don Simpson, Jerry Bruckheimer, Tom Cruise, and Cruise's wife, actress Mimi Rogers. After traveling together in a private plane, the group shared a rented villa in Palermo, on the island of Sicily, where the producers, Skaaren, and Cruise spent hours discussing the film and working on the script.[66]

Back in the United States, excitement continued to build about *Batman*. Skaaren flew to Los Angeles for the film's world premiere. Industry interest in the film was so intense that Warner Bros. scheduled two screenings on the same night, one at the Mann Bruin Theatre and the other at the Fox Westwood Village. The event, which took place on Monday, June 19, four days prior to the film's official opening, offered a snapshot of Hollywood power in the 1980s. In addition to *Batman*'s stars, many other celebrities turned out for the premiere, including Don Johnson and his wife, actress Melanie Griffith; James Brolin, who had had a small role in Burton's *Pee-wee's Big Adventure*; and a who's who of young Hollywood: *Beetlejuice*'s Winona Ryder as well as Christian Slater, River Phoenix, Robert Downey Jr., and Sarah Jessica Parker. Skaaren walked the red carpet prior to the screening, enjoying the evening's celebratory feel and happy to see Jack Nicholson in particular. He and Hamm finally met in person, and the two writers shook hands before the lights went down for the screening.[67] The *Batman* afterparty was held at Twenty/20, a "disco palace" in nearby Century City. Skaaren celebrated with Warner Bros. production exec Lucy Fisher, who had helped to convince him to do the project, and her husband, Doug Wick, with whom Skaaren had partnered on *Flawless*.[68]

Congratulatory telegrams began arriving even before Skaaren left Los Angeles. Various William Morris executives sent notes, including Norman Brokaw, president and CEO of the agency, who praised the film's writing. Executive vice president Leonard Hirshan, who attended one of the two premieres, mentioned the "maddening, ecstatic" crowd that responded so well to the film. William Morris vice president Jim Crabbe presciently noted that the film just might be "the first movie of the 1990s," and agent Carol Yumkas predicted that *Batman* could be "the biggest grossing picture of all time."[69]

Yumkas wasn't far off. A few nights later, *Batman* producers Guber and Peters and Warner Bros. executives Terry Semel and Mark Canton heard that excited fans were lining up with sleeping bags outside movie theaters in Westwood, camping out for tickets the night before *Batman*'s Friday opening. At Canton's birthday party the next evening, he received a personal call from Steve Ross, the chairman of Warner Communications, Inc. Ross was overseeing the delicate merger of Warner and Time, Inc., and he congratulated Canton on *Batman*'s opening. "You may be responsible for making the merger happen," Ross reportedly told an ecstatic Canton.[70] Skaaren received a fax from Doug Wick the day after *Batman* premiered. "Holy Batshit!" wrote Wick underneath an industry chart detailing the box-office grosses for June 23. *Batman* topped the list, followed by *Dead Poets Society*, *Field of Dreams*, *Ghostbusters II*, and *Honey I Shrunk the Kids*. The copy noted that *Batman* had grossed $15.3 million on its opening day.[71] By Monday morning, the news became somewhat more official: estimates of *Batman*'s opening weekend gross on 2,850 screens were between $40 million and $42.5 million, which *The Hollywood Reporter* noted set multiple weekend box-office records. By the time the July 4th holiday weekend kicked off, ten days later, the film would have set another record and officially achieved blockbuster status with its $100 million gross at the box office.[72]

Trade magazine *Variety* ran one of the first advance reviews of the film, praising Jack Nicholson's performance and the Joker's "lavish verbal pirouettes" as well as Anton Furst's strikingly moody production design. "But the uneven Warner Bros. release treats its thin plot too reverentially," noted the review, which also blamed Hamm and Skaaren for failing "to bring the richness and complexity to Batman that would complement the visuals." Cautioning parents against bringing young children to the film, which was rated PG-13, the review predicted that Burton's *Batman* "will find admirers and detractors in equal numbers."[73]

Sometimes the admirers and detractors were one and the same. Mary Cantwell, reviewing the film for the *New York Times*, admitted to being a longtime fan of Batman comics. "I didn't miss Robin," she wrote of the film, whose original screenplay by Hamm introduced the other half of the Dynamic Duo in the film's third act until Skaaren nixed the character. "But I did miss a few things that might have clarified the plot, although the whole thing being inchoate, I'm hard put to describe exactly what those things might have been," mused Cantwell.[74] Pauline Kael called the film "powerfully glamorous . . . with sets angled and lighted like film noir." She also addressed the film's production history, claiming that the 1988 writers strike had damaged Hamm's "promising" script because it interrupted his final pass and introduced other writers like Skaaren into the mix who failed to develop characters adequately "or provide the turning points that were needed." Still, wrote Kael, the film "has so many unpredictable spins that what's missing doesn't seem to matter much. The images sing."[75]

A number of articles about the film repeated Hamm's claim that because he wouldn't work on the script during the 1988 writers strike, which lasted twenty-two weeks from March through August, the producers hired others to tinker with it, including Skaaren. This backstory was usually followed by an unflattering critique of the finished film's narrative structure, with a quote from Hamm that implied his version would have been better. "Hamm's original conception got mangled," wrote Michael Sragow in the *San Francisco Examiner* in August 1989. "As a result, the finished movie—on a narrative level—is ragged and disjointed. . . . But Hamm is still responsible for much of the magic that propelled the finished movie into becoming the top-grossing movie of 1989," Sragow continued, noting that within two months after its release the movie had earned approximately $230 million.[76] Although some of the press accounts indicated that Skaaren worked on the script during the strike, this was not true. However, because the studio approached Skaaren four times about the project before he agreed to work on the script, it is likely that at least one of these requests occurred during the strike.

Skaaren seemed to take much of this critique and Hamm's credit grab in stride. And as the movie continued to rake in profits that summer, more and more people began taking ownership of its success. Producer Jon Peters "blustered to anyone who would listen that he had written, directed, cast, and singlehandedly marketed the film," observed journalists Nancy Griffin and Kim Masters of that period. Skaaren, ever the diplomat on the record concerning Hollywood politics, said later, "I hear a lot of stories of Jon saying he wrote it and directed it and acted in it. And that's just sort of who Jon is, and he's hilarious."[77] As Skaaren told the *Dallas Morning News*, "These projects are not private creations. They're industrial events. And as such they're risky, with a lot of people and a lot of stress involved."[78]

At the time, the stress seemed to be worth it. Although *Batman*'s reviews continued to be mixed, the film's profits poured in. The blockbuster passed the $200 million mark midsummer, and before the end of the year it would easily best all other releases for 1989, including several highly anticipated summer films, such as *Indiana Jones and the Last Crusade* and *Ghostbusters II*. By the end of its theatrical run, during which the film had played on more than 23,000 screens, *Batman* had become the second highest domestic grossing film of all time.[79] What did this mean for Skaaren? *Batman* would become the biggest moneymaker of his career, not only because of the size of the film's profits themselves but also because Skaaren's deal included 1 percent gross profit participation (after breakeven) in addition to his net profit points. This level of profit participation typically was reserved for A-list stars and indicates Skaaren's value within the industry only four years into his Hollywood career.

For Skaaren, the experience of working on *Batman*, and the film's subsequent blockbuster success, seemed to mean just as much as, if not more than, the financial rewards he reaped. Herb Sleeper, who had attended John Marshall High School with Skaaren back in their hometown of Rochester, recalls seeing his former classmate at their twenty-fifth high school reunion in mid-June, shortly before the *Batman* opening. Although Skaaren didn't mention the film or his involvement with it, Sleeper noticed that Skaaren was wearing a small pin in the shape of the Bat symbol on the lapel of his sport coat. Sleeper had heard of the upcoming film, of course, and assumed that Skaaren had been involved with it in Austin in some way, knowing that he had once run the state's film commission. But it wasn't until after the film's release and even Skaaren's death eighteen months later that Sleeper learned how integral Skaaren had been to the comic-book adaptation.[80]

Skaaren flew back and forth to Los Angeles that summer, where he met with Jerry Bruckheimer about the *Days of Thunder* script and other power players like Ned Tanen, who had recently left his post as president of Paramount's Motion Picture Group to return to independent producing. The *Days of Thunder* project had hit a wall due to disagreement between Don Simpson and Tom Cruise over the direction of the story, and Bruckheimer and Skaaren were trying to find a way to defuse the situation. Skaaren's meeting with Tanen was part of his "short range" plan to leverage *Batman*'s success into more lucrative financial deals with the studios. His profile had risen to the extent that veteran publicist Paul Bloch of Rogers & Cowan reached out to offer to represent Skaaren. (By that time, Skaaren had arranged a short-term deal with Cruise publicist Andrea Jaffe.) During that same period Skaaren wrote somewhat loftily about shaping "a Spielbergian role" for himself within the industry.[81] Whether or not this would be possible remained to be seen, but certainly the months immediately following *Batman*'s spectacular release were the time to act.

EIGHT

The Man Hollywood Trusts

When you hire Warren, you pay Warren's deal. If you don't pay his price, he'll work for someone else.

PRODUCER DON SIMPSON

*B*atman publicity responsibilities continued for Warren Skaaren into the fall of 1989 as Warner Bros. prepared to release the film on videocassette. Requests for interviews also arrived. Skaaren had written a feature about Pancho Villa's death mask for *Texas Monthly* back in the early 1980s, and now the magazine wanted to profile him and his recent successes. Writer Emily Yoffe met Skaaren at the Wren Valley house, where the two spent a few hours discussing his career and how he approached a rewrite. Yoffe deftly captured Skaaren as script doctor in the opening to her *Texas Monthly* profile, which has Skaaren relaying a story about finding a diamond on the ground at Dallas's Love Field airport in 1981. "How are you going to use this? I could tell it a thousand ways," he said.[1]

Skaaren did indeed find a heart-shaped diamond in the dirt at Love Field during the time that he was commuting between Austin and Dallas as chairman of the production company FPS. With attorney Amon Burton's help, they reunited the nearly five-carat gem with its owner, a wealthy Oklahoma oilman who had purchased it for his girlfriend. Skaaren intimates insist that lucky things like this happened to him all the time. As Skaaren told Yoffe, however, he saw it as having less to do with luck than with a principle that guided his life. "I pay attention. How many people walked over that diamond at Love Field? It was in plain sight. It's a physical law: pay attention to what piques your curiosity. It's the same for your work."[2]

In the fall of 1989, however, Skaaren was struggling to pay attention. He had met with Tim Burton during one of his trips to Los Angeles that summer to discuss writing the sequel to *Beetlejuice*. It would
be Skaaren's first original script since the unproduced *Crimson Eagle* in
1987. But Skaaren was distracted by the mounting conflict between him
and Helen. The couple had celebrated their twentieth wedding anniversary in March, and Skaaren had written optimistically about their future almost a year earlier. But more than one friend has speculated that
Helen did not share Warren's passion for movies, and *Batman*'s phenom-
enal success upon its opening in June of that year only heightened the
amount of attention Warren was receiving for his movie work. Almost
from the beginning of his screenwriting career in 1984, Skaaren had
been in demand as a rewriter, but with the release of *Batman*, he secured
his place in the elite rank of script doctors who could command seven-
figure paydays and more. The issues between Warren and Helen hadn't
changed much since the early years of their marriage and included mun-
dane differences, such as their incompatibility as travelers and Skaaren's
occasional tendency to stray from the macrobiotic diet Helen favored,
to weightier matters, such as their disagreements over having children.
According to Skaaren's journal, in mid-August, when he asked his wife
what she thought had gone wrong in their marriage, she cited his midlife
crisis; his anger at his mother, Pearl; and their differences as contribut-
ing factors.[3]

The couple separated that same month, with Warren moving out
of the spacious Tuscan villa on Wren Valley. After leaving the house,
Skaaren stayed first in an Austin hotel, then with friends, and eventually
in a rather seedy apartment south of downtown. Sometime in the late
summer or early fall of 1989, he also began seeing Julie Jordan, a woman
he met through his involvement with the macrobiotic community. Jordan supported Skaaren's heightened involvement with different types of
counseling, which he began pursuing with renewed intensity. In addition to spending more time writing in his journal, Skaaren started to explore his inner "selves" in therapy, identifying and giving names to aspects of himself that he felt needed to be acknowledged and nurtured.
"WES" (Skaaren's initials) represented Skaaren as a child, whom he once
described as the boy for whom he wrote action movies like *Top Gun* and
Batman. "I love things that go *zoom!* I loved the Batmobile. I really think
most of my movies are written by an eight-year-old boy," he told writer
Kevin Phinney in 1990. "Ingrid" was the name Skaaren gave to his feminine side, and so on. In the same interview with Phinney, Skaaren also

revealed how his struggle to understand relationships made its way into his screenplays. Describing the work he did on *Batman*, Skaaren said, "I also wrote the scene where Vicki says to Bruce, 'Are we going to try to love each other?' And he says, 'I'd like to, but . . . I've got to go to work.' To me, that encapsulates the issues of masculine and feminine in America right now. Are there going to be relationships?"[4]

Skaaren's turmoil over his personal life was playing havoc with his ability to make decisions about work. He vacillated over taking on the sequel to *Beetlejuice*. A list of pros and cons, his tried-and-true way of dealing with ambivalence, included "money, back in the game, others will have to take care of themselves, my comfort, camaraderie . . . fun, luxury" as positive reasons to take the assignment. He also noted that "Beet is good for me and people," possibly referring to the fact that fans of the original *Beetlejuice* had made their interest in a sequel well known to the executives at Geffen and Warner Bros. (the production and distribution companies, respectively). The negative aspects of working on *Beetlejuice 2*, for Skaaren, included the toll it would take on his already fragile personal life, the fear that he wouldn't be able to satisfy Burton or the executives at Warner Bros., and the nagging suspicion that "Beet is old biz for me." With the added possibility that he would work on a follow-up to *Batman* in the spring of 1990, Skaaren worried that he'd be juggling two demanding projects simultaneously, or at least back-to-back.[5]

He already had turned down the offer to write *Beetlejuice 2* in August, but Burton and/or the studio had approached him again by late September. He was in the process of reconsidering the project when the tensions in his private life escalated. Jordan was going through a personal crisis and turned to him for reassurance. Skaaren was still in contact with Helen and would go to her when she called with a problem, complicating his deepening relationship with Jordan. One evening during this time, Skaaren found himself calling Jordan, who was in New Mexico, from a pay phone in the parking lot of a shopping center. The reality of his chaotic personal life began to sink in. "My car is old and dilapidated. I am in a relatively cheap apartment. I can't go home . . . I am having sexual disfunction [*sic*] with my wife because of guilt and I am tired of it. I'm a rich and powerful man in a fucking parking lot," he wrote in despair. A couple of days later, he had decided to say yes to *Beetlejuice 2*, telling himself, "Do Beet 2 for the soul. . . . As a gift to myself."[6]

The following month Skaaren participated in a screenwriter's seminar on the University of Texas campus. He joined a distinguished list of speakers that included Jack Valenti, founder and head of the Motion Picture Association of America, the trade association that represented the major movie studios and handled ratings for theatrical releases; Horton Foote, whose numerous writing credits included the adaptation of *To Kill a Mockingbird* (1962) and *The Trip to Bountiful* (1985); Ernest Lehman, who had written with Alfred Hitchcock on *North by Northwest* (1959) and worked on the musical blockbuster *The Sound of Music* (1965); and Jay Presson Allen, who had written *The Prime of Miss Jean Brodie* (1978) and done uncredited work most recently on *The Verdict* (1982). With the exception of Lehman, all of the presenters had Texas ties: Valenti had served as President Lyndon Johnson's press secretary, and Foote and Presson Allen had both grown up in Texas. The other writers showed clips from their films and talked about "their reverence for the written word," recalled writer Kevin Phinney, who was in the audience. Skaaren screened the scene from *Top Gun* in which Tom Cruise's Maverick and his best friend, played by Anthony Edwards, serenade Kelly McGillis's flight instructor. "I like to turn the sound down on my movies," Skaaren offered when the clip ran without dialogue or music. "If I can follow the action of the scene without having to hear the dialogue, I know the film is working on a visual level."[7]

At some point during the event, Skaaren ran into an acquaintance, a university professor, and asked about a mutual friend. The faculty member told Skaaren that their friend had passed away two years earlier from skin cancer. Skaaren, who had never pursued the prescribed course of treatment for his own malignant tumor in 1987, began to panic. "I was terrified the whole afternoon because this thing on my eye was hurting. [The story] freaked me out in some way and left me feeling vulnerable."[8]

It was not unusual for Skaaren to be somewhat preoccupied with death. After all, one of his favorite books was Ernest Becker's *The Denial of Death*, which he had discovered around the time he was working on the Freddie Steinmark project in the mid-1970s. But events during the late fall of 1989 seemed only to heighten this preoccupation. In November he spent time in Rochester, moving his aged parents into an apartment within Charter House, an assisted living facility that was affiliated with the Mayo Clinic. Morris was now in his late eighties and in frail health. Skaaren's mother, Pearl, had recently turned eighty-two but seemed as physically strong as ever. Skaaren spent a week with his parents, helping them to get settled; although exhausting, the trip was a good one. His mother in particular seemed to be enjoying her son's success with *Batman*. The film's widespread recognition helped the

Skaarens understand what their son did for a living. Indeed, as Pearl began to meet fellow retirees living in Charter House, she would often introduce herself as "Batman's grandmother."[9] For the first time in a long
while, the forty-three-year-old Skaaren felt that his parents treated him
as an adult, and he took tremendous pride in the fact that his income
could support them in what was considered one of the finest retirement
communities in the country.[10]

Death was also the focus of *Beetlejuice 2*, which was Skaaren's main
project at the end of 1989. The two-page synopsis for the proposed film
focuses on Leo, a composer of operas, and his girlfriend, Julia, a soprano,
whose romance ends tragically when Leo accidentally falls to his death
from atop the Eiffel Tower while proposing to Julia. Leo's entrance into
the afterlife makes it possible for Beetlejuice to escape, and he sets his
sights on Leo's distraught fiancée. Skaaren and Burton discussed the
project fairly often throughout November and December. A slight hic-
cup occurred during negotiations when it appeared that The Geffen
Company was arranging to have another writer, Jonathan Gems, also
work on the project. Skaaren panicked and was ready to back out of the
deal when a flurry of phone calls and faxes from David Geffen and Tim
Burton smoothed over the situation and affirmed Skaaren's status as sole
writer on the project. Leveraging *Batman*'s success, Mike Simpson negotiated a million-dollar fee for his client, not including a series of front-
and back-end participation bonuses.[11]

Given the success of *Beetlejuice* upon the film's release in 1988, executives at Geffen, the film's production company, were eager to capitalize on fans' sustained interest in the characters. Merchandise, comic
books, and an animated television show had only heightened this interest in the Beetlejuice character in particular. Skaaren and Burton met
with Geffen president Sean Daniel and company executive Eric Eisner
in December prior to Skaaren's committing a first draft to paper. Burton liked Skaaren's idea that Leo's character would be reincarnated after his death, pitting him against Beetlejuice in a competition of sorts for
Julia's affections. Daniel and Eisner were more interested in laying out
certain factors that they wanted Skaaren to keep in mind as he wrote.
The Geffen executives noted that much of the audience for *Beetlejuice*
was young and prone to repeat viewings, and that the television series
and merchandise related to *Beetlejuice* could only help build momentum for the follow-up. Daniel mentioned that Winona Ryder, who had
played Lydia in the original, might be cast in the sequel. He and Eisner also teased the possibility that another major character could return

in a cameo. According to notes from the meeting, Michael Keaton, who would reprise his lead role, wanted the character to be heroic in *Beetlejuice 2*, perhaps with a desire to "make something of himself." Comparisons were even made to Steven Spielberg's *E.T.* (1982), with Skaaren dutifully noting someone's suggestion that perhaps Beetlejuice could have a dog as a friend to humanize the character. Daniel and Eisner returned again and again to the fans' expectations regarding the titular character. "The audience's crazed desire to see him again should be built on and dragged out," they told Skaaren, encouraging him to create "one of the great entrances in all history."[12]

Skaaren plunged into research for *Beetlejuice 2*, happily distracting himself from the trouble in his personal life. He researched the latest operas and familiarized himself with the newest production trends, such as the move toward staging "modern" operas directed by outsiders like theater director Peter Sellars and written by The Police's Stewart Copeland.[13] As Skaaren began to sketch out the script's main beats and story arc, Denise DiNovi, head of Tim Burton Productions, sent him a file of fan mail related to the animated television series. Skaaren seemed particularly interested in a letter from a twenty-five-year-old mother who watched the show and wrote that Beetlejuice "was such a bastard in the movie, but I like him as this nice sort of 'hero against his will' character" in the television series.[14] Skaaren weighed the fans' interest carefully as he sketched out characterizations prior to writing an outline. Burton described Beetlejuice as a "regular guy even though he's a demon from hell." He encouraged Skaaren to "treat him like a real character" and ask questions about Beetlejuice's background before he died and to explore how and when he died, mining each of these scenarios for humor and satire.[15]

"We struck an archetypal note with him that was unique," Skaaren said of the Beetlejuice character while he was in the midst of working on the sequel. "I want to keep on perfecting that. In America, no one has shed any light on the Trickster lately, although American Indian cultures know that kind of figure very well."[16] In preparation for the first draft of the sequel, now called *Beetlejuice in Love*, Skaaren plumbed old favorites by author and mythologist Joseph Campbell and psychologist Carl Jung, fleshing out Beetlejuice's psychological profile. From Jung, he noted that "the hero's task has an aim that goes beyond biological and mental adjustment. It is to liberate the anima as that inner component of the psyche which is necessary for any true creative achievement." With Beetlejuice, Skaaren saw the opportunity to explore the push-pull nature of one's conscious and unconscious desires. And given the upheaval in his private life during that time, Skaaren was in an ideal position to do this. Immersed in therapy and other types of counseling throughout the fall of 1989, Skaaren reminded himself to write from his "feminine" side while working on *Beetlejuice in Love.*

By the end of 1989, screenwriter and script doctor Robert Towne had agreed to work on the stalled *Days of Thunder* script with Tom Cruise, Don Simpson, and Jerry Bruckheimer. (Towne, whom Skaaren had met in 1988 at Jack Nicholson's house, where the two friends were working on the script for *The Two Jakes* [1990], would go on to receive writing credit on the first two *Mission: Impossible* films, projects that Skaaren also had been working on before his death.) Multiple and conflicting accounts exist about how and when Towne took over the writing of the *Days of Thunder* screenplay. Skaaren, who remained a consultant on the project throughout its production and into the summer of 1990, maintained that he met privately with Bruckheimer to discuss the creative impasse between an "inflexible" Cruise who wanted "an increasingly talky movie" and a fuming Simpson who was becoming more and more disinterested in Cruise's version of the film. Skaaren also admitted to having inside information that Cruise was "getting heavy outside pressure" to abandon the project for a weightier film. According to Skaaren, it was his decision to leave the project under the guise of bringing in a new point of view that might defuse the tension and bridge the divide between Cruise and Simpson. "I left under the most favorable terms with all involved," Skaaren wrote in his Statement of Contribution submitted to the WGA in 1990.[17] But in a *Rolling Stone* interview with Cruise shortly after *Days of Thunder*'s release in the summer of 1990, it was suggested that Skaaren left the project after the "sheer exhaustion" of writing seven drafts. "There was frustration that the script wasn't getting there," Cruise was quoted as saying, adding that he was eager to go into production on the project.[18] Skaaren's assistant, Linda Vance, recalls the writer's own annoyance. "Warren just got totally disgusted by the time he was on his last draft. . . . I remember him saying, 'I can't go on much longer. This is good writing, and they've got to accept it or not'," says Vance of the period when Skaaren completed his seventh and last draft of the script in the summer of 1989.[19] Towne, for his part, maintained that he agreed to come on to the project if he could start "from scratch" on the script, a point that Skaaren would eventually dispute during the 1990 screen-credit arbitration.[20]

Although Skaaren stayed in touch with the producers as Towne began working on *Days of Thunder*, and offered comments on Towne's re-writes when asked, he was essentially free to devote himself to *Beetle-juice in Love*. And as 1989 came to a close, Skaaren took time to reflect on the year and his goals for the coming months. He wrote that he hoped to return to the Wren Valley house, where Helen remained while he lived elsewhere during the separation. He wanted to redecorate his of-fice, return to Norway to explore his parents' roots and by extension his own Scandinavian heritage, and figure out if a move to New Mexico was something that might make sense at this point in his life.[21] Warren spent the holidays in Santa Fe, and he wrote to Helen back in Austin about his deep attachment to the place. "I seem to be connected to the mountains of New Mexico. I dream of them every week. I take great joy in simply being there. . . . They heal me wordlessly."[22] Privately, he wrote about his cancer scare in the fall of 1987, describing it as a gift that "showed me the way to a new set of relationships in the world."[23] In Santa Fe on New Year's Eve, Warren marked the transition into 1990 at a friend's party, admitting later that he had traveled to New Mexico partly to avoid having to choose to spend the holiday with either Helen or Julie. As the clock struck midnight, he watched his friends kiss and hug one another and thought, "This is it. This is exactly where I am. Alone on New Year's Eve, starting the 90s alone. In a crowd of drunks."[24]

Back in Austin in early January, Skaaren continued to work on an extended outline and flow charts for *Beetlejuice in Love*. He also did an interview for the *Chicago Tribune* about *Batman*, which was still in the news thanks to its ongoing financial success on videocassette and its rec-ognition during awards season, including a Golden Globe nomination for Jack Nicholson's performance and an Academy Award nomination for Anton Furst and Peter Young's production design.[25] *Premiere* maga-zine even gave the film a nod, citing the Joker's line, "What kind of world do we live in where a man dressed up as a bat . . . gets all my press?" as one of the "Best Lines of 1989" and crediting Skaaren and Hamm.[26] In an article titled "How to Write a Screenplay," for which he was interviewed by a women's magazine, Skaaren managed to remain diplomatic even as he called out Jack Nicholson for stealing his credit. "Jack Nicholson once was asked who wrote the line, 'What this city needs is a good enema.' He said he did. That meant I did a good job. You have to make every-one think that their part comes out of them, or they won't be able to act it well."[27]

But Skaaren spent the majority of his time taking stock of his life and beginning to consider the possibility of divorce. While he admitted to himself that the prospect of ending his marriage scared him because it could mean the potential "loss of my fortune," his deeper fear had to do with being alone. He had come to realize, with the help of hours and hours of therapy, that the relationships he had with the primary women in his life were damaging and needed to change. And it would be up to him to make that change for himself. "No one I ever choose to be with again will need me so desperately like my mother and like Helen and I must grieve the loss of that projection," he wrote while still in Santa Fe. And yet, Skaaren also recognized how both relationships had motivated him in his work, adding, "I have flourished under it."[28] Indeed, one of the inner "characters" Skaaren identified around this time was someone he called "Working Warren," a version of himself who was "competent, smart, effective, aggressive" but whose fatal flaw was his inability to know when to stop working.[29] As a gift to himself, Skaaren began to take flying lessons in January. He described the process of learning to pilot an airplane as similar to the emotional free fall he was experiencing in his personal life. Both required "flying through danger with thought and preparation."[30]

It's not surprising given the level of intensity in Skaaren's personal life that references to some of his experiences made their way into the screenplay for *Beetlejuice in Love*. He satirized the numerous counseling and group therapy sessions he underwent in one particularly funny scene in which Beetlejuice is forced to undergo grief counseling shortly after his arrival in the afterlife. "It's a wretched herd of dead humanity," muttered Beetlejuice after sizing up his fellow group participants.[31] In a later draft Skaaren added a "rich dowager type" character, Mrs. Goodin, whose financial support is funding the opera in which Leo's girlfriend, Julia, is performing. After presenting a check to the director of the opera foundation, Mrs. Goodin remarks, "It's peanuts to me, but it keeps this dump afloat. I've got some medical news. I've got a malignant wart on my chest." When the opera director expresses his concern, Mrs. Goodin responds, "No problem, but Kyle and I are going to live it up from now on, we're going skydiving this afternoon, aren't we Kyle?" As Natasha Waxman has observed of the passage, which seems to be a reference to Skaaren's own malignant chest mole diagnosed two and a half years earlier, the acknowledgment of his cancer was covert at best.[32] In retrospect, however, Mrs. Goodin's final line in the scene seems the most prescient: "The point is I may live forever or I could croak in a year."

In August 1989, when Skaaren was debating whether or not to work on the *Beetlejuice* follow-up, one of his worries about the project was that his work wouldn't be good enough to please Burton and the executives at Geffen and Warner Bros. Still, he enjoyed working with Burton despite their differences, which he discussed in an interview that year for a comics magazine. "I'm sort of a boring middle-America guy and Tim's very hip. But when it comes to our senses of humor, and the kind of craziness we both appreciate in a non-linear progress of stories, we're very much together."[33] For Skaaren, one of the most challenging aspects of the *Beetlejuice in Love* script was how to conceive of a tangible way to show the characters moving between the present-day setting of the story ("the upperworld") and the afterlife ("the underworld"). Skaaren imagined a kind of membrane that separated the two worlds, and he struggled to describe it well enough in early drafts so that it would function as both a plausible story element and, later in production, an impressive visual effect. Once Burton expressed his enthusiasm for the idea, Skaaren put even more pressure on himself to clarify the concept.[34]

By the spring of 1990, while Skaaren was working on *Beetlejuice in Love*, Jerry Bruckheimer and Don Simpson were in South Carolina on the set of *Days of Thunder*, which had begun production in March. Skaaren had read through Robert Towne's shooting script (dated February 1990) and carefully noted similarities between Towne's work and his own, earlier drafts in preparation for the screen-credit arbitration, which would be automatically triggered because of the Writers Guild of America rules concerning credit when multiple writers were involved on a project. In Towne's final draft, the race announcers were a prominent narrative feature, a device that Skaaren had championed early on as a means to convey expository information and to help audiences quickly grasp race culture in general. Cruise had balked at the idea in 1989, however, and those sections had been minimized in Skaaren's subsequent drafts. While some details had changed in the script, the story's major beats remained similar to Skaaren's early structure. Despite an abundance of montage sequences, however, Towne's script seemed more sophisticated than Skaaren's drafts, starting with the change of Cruise's character's love interest from the owner of a club frequented by drivers and their pit crews to an ophthalmologist who helps his character overcome a potentially career-ending eye injury.[35]

In April, Skaaren received a letter from the WGA notifying him, Robert Towne, and Donald Stewart (the other writer who worked on *Days of Thunder*) that screenwriter Eric Hughes was challenging Paramount's proposed story credit and claiming that he should be included in the credits arbitration.[36] Hughes, whose previous credits included *Against All Odds* (1984) and *White Knights* (1985), believed that Towne's final shooting script was very similar to an unproduced screenplay about car racing that he had written for Paramount. Thus, the WGA announced that it would conduct a preliminary arbitration to determine if, in fact, Hughes should be included in the automatic arbitration triggered by the fact that two or more writers had worked on *Days of Thunder*. Skaaren flew to Los Angeles in early May to testify as part of the proceedings surrounding credit determination for the film. While Hughes's claim was eventually dismissed, his challenge of the WGA and, by extension, of the megastar Cruise, whom Paramount had proposed to receive story credit, caught the interest of the trade press. *Variety* interviewed Skaaren about the situation, and he was careful to point out that an arbitration would take place even if Hughes had not challenged Paramount's proposed credit. "It's getting to be more and more complex, especially on these big, complicated and expensive movies," Skaaren admitted to *Variety*'s Will Tusher. "A lot of people get involved . . . and it's a legitimately complicated thing to determine credits. The Writers Guild does its best, but it's not easy on all of us. That's for sure."[37] The following day *Variety* ran another story, this time featuring a quote from writer Donald Stewart, who took credit for the original screenplay for the film. "[The movie] is what it is today from that," Stewart told Tusher.[38]

In mid-May Skaaren and the other writers received official notification that the *Days of Thunder* screenplay credit would be arbitrated by the WGA. Skaaren set to work preparing his final Statement of Contribution, which by WGA rules was due to their office within twenty-four hours of his receipt of the initial notification. The final document ran to twenty-six pages and carefully laid out his multiyear involvement in the film, from his first meeting in early 1987 with Tom Cruise in a Chinese restaurant to his decision in November 1989 to remove himself as a writer on the project. While Skaaren's statement was as detailed as any he had written over the approximately five years he had been working as a rewrite man, this one in particular seemed a bit more urgent, even slightly reckless, in its tone and content.

He referred to Don Simpson as "very vociferous," and while the outspoken producer had surely been called much worse in print, it was uncharacteristic of Skaaren to be anything but diplomatic regarding his Hollywood peers. "Ours was an intense, hands-on development process," Skaaren explained in his statement, promising to "show the inside history of the battle between [Tom] Cruise and Simpson during my drafts and how many of those experiments led to Towne's final draft."[39]

One of the "inside" details that Skaaren chose to share in his statement concerned the backstory to the development of Cruise's love interest in the script, who initially was a nurse in Skaaren's October 1988 outline before she became a club owner. "Cruise insisted his character be a divorcing man (interesting to note that shortly after I left, Cruise became a divorced man himself, at which point he dropped the insistence on this theme in the script. Ah how life and art intermingle!)" wrote Skaaren.[40] The intimate nature of this revelation may not have been a big deal in an industry that thrived on gossip, but it was unlike Skaaren to share such observations, particularly in a situation in which he did not know the identity of those who would be reading his statement. But details such as these did emphasize his privileged position on the project during its development.

In his opening letter to the arbiters, Skaaren mentioned how "the studio publicity machine and the vociferous Don Simpson . . . have filled the press with the notion that Towne somehow 'deserves' sole credit for his rewrite." Indeed, Simpson was quoted in Army Archerd's column "Just for Variety" as saying, "Whatever's on screen came out of his [Towne's] mind, heart and soul. He kept writing until one week before we finished. I never saw anyone that talented work that hard."[41] Ironically, it was Skaaren whom Archerd had championed in his column five years earlier during the *Top Gun* screenwriting credit debate. As Skaaren acknowledged in his statement to the WGA arbiters, "I've been the last writer on other films and I remember the intense camaraderie that's formed by the heat of battle. That's obviously the case with Mr. Simpson and Mr. Towne. But a larger view is required by the WGA."[42]

A month before *Days of Thunder* was released in late June 1990, the WGA Arbitration Committee had made its decision. The *Sarasota Herald-Tribune* ran an article about the film on opening weekend, noting that "production was further complicated by a contentious screenplay credit arbitration, which Towne and Cruise, who co-created the story, eventually won."[43] Skaaren had received $750,000 for his work on *Days of Thunder*. Agent Mike Simpson and L.A. attorney Harold Brown had spent much of the summer and fall of 1988 working out the finer points of Skaaren's profit participation on the film. Although the WGA's decision meant that Skaaren lost out on a screenwriting credit, his deal still entitled him to 1 percent of the film's adjusted gross receipts beyond a cash breakeven amount that he would also receive.[44] The film, which earned mostly mixed to negative reviews, did strong business on its opening weekend and ranked in the top spot at the box office. It had earned more than $82 million at the domestic box office by the end of the year.[45] According to Skaaren's deal, and factoring in the film's foreign receipts, he was entitled to approximately $150,000 of the film's profits.

Skaaren's personal life continued to be in flux. He and Helen remained separated, although they stayed in occasional contact. Julie Jordan was also still in his life, and they saw each other frequently. By this time, Skaaren was living in a dingy rental in South Austin, an apartment that friends recall as being almost the antithesis of the lovely, tastefully decorated Wren Valley villa. Sometime in the spring of 1990, Skaaren had begun to experience recurring back pain. He sought treatment from chiropractors and acupuncturists and began taking a combination of herbs on a regular basis, but the pain continued. When Linda Vance wasn't driving him to medical appointments, Jordan would accompany him to sessions with alternative healers. Concerned about his health, Jordan had consulted an astrologer that spring and asked for a reading of Skaaren's chart without his knowledge. The astrologer told Jordan that the man in question was about to face a difficult time. Although he was used to "operating" as a "free agent," said the astrologer, this man would feel "a lot of strings" tying him down.[46]

Conclusion

I've been dead once; it's very liberating.

THE JOKER, *BATMAN* (LINE WRITTEN BY WARREN SKAAREN)

B y July 1990 Warren Skaaren had completed a first draft of *Beetlejuice in Love*. This final version of the multiple "scratch" drafts that Skaaren had written throughout the spring hadn't changed much from the initial concepts that he and Tim Burton had discussed the previous summer. Reincarnation was a dominant theme, and the story still pivoted on a romantic triangle involving Beetlejuice, an opera singer, and her recently deceased fiancé. Skaaren had given an early draft to Diane Haug, a woman with whom he had been friends since the 1970s. By 1990 Haug had left Austin for New Mexico, and she had experience in palliative and hospice care, so Skaaren solicited her feedback on the script's death images.[1] Gone was the reference to a minor character's malignant chest mole, which echoed Skaaren's own cancer diagnosis three years earlier. The script mined Beetlejuice's wacky characteristics and even featured a chorus singing a "We are the World"–style song in tribute to the character. Despite its quirkiness and weak spots, Skaaren's draft had a charmingly playful, almost wistful quality. On July 10 he sent copies of the bound script by express mail to Burton and David Geffen in Los Angeles.[2]

A week later, Skaaren made an urgent call to his assistant. His back pain had intensified, and he had gone to his chiropractor. After doing an initial exam, the doctor recommended that Skaaren have an MRI. Skaaren asked Linda Vance if she could take him to the appointment that afternoon. After they arrived at the imaging center and

Skaaren was taken to be prepped for the exam, Vance settled into working a crossword puzzle. More than an hour passed, so she went to check on Skaaren's progress. She found him in a dark room with a couple of doctors, peering at a series of X-rays. "Linda, I'll be a bit longer than I thought," Skaaren told her.

More time passed. Vance was startled when a car drove up outside the reception area and a man dressed in a business suit got out and rushed through the waiting room and toward the exam area where Skaaren was huddled with his doctors. Another hour went by. Finally, Vance asked one of the nurses at the front desk to check on Skaaren. "They're bringing him out now," the nurse said when she returned. Behind her, Skaaren was being pushed down the hall in a wheelchair. His face was ashen and drawn. "It was not the Warren that I had taken in," Vance said later.[3]

As they left the imaging center and began to drive toward the Wren Valley house at Skaaren's request, he asked Vance to pull over. "What's going on, Warren?" she asked. Skaaren told his assistant that he needed to think. They sat in silence for about five minutes. "Well, I think I'll head toward home, and you let me know if there's any change," Vance said as she began to drive. At one point, Skaaren told her to go to his bank, giving her his ATM card and instructing her to withdraw $500. When she returned to the car, he said, "Boy, it's been a tough year, hasn't it?" Vance assumed he was referring to his and Helen's separation, which had occurred almost twelve months earlier. When Vance agreed, he continued, "Yeah, and now this." Vance still had no idea what had happened with his MRI, and she asked Skaaren if he wanted to discuss it. "No," he replied, so she turned the key in the ignition and drove him home.[4]

Once inside, Skaaren continued to waffle. First he asked Vance to stay and make some calls, and then he sent her home with instructions to rent a van. "I've got to go to Houston tomorrow and see some doctors" was all he'd tell her. While she scoured the city for available transportation, Skaaren made calls to a few close friends, including Blake Gould, a macrobiotic specialist who had counseled Skaaren after his 1987 cancer diagnosis. Later that evening Skaaren checked in with Vance, who had had no luck in renting a van. "We've got to fly," Skaaren insisted, and he asked her to secure a private plane so that they could fly out in the morning.

By 10 A.M. on July 19, Skaaren and Vance were en route to Houston. Midway through the thirty-minute flight, Skaaren turned to Vance. By this time Vance knew that they were headed to The University of Texas

MD Anderson Cancer Center. Vance had suspected Skaaren's cancer diagnosis, but what he said next floored her. "Three and a half years ago, I had this mole on my chest, and it became infected. It turned out it was melanoma. Now they say I've got tumors in my spine," Skaaren said as he began to cry. Vance was speechless. Not only was she trying to process his current diagnosis, but she was dumbfounded that he had been diagnosed three years earlier, shortly after she started working for him on a daily basis. She had never known.[5]

A limousine was waiting for Skaaren and Vance on the tarmac in Houston. Vance had made the transportation arrangements, but it was Skaaren's reputation as the screenwriter of *Batman* that fast-tracked his admittance to MD Anderson and helped to secure a private suite on an upper floor reserved for heads of state and other high-profile patients. Four doctors—two senior and two junior physicians—attended to Skaaren, examining the X-rays that Vance had carried under her arm from Austin. They sent Skaaren for additional scans, then visited him in his room afterward. The experts at MD Anderson did not sugarcoat their prognosis. Skaaren's cancer had metastasized and spread to his spine and his thorax. He needed emergency surgery. Without it, he had only a 1 percent chance of survival. Skaaren, ambivalent at best about Western medicine, resisted the idea. "He did not like what he was hearing, and he didn't seem to have any faith in them," said Vance. When Amon Burton arrived later that day, he listened to Skaaren's protestations and about how he was going to beat the disease, then asked, "So why'd you come down here if you're not going to have this done?"[6]

While Skaaren underwent additional tests to prep him for his surgery the following day, Vance and Burton got dinner in MD Anderson's cafeteria. They commiserated about their shock—not only regarding Skaaren's current diagnosis but also over the fact that neither one had been privy to his 1987 cancer scare. They discussed, too, the trouble brewing on the horizon. Earlier that afternoon, Skaaren had spent the time between medical tests on the phone, taking calls from Helen, who was still in Austin, and reaching out to Julie Jordan. Both women were planning to arrive in Houston the following day. Returning to Skaaren's hospital room, Burton produced a series of legal documents from his briefcase. One was a medical directive asserting Skaaren's wish not to be kept alive on a ventilator or to have similar life-extending measures taken should the situation arise. Vance and a visitor meeting with another patient in a room nearby acted as witnesses.[7]

Vance and Burton remained with Skaaren until he was taken into the operating room the following day, July 20. By that time Helen and her sister, Liz Viola, had arrived from Austin. Julie Jordan was also on her way. Vance and Burton flew back home to tend to Skaaren's business while he underwent the operation to remove the tumors pressing on his spine. For the next five days, Vance held down the fort at Skaaren's office at the Wren Valley house, returning phone calls and answering mail while under strict orders from her employer not to discuss what was happening with anyone, even his agent, Mike Simpson. Back in Houston, Skaaren spent those five days recovering from surgery with Helen and Julie at his side. He was also in constant phone contact with Blake Gould. Skaaren checked in regularly with Vance, beginning and ending the day with phone conversations that helped him keep track of his work commitments and allowed him to vent about his diagnosis. During the weeklong course of Skaaren's treatment in Houston, Vance began to realize how deeply invested he was in the macrobiotic lifestyle. "Right there he was making the decision . . . he was having traditional medicine done to him but he was also immersed in this other, nontraditional healing right from the start."[8]

Skaaren's doctors released him from the hospital a week later, and Vance flew to Houston at Skaaren's request to drive Helen's car back to Austin. He would return by private plane, accompanied by his estranged wife and his girlfriend. "They all got in the plane to fly back to Austin, the three of them squabbling about where everyone was going to sit," Vance recalled about a year later.

Skaaren wanted to return to his house on Wren Valley, which he had vacated nearly a year earlier when he and Helen separated. While Amon Burton negotiated with Helen to arrange Warren's return to the house, where he requested to live by himself, Warren spent the first few weeks after his surgery staying with friends in North Austin. Acquaintances and intimates from the macrobiotic community visited often. "It became the most important thing surrounding him. If you believe in all of that, then you're going to try it all, and he did. We had everybody from shamans to feather people," says Vance of the variety of healers and practitioners whom Skaaren sought out during this time.[9] Eventually Helen moved out of Wren Valley and Warren moved back in, choosing to set himself up in the first-floor guestroom just off the house's warm and inviting kitchen. The negotiations and tense interpersonal dynamics that arose during Skaaren's time in Houston set the tone for his return to

Austin. "It was six months of absolute madness, of these power struggles that went on around Warren as he was dying," said Vance. "And it got worse."[10]

One of Skaaren's first decisions upon his return to Austin was to make plans to attend a macrobiotic conference in Vermont. He and Jordan traveled to New England together, staying in a bed-and-breakfast and meeting up with Blake Gould in addition to attending conference events. Skaaren's doctors at MD Anderson had prescribed steroids as part of his postsurgical recovery, and while Skaaren was taking the drugs, he was eager to pursue homeopathic alternatives for his cancer diagnosis. He also used natural treatments, such as barley plasters, which Jordan applied to his back twice a day for three hours at a time. As with the steroids, the plasters were meant to minimize inflammation particularly around the site of Skaaren's surgical wound. He wore a corset to give support to his back in addition to taking the steroids. Although Skaaren insisted on making the trip to explore macrobiotic options by meeting with Gould and attending the conference, he still was in tremendous pain postsurgery. At one point, he asked Jordan to go to a nearby store to buy a bottle of Advil. When she returned, Skaaren took two pills and began to cry. "We just knew it was the beginning of something," said Jordan. "Warren took two Advil, which was nothing. [But] I just cried my heart out on the bed because I saw then that drugs were the path that we were going to be taking."[11]

In reality Skaaren's treatment path was murky at best. Over the next five months, that path would take many twists and turns as Skaaren ran hot and cold about how to deal with his cancer diagnosis. Jordan and others were part of the "life squad," a team of friends and new acquaintances who embraced the healing power of macrobiotics and other alternative therapies. "We were one hundred percent geared toward Warren living," said Jordan of the group, some of who had met through the local re-evaluation counseling (RC) sessions that Skaaren had attended fairly regularly over the previous years. One of the beliefs championed by this particular type of counseling, according to Jordan, was that if a person was able to "discharge the beliefs and the fears around the pain," one could discover the "core" of the pain and thus weaken or even abolish its source.[12]

Brian and Kaye Connors knew Jordan through macrobiotic circles, and when she could no longer manage all of Skaaren's meals herself, she asked them to help out. The Connorses had met at a macrobiotic center in Northern California. While studying there, they had also learned about caring for and healing people with serious illnesses through macrobiotic diet and alternative practices. The Connorses had recently arrived in Austin, and when their house-sitting gig ended in mid-fall, they began taking care of Skaaren. Their first meeting was a relaxed conversation that took place around the Skaarens' kitchen table. "He seemed very genuine in his need for life energy," Brian Connors recalled. "He was looking for something special that he wanted in his life. He wasn't necessarily looking for, say, techniques to heal him. He was looking for a more complete experience. He was looking for companionship as much or more than just trying to be healed."[13]

Others, like longtime assistant Linda Vance and attorney Amon Burton, were more focused on helping Skaaren get his house in order, literally and figuratively. To Vance, for instance, the comings and goings of those on the "life squad" seemed at times to be sapping Skaaren's energy more than anything. "He had this whole other group pulling on him and telling him that he could be healed if he would do what they wanted him to do. And some of it was legit, but I'm not sure at that time that it was going to help," said Vance of the various herbal medicines, acupuncture therapy, massage treatments, and healing sessions being administered to Skaaren by several different individuals, including a shaman who was treating Skaaren long-distance from Hawaii.[14]

Lee Walker had become close to Skaaren after his diagnosis. He was a few years older, but he and Warren shared a number of similarities. Both men were tall, although at 6'9" Walker trumped Skaaren by nearly half a foot. They were voracious readers and later discovered that they both loved *A Pattern Language*, about architecture, community, and urban design. Walker had dealt with back pain, too, and had only recently recovered from a lengthy illness that had effectively forced his resignation as the first president of Dell Computer Corporation. At one point Walker, who visited almost daily, assembled Vance, Burton, and Jordan to discuss the possibility of having Skaaren meet with a medical expert who had treated Walker years earlier. Walker admired what he saw as Skaaren's childlike sense of exuberance about life, which manifested itself in his intense curiosity about a variety of subjects and people. But he also worried that this aspect of Skaaren's personality was incapable of making realistic choices regarding his cancer treatment. "Warren the child had sought out what I think might be charitably called a lot of magic in trying to treat the melanoma," he observed later.[15] But Jordan insisted that Skaaren's choice to surround himself with like-minded people from the macrobiotic and New Age communities was ultimately beneficial. "It was a triumph for him to be in his house and to have some feeling of a family around him," she said of that time.[16]

Beginning a new journal in September 1990, Skaaren wrote on the first page, "What a gift to learn how to rest." Still, he approached his illness much like he did his writing work, making lists and focusing his energy. "Decide to get well. Get help. Approach treatment with enthusiasm," he wrote.[17] On a to-do list for that period, interspersed among the business items regarding *Beetlejuice in Love* meetings and the *Batman* sequel, was a list of "healing modalities" that included oxygen, remedial yoga, visualizations, and RC, or cocounseling, sessions. He noted that he wanted to "optimize my healing schedule," but on some level he also seemed to acknowledge the gravity of his diagnosis given that his list also included questions about his will, his budget, and his parents.[18] Vance continued to help Skaaren manage his work schedule, which consisted mostly of postponing meetings in Los Angeles related to the *Beetlejuice* project. She was still under strict instructions not to reveal the truth about Skaaren's health. Instead, she would field calls by telling people that he was taking an extended break. "People generally were okay with it," recalls Vance, "because Warren had never taken a long vacation, so he was due one."[19] Still, agent Mike Simpson thought it was unusual. "He was supposed to come out for a business meeting for *Beetlejuice in Love*, and it always kept being, 'Oh, I can't come next week.' And this was so unlike him. Something was up. I just couldn't tell what it was."[20]

After the Connorses joined the "life squad" to care for Skaaren, his days took on a fairly predictable schedule. Kaye would wake him up, usually giving him a toe or leg massage to help him prepare to get out of bed. Within a month or two of his visit to MD Anderson, Skaaren had instructed Vance to lease a hospital bed specially made for burn victims. The bed, which used an air compressor to gently rotate the patient's body to avoid bedsores, cost thousands of dollars per month. Kaye Connors or Julie Jordan would help with Skaaren's shower, and then he would hobble on crutches to the kitchen for breakfast, where they would talk about how he had slept and how he was feeling that day. Jordan, Kaye Connors (and occasionally husband Brian), and visiting Irish cook Mary Kett prepared meals featuring mostly whole grains, beans, and seed vegetables for Skaaren. But as Brian Connors observed, the meals he ate seemed less important to Skaaren than how they looked or with whom he shared them. "Warren liked the presentation of the food more than he liked the food. And if you had everybody at the table, and you had 'the family' there and the love put into it. . . . it was more of a nurturing experience than even what was on the plate."[21]

Initially, Skaaren pursued both traditional and nontraditional healing protocols after his surgery. Over the course of two weeks, Vance took him for regular radiation treatments, and Skaaren insisted that he eat a macrobiotic lunch before each appointment. After his appointment, Vance would drive him back to Wren Valley, where an acupuncturist or massage therapist would be waiting for him. But as his condition worsened throughout October and November, Skaaren lashed out, directing his anger toward traditional medicine. Longtime friends like Bob Rynearson, a practicing psychologist, felt that hostility directly. "He began to become frightened of me and frightened of science. He began surrounding himself with these really crazy people who took over his life. And pretty much shut out the rest of us. He was just terrified of dying. All of these people around him were just protecting him from death, and I was reminding him of death."[22]

Occasionally Rynearson would make the hour-long drive from Temple to Austin to visit with Skaaren, and they often would discuss Skaaren's emotional state. After one visit in early October, Skaaren wrote that Rynearson had advised him to "deal with my guilt and rage" and his need to protect others, particularly women, in his life.[23] According to more than one intimate, Skaaren directed some of this rage toward Helen, his estranged wife, because of what he saw as her encouragement to pursue nontraditional healing of his malignant chest mole in 1987. "He was very angry at Helen. He blamed Helen for his illness. And that's not okay and not right, but he did," recalls Kaye Connors.[24] Skaaren made it clear to those around him that Helen was not welcome. "If her name was mentioned, he protested greatly," one friend recalled.[25]

Vance not only ran interference with Skaaren's Hollywood connections but also interceded on his behalf with family members, friends, and others who tried to get in touch. "It was his choice to lock out people he had known all of his life and invite people he had only known for six months or eighteen months or two years. He didn't talk to relatives on the phone, he didn't want them to come see him," said Vance of people like Jerry Hall, whom Skaaren had been close with during his film commission years.[26] Hall happened to reach out to Skaaren that summer. "Warren always, always returned my phone calls," said Hall years later. "I called him about something, and he called me back from MD Anderson. I began to put one and one together, but I didn't say anything ever, at all, about it." Hall tried to see Skaaren throughout the fall, but Vance put him off at Skaaren's request.[27] In the course of a few weeks, the Wren Valley house went from a tranquil space that fed Skaaren's creativity to a bustling hive of energy and foot traffic. "It was like this stage play and there were all these actors, and they were coming and going. They would just show up out of the blue," said Vance of the noticeable shift at the house. "Everyone that was around him, they all loved him. There wasn't a single person that didn't love Warren, that didn't try in their own way to do everything they could to help him. [But] they weren't always going in the same direction."[28]

Around Thanksgiving, Skaaren's condition seemed to worsen. His pain increased to such an extent that he requested to go to the hospital and was sent home with a morphine drip. Skaaren struggled with the decision to resort to drugs even though it brought him physical relief from the constant and almost unbearable pain in his back and legs. Skaaren confided in Jordan, for instance, that he was taking only enough morphine to keep the pain at bay. "If the drugs took the pain away, I have nothing but gratitude for the drugs. Thank god for morphine," Jordan said shortly after his death. Only later did she realize that Skaaren probably harbored some guilt, thinking that he was disappointing those on the "life squad" who had favored a drug-free approach to healing. "In some way, all of us were interfering with him," Jordan said later.[29] By November Brian and Kaye Connors were living in the house and taking care of Skaaren's meals, the laundry, and general housekeeping. They saw firsthand how the morphine both helped and hindered Skaaren's condition. "He almost overdosed on it at first because it felt so good to have it," recalled Kaye. "I understand why he wanted to go on the morphine, but it really accelerated things."[30]

In September, a mutual acquaintance from Austin had been visiting Diane Haug in New Mexico and saw a photo of Skaaren on her bulletin board, prompting the friend to mention a rumor circulating that Skaaren was seriously ill. Haug had moved to New Mexico in part to specialize in a type of palliative care that involved breath work and other alternative healing techniques. Haug called Skaaren immediately, and they stayed in touch by phone until she could travel to Austin in November.

As with so many of the women who came into contact with Skaaren, Haug felt a strong connection to him. Like Jordan, she shared his Norwegian background, and they teased one another that they had been siblings in another life. During their lunch in the spring of 1990, they had spoken about Skaaren's love of New Mexico and his deep interest in moving there one day. Haug's choice to live alone and in a remote, rugged part of the state seemed to appeal to his craving for independence. After Haug learned of Skaaren's diagnosis that fall, their conversations dealt with his fear and frustration surrounding his illness. "His plea to me was, 'Help me access what I know is available to me on some level but feel very estranged from. Help me reconnect with my own ability to heal myself. I know that I have the power to do that, and I feel really far away from it right now.'"[31]

But when Haug finally arrived that November, her experience with other terminally ill patients told her that Skaaren had at best six weeks left to live. Still, she became swept up in the energy of the "life squad" and Skaaren's own will to heal. She focused her efforts on helping him deal with his constant physical pain. Together they did breathing exercises and guided meditation, particularly at night, when Skaaren's fear and pain seemed to be at their worst. Haug also sensed that her role at that point was to be as honest as possible with him given what she knew about the process of dying. On Haug's second night with Skaaren, he asked her to tell him what she saw. Instead of telling him that she thought he was dying, she shared her deep belief that healing had nothing to do with the outcome of the physical body. An environment that entertains the possibility of dying, she told Skaaren, is probably the best environment in which to heal.[32]

By December, one of Skaaren's greatest fears was that those caring for him at home would not be able to help him manage his pain. The tumors had metastasized from his spine to his hips, trunk, and lungs. He vacillated about going to the hospital, but Haug told him in so many words that if he were admitted to the hospital at that point he probably would not be returning home. Skaaren's doctor, Mike Williams, agreed to make a home visit on the morning of Sunday, December 23. Tremendously debilitated by the chronic pain, Skaaren had been weak and unable to communicate, but he summoned the strength to have his hair combed and was sitting up when Williams walked into his room. After a brief exam and private conversation, Williams emerged from Skaaren's bedroom. A small group including Haug and the Connorses had gathered in the living room. When they asked Williams for his prognosis, his response was grim. "I don't think Warren's going to be living through the New Year," he told them. "I think we're at the end stage here."[33]

Over the next several days, the man who seemed to believe he could heal himself began to address the reality that he was dying. He asked for Haug's help in planning a series of "interesting conversations" with key people in his life, including his mother, who flew in from Rochester. Unaware of the severity of their son's illness, the elder Skaarens were devastated when they received Amon Burton's call. Morris was too frail to travel, so Pearl made the trip alone to Austin. Mrs. Skaaren's diminutive size and sweet disposition surprised more than one Skaaren intimate who had been expecting the domineering, cold, and unkind mother that Skaaren had so often described when recounting his childhood. At Skaaren's request, Haug was present for his final conversations with his mother and even with his wife, Helen. "Warren started finishing some of that business," said Haug, referring to the difficult and unresolved relationships he had had with the primary women in his life.[34] Skaaren had wanted to have a similar conversation with Julie Jordan, who was no longer living at the house. In November, he had broken off their intense romantic relationship. "When he realized and took in that he was going to die, he called me and asked me to come up," recalled Jordan. When she arrived at the house, Haug pulled her aside to brief her on Skaaren's condition, but by the time Jordan got into his bedroom, he had slipped back into a morphine haze. "He could never say to me what he wanted to say," Jordan said. "And I always wondered what it was."[35]

A couple of weeks earlier, Amon Burton had gone against his friend and client's wishes and placed a call to Mike Simpson at William Morris. "I've told Warren he has to call you and tell you what's going on. He's got cancer," Burton said to Simpson. "And Mike," he continued, "you have to know this because your reputation's at stake and so is Warren's in terms of his commitments. But he'd kill me if he knew I was making this call." Burton's news blindsided Simpson, whose own father had passed away from the disease, but it also explained the previous months of unreturned phone calls and excuses from his otherwise reliable client. When Skaaren finally did call Simpson, he downplayed his illness, telling his agent that he was in the hospital for tests but that he'd be out in a few weeks. They spoke on the phone a few more times, but the conversations revealed the reality that Skaaren was in the final weeks of his life. "My father had died of cancer, and I knew how it was in the end. Warren was sort of becoming delirious and not making sense," said Simpson.[36]

Burton also arranged for Austin folk singer-songwriter Tish Hinojosa to play for Skaaren on Christmas Eve. Hinojosa stood at the end of Skaaren's bed with her guitar and serenaded him with several songs. When she began to sing "The First Noel," Skaaren suddenly joined in, his distinctive baritone deceptively strong for someone who had only days to live. The household, which for months had bustled with the energy of the "life squad," seemed to slow down momentarily as those in the Wren Valley house came into the room to listen to Hinojosa's performance. Also present was Burton's college-aged daughter, Amy, whom Skaaren had grown close to, as he had with several of his other good friends' children. In February of that year, Skaaren had written to Amy while she was studying abroad in London, describing his work on *Beetlejuice in Love* ("I am engaged in loosing Beetlejuice once again on an unprepared world") and recounting the *Days of Thunder* arbitration, writing, "I don't know if I even want my name on it. . . . Tom [Cruise] and I remain good friends but studio politics weighed heavily on both of us." He also hinted at his and Helen's separation, telling Amy that he was spending a lot of time alone: "I think all marriage contracts should specify a month off for each five years married."[37]

Earlier on Christmas Eve, Skaaren had made a rare trip outside of the house for an impromptu ride with a group of male friends that included Amon Burton, Lee Walker, and Tom Giebink. Skaaren, groggy from the morphine, had wanted to get out of bed and insisted that someone bring him a director's chair. Those in the house played along, telling him that the chair wasn't available but arranging to get a stretcher so that he could be lifted and transported out of the bedroom. Initially the Connorses and others had brought him into the living room to see the thirteen-foot-tall Christmas tree that Kaye had been decorating in the weeks leading up to the holiday. But Skaaren insisted they go farther, so they wheeled the stretcher out onto the porch. The late December air was crisp under a vivid blue sky. When the men started to bring Skaaren back into the house, he indicated that he wasn't ready. "Let's go for a ride," he told them. His male friends quickly removed a seat from Giebink's van to make room for the stretcher, and they all piled in around Skaaren. The overstuffed van made it up the Skaarens' steep driveway and onto Redbud Trail, the winding main road that connected the rolling hills of Westlake to the Austin neighborhoods just west of the state capitol. The van traveled a short distance down Redbud as everyone sang Christmas carols. "I'm tired," Skaaren told his friends, so the men turned around and brought him home.

"That day as much or more than the other days, Warren amassed that group of people there together to get what he wanted," Brian Connors said of Skaaren's "directing" of the experience. "We were all somewhat exhausted emotionally and physically from everything that had been going on. It just took every person that was there, it just took a piece of everybody's energy to make that happen. It was the whole collective group that Warren brought together. He was still in control and he knew what he was doing."[38]

Over the next few days Skaaren drifted in and out of consciousness. The relative flurry of activity in the days leading up to Christmas seemed to make way for a kind of peace in the house. It was a feeling that Haug sensed in Skaaren himself despite the inherent fear he had often expressed about his impending death. The people closest to Skaaren in those final weeks had seen to every last detail to ensure that his passing would be as peaceful as possible. Following his wishes, a cremation carton had been delivered to the house and was stashed away until the appropriate time. Arrangements had been made with the county medical examiner to waive the mandatory postdeath visit, and the mortuary had been alerted not to expect a body until as many as eight hours after Skaaren's passing.[39]

Sometime between December 27 and December 28, Warren Skaaren slipped into a final coma. Vance, Haug, and a few others took turns sitting at his bedside. Skaaren died shortly before five o'clock in the afternoon on Friday, December 28. Vance had returned home to change clothes before going back to Wren Valley. Brian Connors had left to run an errand, and Kaye was in the kitchen cooking. Lee Walker and Helen Skaaren were in the living room, but the only person in the bedroom with Warren was a nurse named Julia who witnessed Skaaren taking a soft, final intake of breath.[40] When he died, Julie Jordan was at home in her kitchen, slicing an onion. A feeling of stillness surrounded her. "I felt like everything was all right, and I am loved. I knew then that he had died," she said months later. "I think that's what he wanted to tell me [at our final meeting], that he had loved me. That was all."[41]

The hours immediately following Skaaren's death unfolded like a scene in one of his rewrites for Tim Burton. A few of the women in the house quietly tended to his body. They rubbed Skaaren with a fine, chalk-like clay—"holy dirt" from El Santuario de Chimayo, a sacred site near Santa Fe thought to have healing properties. On his forehead they sprinkled holy water sent by Mary Kett, the Irish macrobiotic cook. His body was covered in a white, embroidered sheet, and Italian lace—a gift from another close friend—was draped nearby. A Tibetan prayer flag hung from the bar above his bed. Candles and Gregorian chants added to the peaceful ambience, which seemed to reflect Skaaren's cornucopia of spiritual interests. "It was the most holy thing I had ever experienced," said Kaye Connors months later. "Warren's body was still there, but Warren certainly was not there. His spirit had gone."[42] Phone calls were made, and friends were invited to come to the house. Dancer and performance artist Heloise Gold, with whom Skaaren had written a one-woman show earlier that year, was struck by the contrast of that peaceful evening with the chaos of the months immediately preceding it. "His death was extremely complicated, it was a drag to be around in some ways," said Gold of Skaaren's strong desire to hide his illness from so many. "He had a cool smile on his face after he died. He looked like a fourteen-year-old boy, a real innocence and sweetness. We hadn't seen a smile like that on his face in a long time."[43]

Friends continued to gather in the Wren Valley house throughout the evening, sitting in the bedroom with Skaaren's body or out in the sunken living room by the fire. At almost exactly midnight, two men in dark suits rapped on the house's large mahogany front doors. Amon Burton invited the mortuary representatives inside, but he also made it clear that when the time came, Skaaren's friends were going to be transporting the body out of the house and into the waiting hearse. Inside Skaaren's bedroom, a group assembled to lift the body into the cremation carton resting on the same rolling stretcher that had carried Skaaren outside for the Christmas Eve ride earlier that week. Personal effects and special tokens like Native American prayer feathers were tucked around the body. Passing with the stretcher into the cool December air, his friends were struck by what they saw. A long, dark hearse stood waiting in the driveway, its distinctive tail fins and chrome accents calling to mind the Batmobile. Fog had rolled in after midnight, adding to the eerily cinematic effect.[44]

The small group huddled together as the hearse climbed the steep driveway and bore Skaaren's body away. They gathered inside for a final meal together, sharing a few beers left in the refrigerator and some Norwegian holiday bread sent by Pearl Skaaren earlier in the week. It wasn't exactly the bread and the wine, but the repast felt like a communion of sorts as they toasted Skaaren. After the six months of fear, anxiety, anger, and grief that had pervaded the Wren Valley house, the hours following Skaaren's death gave way to a remarkable sense of calm felt by many in the "life squad" that night.

During Skaaren's illness, Vance had collected quotations from well-known people throughout history, copied them onto slips of different-colored paper, and put them in a glass bowl. The positive-minded sayings were meant to focus Skaaren's thoughts and buoy his spirits. He would begin each morning by choosing a slip from the bowl, and that quote would be his thought for the day. On the morning of Skaaren's death, Vance had pulled one final slip from the jar, the first line from a poem by John Keats: "A thing of beauty is a joy for ever."[45]

[   ]

In January 1991, a month after his death, one of Skaaren's final interviews appeared in the women's magazine *Mirabella*. The issue had gone to press before news of Skaaren's death had been released, and writer Gene Stone's introduction refers to Skaaren as among "the preeminent writers in the field." Diane Keaton, that month's cover subject, had been one of the first stars Skaaren had worked with early in his Hollywood career. They met several times in New York, with Skaaren writing a treatment for a comedy that was never produced. Interviewed for *Mirabella* on the subject of how to write a screenplay, Skaaren extolled the virtues of the three-act structure and the necessity of feeling connected to one's material. For instance, he said, Maverick's relationship with Viper, his "hero-father" in *Top Gun*, kept Skaaren going through the script's countless revisions. "That particular familial theme fascinates me, so I could endure the endless rewrites. You have to love the theme or you lose the thread." Of script-doctoring Skaaren said, "If you are very, very lucky, maybe 60 percent of your work will appear on the screen."[46] Months later, Larry Ferguson's years-long suit against the Writers Guild for sole screenplay credit on *Beverly Hills Cop II* was decided once and for all by a California appeals court: the credits remained as dictated by the Guild's arbitration, giving Ferguson and Skaaren shared screenplay credit.[47]

By the time of Skaaren's memorial in late January 1991, Geffen and Warner Bros. had hired screenwriter Michael McDowell, the first writer of *Beetlejuice* with whom Skaaren ultimately shared writing credit for the film, to replace Skaaren on *Beetlejuice in Love*. "There's a part of Warren that would find that irony really neat, and there's a part that would hate it," mused Skaaren's agent, Mike Simpson, at a small gathering after the Austin memorial.[48] At the same event, Tim Burton pondered Skaaren's fate, making reference to Skaaren's purgatory scene from *Beetlejuice*, in which newly deceased characters wait to receive further instructions from a caseworker in a depressing environment not unlike a motor vehicle registration office. In his notes, Skaaren had dubbed it "the bureaucratic limbo" scene.

"He's perhaps down there holding his number right now. Or up there," Burton cackled, acknowledging the possibility that Skaaren could be on his way either to hell or to heaven. "Holding his number, waiting to see his caseworker. Won't he be surprised."[49]

Notes

This book draws extensively from the primary materials housed in Warren Skaaren's archive at the Harry Ransom Humanities Research Center. It also features quotations and background material taken from dozens of interviews with Skaaren's friends, colleagues, and associates. Biographical details and other background information have been sourced from interviews (and, when necessary, verified with other sources) unless otherwise noted. When thoughts are attributed to an individual, they are also drawn from interviews and primary materials. The research for this story also includes primary materials from personal collections and other public archives, as well as secondary materials such as newspaper articles and books. The following abbreviations appear throughout the Notes to distinguish the source of quotations or specific information.

WAX Natasha Waxman, *Warren Skaaren, Screenwriter: His Life, Films, and Letters*. Austin: Harry Ransom Humanities Research Center, University of Texas, 1991.

WSC The Warren Skaaren Collection, Harry Ransom Humanities Research Center, The University of Texas at Austin.

INTRODUCTION

1. Ron Bozman, videotape of memorial service for Warren Skaaren, The Warren Skaaren Collection, Harry Ransom Humanities Research Center, The University of Texas at Austin (hereafter WSC).

2. Heloise Gold, videotape interview by Tom Giebink, ca. 1991, WSC.

3. Ron Bozman, videotape interview by Tom Giebink, ca. 1991, WSC.

4. Robert Wise, videotape of memorial service, WSC.

5. Mike Simpson, videotape interview by Tom Giebink, ca. 1991, WSC.

6. Tom Cruise letter read by Mike Simpson, videotape of memorial service for Warren Skaaren, WSC.

7. Michael Douglas letter read by Mike Simpson, videotape of memorial service for Warren Skaaren, WSC.

8. Mike Simpson, videotape of memorial service for Warren Skaaren, WSC.

9. Tim Burton, videotape interview by Tom Giebink, ca. 1991, WSC.

10. Kevin Phinney wrote "Death of a Screenwriter," *Premiere*, March 1991, 98–99.

11. Roderick Mann, "Vidal Sues to Get Credit on 'Sicilian,'" *Los Angeles Times*, February 14, 1987, http://articles.latimes.com/1987-02-14/entertainment/ca-2975_1 _gore-vidal. Accessed October 4, 2011.

12. "L.A. Ruling Favors Vidal in WGA/'Sicilian' Suit,'" *Variety*, November 11, 1987, 6.

13. Tad Friend, "Credit Grab," *The New Yorker*, October 20, 2003, 160.

14. Ibid., 163.

15. Ibid., 162.

16. Ibid., 163.

17. David Robb, "'Jurassic World' Credits Resolved," *Deadline Hollywood*, April 7, 2015, http://deadline.com/2015/04/jurassic-world-script-credits-resolved -colin-trevorrow-speaks-on-arbitration-process-1201406086/. Accessed August 20, 2015.

18. Friend, "Credit Grab," 167.

19. Tom Stempel, *Framework: A History of Screenwriting in the American Film* (Syracuse, NY: Syracuse University Press, 2000), 185.

20. Beverly Walker, "Limbo Land," *Film Comment*, February 1987, 37.

21. Ibid., 35.

22. *Screen Credits Manual*, Writers Guild of America, 1984, WSC.

23. Friend, "Credit Grab," 162.

24. Shawn K. Judge, "Note & Comment: Giving Credit Where Credit Is Due? The Unusual Use of Arbitration in Determining Screenwriting Credits," *Ohio State Journal on Dispute Resolution* 13.221 (1997): 260.

25. Ibid.

26. Ibid.

27. *Screen Credits Manual*, Writers Guild of America, Sec. III.B.7.

28. Stempel, *Framework*, 218.

29. Julie Jordan, videotape interview by Tom Giebink, ca. 1991, WSC.

30. Linda Vance, videotape interview by Tom Giebink, ca. 1991, WSC.

31. Kaye and Brian Connors, videotape interview by Tom Giebink, ca. 1991, WSC.

32. Linda Vance, videotape interview by Tom Giebink, ca. 1991, WSC.

33. Ibid., and Julie Jordan, videotape interview by Tom Giebink, ca. 1991, WSC.

34. "BJ2 notes," ca. 1989, WSC.

35. Ron Bozman, videotape of memorial service for Warren Skaaren, ca. 1991, WSC.

36. Julie Jordan, videotape interview by Tom Giebink, WSC.

CHAPTER ONE

1. All dialogue from Warren Skaaren's first rewrite of *Top Gun* dated May 6, 1985, WSC.

2. Clyde Skaaren, Author's Interview, March 20, 2014.

3. This detail and successive information about the Rauk family and its multi-generational history is from Kaye Rauk's fifty-nine-page document in the WSC, which she sent to Pearl Skaaren and other Rauk relatives in 1979.

4. Jon Gjerde and Carlton C. Qualey, *Norwegians in Minnesota* (St. Paul: Minnesota Historical Society Press, 2002), 1, 3.

5. Sharon Thoreson, "Sigrid Rauk Found Dream Home," undated newspaper article included in Kaye Rauk's family history, WSC.

6. Undated audio recording of Warren Skaaren interviewing his parents, WSC.

7. Warren Skaaren, journal entry, ca. 1988, WSC.

8. Gjerde and Qualey, *Norwegians in Minnesota*, 29.

9. Warren Skaaren, undated letter written after 1986, WSC.

10. Clyde Skaaren, Author's Interview, March 20, 2014.

11. Warren Skaaren, "Stuff Coming Up" (therapy notes), November 24, 1987, WSC.

12. Harriet W. Hodgson, *Rochester: City of the Prairie* (Rochester, MN: Windsor Publications, 1989), 10. This and the following historical information about Rochester is drawn from Hodgson's book unless otherwise noted.

13. Herb Sleeper, Author's Interview, May 2012.

14. Gjerde and Qualey, *Norwegians in Minnesota*, 70.

15. Pearl Skaaren, videotape interview by Tom Giebink, ca. 1991, WSC.

16. Ibid.

17. Birth certificates, 1946, WSC.

18. Clyde Skaaren, Author's Interview, March 20, 2014.

19. Ibid.

20. Bob Rynearson, Author's Interview, February 22, 2013.

21. Pearl Skaaren, videotape interview by Tom Giebink, ca. 1991, WSC.

22. Warren Skaaren, "Journal 1990," WSC.

23. Warren Skaaren, "Stuff Coming Up" (therapy notes), February 2, 1988, WSC; Stanley Kusunoki, untitled interview in *Rochester Post Bulletin*, May 10, 1986, 11C.

24. Bob Rynearson, Author's Interview, February 22, 2013.

25. Ibid.

26. Tom Giebink, videotape interview by Diane Haug, ca. 1991, WSC.

27. Clyde Skaaren, Author's Interview, March 20, 2014.

28. Lee Walker, videotape interview by Tom Giebink, ca. 1991, WSC.

29. Kaye Connors, Author's Interview, April 11, 2014; Diane Haug, videotape interview by Tom Giebink, ca. 1991, WSC.

30. Pearl Skaaren, videotape interview by Tom Giebink, ca. 1991, WSC.

31. Herb Sleeper, Author's Interview, May 2012, and Sleeper, e-mail response, April 9, 2014.

32. Pearl Skaaren, videotape interview by Tom Giebink, ca. 1991, WSC.

33. Warren Skaaren, essay for Rochester Junior College promotional campaign, ca. 1989, WSC.

34. Herb Sleeper, Author's Interview, May 2012.

35. Tom Giebink, videotape interview by Diane Haug, ca. 1991, WSC, and Bob Rynearson, videotape interview by Tom Giebink, ca. 1991, WSC.

36. Warren Skaaren, essay for Rochester Junior College promotional campaign, ca. 1989, WSC.

37. Warren Skaaren, undated "HRC" speech, WSC.

38. Ibid.

39. Ibid.

40. Squire Shop advertisement, *Rochester Post Bulletin*, August 25, 1967, 5. Courtesy of the Olmsted Historical Society.

41. Pearl Skaaren, videotape interview by Tom Giebink, ca. 1991, WSC.

42. Ron Bozman, videotape interview by Tom Giebink, ca. 1991, WSC.

43. Natasha Waxman, *Warren Skaaren, Screenwriter: His Life, Films, and Letters.* Austin: Harry Ransom Humanities Research Center, University of Texas, 1991 (hereafter WAX), 12.

44. Letter to Robert Wise, "Sun Oct 16," 1966, WSC.

45. Warren Skaaren quoted in *Rice Thresher* (Houston, Texas). Coyner, Sandy, editor, vol. 54, no. 27, ed. 1, Thursday, May 4, 1967, Newspaper, May 4, 1967; digital images (http://texashistory.unt.edu/ark:/67531/metapth245003/: accessed May 6, 2014), University of North Texas Libraries, The Portal to Texas History, http://texas history.unt.edu; crediting Rice University: Woodson Research Center, Houston, Texas.

46. Warren Skaaren in *Rice Thresher* (Houston, Texas). Phil Garon, ed., vol. 55, no. 22, ed. 1, Thursday, March 21, 1968, Newspaper, March 21, 1968; digital images (http://texashistory.unt.edu/ark:/67531/metapth245025/: accessed May 5, 2014), University of North Texas Libraries, The Portal to Texas History, http://texashistory .unt.edu; crediting Rice University: Woodson Research Center, Houston, Texas.

47. Warren Skaaren, "Stuff Coming Up" (therapy notes), February 2, 1988, WSC.

48. "WS Story," November 10, 1987, WSC.

49. Dennis Bahler, "Pitzer Goes to Greener Pastures," *Rice Thresher* (Houston, Texas). Phil Garon, ed., vol. 56, no. 22, ed. 1, September 12, 1968, 1. Newspaper, Septem-

ber 12, 1968; digital images (http://texashistory.unt.edu/ark:/67531/metapth245025/: accessed May 7, 2014), University of North Texas Libraries, The Portal to Texas History, http://texashistory.unt.edu; crediting Rice University: Woodson Research Center, Houston, Texas.

50. Marisa Cigarroa, "Former Stanford President, Renowned Chemist Ken Pitzer, Dies," Stanford News Service, January 6, 1998, http://news.stanford.edu/pr /98/980107pitzer.html. Accessed May 6, 2014.

51. Bahler, "Pitzer Goes to Greener Pastures," Rice Thresher (Houston, Texas). Phil Garon, ed., vol. 56, no. 22, ed. 1, September 12, 1968, 1. Newspaper, September 12, 1968; digital images (http://texashistory.unt.edu/ark:/67531/metapth245025/: accessed May 7, 2014), University of North Texas Libraries, The Portal to Texas History, http://texashistory.unt.edu; crediting Rice University: Woodson Research Center, Houston, Texas.

52. Warren Skaaren quoted in "Oral History Transcript," 7, from interview conducted with Polly Moore, September 15, 1969. Masterson Collection, Rice University, Woodson Research Center.

53. Terry O'Rourke, "Faculty Requests Reconsideration of Appointment," Rice Thresher (Houston, Texas). Phil Garon, ed., vol. 56, extra, ed. 1, February 22, 1969, 1. Newspaper, February 22, 1969; digital images (http://texashistory.unt.edu /ark:/67531/metapth245025/: accessed May 7, 2014), University of North Texas Libraries, The Portal to Texas History, http://texashistory.unt.edu; crediting Rice University: Woodson Research Center, Houston, Texas.

54. Dennis Bahler, "The Creation of a 'Community' and Unmaking of a President," Rice Thresher (Houston, Texas). Dennis Bahler, ed., Rice Thresher (Houston, Texas), vol. 56, no. 22, ed. 1, Friday, February 28, 1969. Newspaper, February 28, 1969; digital images (http://texashistory.unt.edu/ark:/67531/metapth245051/: accessed May 14, 2014), University of North Texas Libraries, The Portal to Texas History, http://texashistory.unt.edu; crediting Rice University: Woodson Research Center, Houston, Texas.

55. Ibid.

56. See WAX, 14–15; "Oral History Transcript," 19, 33, Masterson Collection, Rice University, Woodson Research Center; "College Meetings Ask Commitment to Sustained Protest," Rice Thresher (Houston, Texas). Phil Garon, ed., vol. 56, extra, ed. 1, February 22, 1969, 3. Newspaper, February 22, 1969; digital images (http:// texashistory.unt.edu/ark:/67531/metapth245025/: accessed May 7, 2014), University of North Texas Libraries, The Portal to Texas History, http://texashistory.unt.edu; crediting Rice University: Woodson Research Center, Houston, Texas.

57. Bahler, "The Creation of a 'Community' and Unmaking of a President," Rice Thresher (Houston, Texas), February 28, 1969, 1.

58. Ibid.

59. WAX, 15.

60. See Nancy Boothe, "Documenting an Administrative Crisis: Rice's 4-Day Presidency," 5, and Dennis Bahler, "The Creation of a 'Community' and Unmak-

ing of a President," *Rice Thresher* (Houston, Texas), 7. Dennis Bahler, ed., vol. 56, no. 22, ed. 1, Friday, February 28, 1969. Newspaper, February 28, 1969; digital images (http://texashistory.unt.edu/ark:/67531/metapth245051/: accessed May 14, 2014), University of North Texas Libraries, The Portal to Texas History, http://texashistory.unt.edu; crediting Rice University: Woodson Research Center, Houston, Texas.

61. "Statement of Warren Skaaren to KOWL, Feb 25 1969; 7:00 PM," WSC.

62. W. S. Dowden letter, February 26, 1969, WSC.

63. Text of Rice University Service Award, 1969, WSC.

64. Warren Skaaren quoted in "Oral History Transcript," 24, from interview conducted with Polly Moore, September 15, 1969. Masterson Collection, Rice University, Woodson Research Center.

65. "WS Story," November 10, 1987, WSC.

66. Ibid.

67. Jerry Hall, Author's Interview, December 12, 2003.

68. Taken from various versions of Skaaren's résumé, ca. 1969–1971, WSC.

69. "WS Story," November 10, 1987, WSC.

CHAPTER TWO

1. "Around the State," *Texas Monthly*, September 1977, 19.

2. Jerry Hall, Author's Interview, December 12, 2003. Warren Skaaren's sketches and promotional ideas for *The Texas Chain Saw Massacre* can be found in the WSC.

3. Quoted in Alison Macor, *Chainsaws, Slackers, and Spy Kids: Thirty Years of Filmmaking in Austin, Texas* (Austin: University of Texas Press, 2010), 13.

4. Warren Skaaren letter to John de Menil, February 12, 1970, WSC.

5. Ann Richards, Author's Interview, December 4, 2003.

6. "Letter to Larry," Warren Skaaren, July 27, 1970, WSC.

7. "TFC Memo," Warren Skaaren, October 27, 1971, WSC.

8. "NM Film History," http://www.nmfilm.com/uploads/FileLinks/0c78aae101f44fcbb8933db2a6148343/jan_2013.htm#history. Accessed June 2, 2014.

9. Various published accounts have described Skaaren's proposal as being forty pages in length, but Skaaren himself wrote that it was a "14-page report." See "TFC Memo," Warren Skaaren, October 27, 1971, WSC.

10. "TFC Memo," Warren Skaaren, October 27, 1971, WSC.

11. Ibid. See also *The Valley Morning Star*, May 25, 1971, 3, and Paul Tinmon, "Texas Film Plans Revealed," *Amarillo Globe-Times*, May 24, 1971, 11.

12. Joy Davis, Author's Interview, August 7, 2014.

13. "TFC Memo," WSC; O'Dil quoted in "Thirty Years on Location," Marc Savlov, *Austin Chronicle*, June 15, 2001, n.p.

14. Jack Keever, "New Film Body Director Sees Success for Texas," untitled paper, n.p. and n.d., WSC.

15. David Foster quoted in Marshall Terrill, *Steve McQueen: The Life and Legend of a Hollywood Icon* (Chicago: Triumph Books, 2010), 351.

16. Quoted in Macor, *Chainsaws, Slackers, and Spy Kids*, 14.

17. Warren Skaaren, handwritten note, WSC.

18. Terrill, *Steve McQueen*, 347–349.

19. Ibid., 350. See also Marc Eliot, *Steve McQueen: A Biography* (New York: Crown Archetype, 2011), 248–255; and Ali MacGraw, *Moving Pictures: An Autobiography* (New York: Bantam Books, 1991), 91–92.

20. David Foster, Author's Interview, July 28, 2003, and Terrill, *Steve McQueen*, 352. See also Foster quoted in untitled newspaper article ca. 1972, WSC.

21. Davis, Author's Interview, August 7, 2014.

22. Jeff Millar, "Warren Skaaren, Movie Mogul," *Texas Monthly*, July 1973, 60.

23. Excerpt from Gordon Dawson letter to Warren Skaaren, WSC. Photograph of Sam Peckinpah, Ali MacGraw, and Warren Skaaren in *Starlight* magazine, WSC.

24. Davis, Author's Interview, August 7, 2014.

25. Skaaren, "WS Story," November 10, 1987, WSC.

26. Ibid. For information about foster children, see résumé of Warren Skaaren, ca. 1974, WSC. For medical information, see paperwork in personal folders, WSC.

27. Terrill, *Steve McQueen*, 370.

28. Millar, "Movie Mogul," 61.

29. *Variety*, April 13, 1973, n.p.

30. Foster quoted in Macor, *Chainsaws, Slackers, and Spy Kids*, 14. Skaaren quoted in Millar, "Movie Mogul," 60.

31. Typewritten letter to Norman, dated May 29, 1973, WSC.

32. Ibid., 2–4.

33. Parsley quoted in Ellen Farley and William K. Knoedelseder Jr., "The Real Texas Chain Saw Massacre," *Los Angeles Times*, September 5, 1982, 4. See also Macor, *Chainsaws, Slackers, and Spy Kids*, 21.

34. Henkel quoted in Macor, *Chainsaws, Slackers, and Spy Kids*, 21.

35. Hall, Author's Interview, December 12, 2003.

36. Kim Henkel letter to Warren Skaaren, October 9, 1973, WSC.

37. Incorporation papers, The Skaaren Corporation, WSC.

38. Henkel quoted in Macor, *Chainsaws, Slackers, and Spy Kids*, 34.

39. Parsley quoted in Farley and Knoedelseder, "The Real Texas Chain Saw Massacre," 6.

40. Ibid. See also Macor, *Chainsaws, Slackers, and Spy Kids*, 34–35.

41. "Skaaren Resigns as TFC Director," *FilmTexas!*, March 1974, 1. Davis, Author's Interview, August 7, 2014. Untitled document, WSC. See longer excerpt in WAX, 19.

42. Minutes from MAB directors meeting, March 26, 1974, WSC. For various drafts of Skaaren's contract, see documents in WSC. Skaaren quoted in Farley and Knoedelseder, "The Real Texas Chain Saw Massacre," 6.

43. David Foster, Author's Interview, July 28, 2003.

44. For details of Foster's contract see documents in *Chain Saw* folders, WSC. See also Farley and Knoedelseder, "The Real Texas Chain Saw Massacre," 6.

45. Undated letter, WSC. Foster quoted in Macor, *Chainsaws, Slackers, and Spy Kids*, 36.

46. See document written by Skaaren and titled "Some thoughts about Ted Zephro's proposal," WSC.

47. The history of Bryanston Distribution and the Peraino family's involvement is detailed in a three-part series by Ellen Farley and William Knoedelseder Jr. titled "Family Business" and published in the *Los Angeles Times* in June 1982. Part Two recounts Louis Peraino's "legitimate" career in Hollywood ca. 1974–1976. See Ellen Farley and William Knoedelseder Jr., "The Hollywood Years," *Los Angeles Times*, June 20, 1982, 3–9.

48. Skaaren quoted in Farley and Knoedelseder, "The Real Texas Chain Saw Massacre," 6.

49. See various drafts of contracts (dated March–April 1974) and other supporting documents, WSC.

50. "The grapevine on Joe and Lou Peraino," typed document, WSC.

51. Letter from Arthur Klein to Philip Vitello, August 15, 1974, WSC.

52. Farley and Knoedelseder, "The Hollywood Years," 4. See also Fred Beiersdorf, Author's Interview, January 8, 2004.

53. Contract details included in letter from Tobe Hooper to cast, crew, and investors, September 4, 1974, WSC. See also Farley and Knoedelseder, "The Real Texas Chain Saw Massacre," 6.

54. Tobe Hooper letter and memorandum, September 4, 1974, WSC. Warren Skaaren contract, revised and signed, November 7, 1974, WSC.

55. Ellen Farley and William Knoedelseder Jr., "Family Business, Episode One: The Pornbrokers," *Los Angeles Times*, June 13, 1982, 12.

56. *Miller v. California*, 413 U.S. 15 (1973).

57. The advertisement appeared in *Variety* on September 4, 1974.

58. Beiersdorf, Author's Interview, January 8, 2004.

59. Farley and Knoedelseder, "The Hollywood Years," 5.

60. Financial statements, December 1, 1974, WSC.

61. Skaaren phone logs, February 1975, WSC. Skaaren letter to Arthur Klein, ca. 1975, WSC. Henkel letter, April 28, 1975, WSC.

62. Skaaren letter, May 22, 1975, WSC.

63. Ibid.

64. Skaaren letter to Arthur Klein, ca. 1975, WSC. See also Skaaren letter to unidentified recipient, August 15, 1975, outlining the terms should The Skaaren Corporation produce the sequel. Recorded phone call with Henry Holmes, undated, C2842, WSC.

65. Nicholas Gage, "Organized Crime Reaps Huge Profits from Dealing in Pornographic Films," *New York Times*, October 12, 1975, 1, 68.

66. Farley and Knoedelseder, "The Real Texas Chain Saw Massacre," 7.

67. Skaaren letter to Arthur Klein, March 16, 1976, WSC.

68. "50 Top-Grossing Films," *Variety*, December 29, 1976, 9. David Foster letter, January 26, 1977, WSC.

69. Farley and Knoedelseder, "The Real Texas Chain Saw Massacre," 7. For more detail about *The Texas Chain Saw Massacre*'s ongoing legal battles, see Macor, *Chainsaws, Slackers, and Spy Kids*, 44–47. Hall, Author's Interview, December 12, 2003.

70. Skaaren letter to Arthur Klein, ca. 1975, WSC.

CHAPTER THREE

1. Skaaren letter to Bill Wittliff, ca. 1974, WSC.

2. Skaaren letter to Arthur Klein, ca. 1974, WSC.

3. Bobby Bridger, Author's Interview, March 22, 2012.

4. Bill Wittliff, Author's Interview, November 10, 2003.

5. *Spooks* treatment, May 10, 1973, WSC.

6. Letter from Mark Saha, October 25, 1974, WSC.

7. Walter "Yukon" Yates, *Breakaway* (Austin: Post River Productions, 2011), 255.

8. Skaaren letter to Walter Yates, August 16, 1975, WSC.

9. See letters and agreements relating to *Breakaway*, August 1975 to November 1975, WSC.

10. Skaaren letter to Walter Yates, August 16, 1975, WSC.

11. Bobby Bridger, *Bridger* (Austin: University of Texas Press, 2009), 225.

12. Yates, *Breakaway*, 256–257.

13. Ibid., 257.

14. Bridger, Author's Interview, March 22, 2012.

15. Ibid.

16. "Breakaway Premiere Synopsis and Contact Notes," WSC.

17. Bridger, Author's Interview, March 22, 2012.

18. *Breakaway* print advertisement, *Austin American-Statesman*, March 26, 1978, 43.

19. Yates, *Breakaway*, 260.

20. Eldon S. Branda, "STEINMARK, FREDDIE JOE," Handbook of Texas Online, published and uploaded by the Texas State Historical Association on June 15, 2010, http://www.tshaonline.org/handbook/online/articles/fst32. Accessed August 28, 2014.

21. Letter to "Freddie Steinmark" project investors, WSC. See also "Agreements for Steinmark 1972–1982" (2 of 2), WSC.

22. Trips detailed in expense reports related to "Freddie," ca. 1978, WSC. "Freddie" treatment details, WSC.

23. Notes from meeting with Fred Akers, February 23, 1979, WSC.

24. Handwritten notes and transcripts of phone conversations with members of the Steinmark family, WSC.

25. Ibid.

26. Jim Dent, *Courage Beyond the Game: The Freddie Steinmark Story* (New York: Thomas Dunne Books, 2011), 288.

27. Notes written by Skaaren after visiting Steinmark family, January 1979, WSC.

28. Bill Downs, letter to Richard Hassanein, October 11, 1979, WSC.

29. Stephen Girard letter, February 22, 1980, WSC.

30. Fred and Gloria Steinmark letter, ca. December 22, 1980, WSC.

31. Letter to investors, ca. April 1981, WSC.

32. Alex McNeil, *Total Television: The Comprehensive Guide to Programming from 1948 to the Present* (New York: Penguin Books, 1996).

33. Bob Montgomery letter to William Morris agent Len Hirshan, June 20, 1984, WSC.

34. Notes and agreement with Fred Fox, May 12, 1982, WSC.

35. Byron Farwell, *The Gurkhas* (New York: W. W. Norton, 1984).

36. Undated article, *Austin American-Statesman*, ca. 1982, WSC.

37. Research notes ca. 1982, *Of East and West*, WSC.

38. Amon Burton, Author's Interview, September 11, 2014.

39. Letter to John Boehle, ca. 1990, WSC.

40. *Of East and West* treatment, ca. 1983, WSC.

41. Story details, *Of East and West* outline, ca. 1983, WSC.

42. Warren Skaaren, "Pancho Villa's Last Gasp," *Texas Monthly*, December 1983, 234.

43. Writer's Agreement between Warren Skaaren and *Texas Monthly*, October 27, 1983, Southwestern Writers Collection, Texas State University–San Marcos.

44. Margery Graham letter to Mike Levy, December 10, 1983, and Sandra Day O'Connor letter to Mike Levy, November 22, 1983, Southwestern Writers Collection, Texas State University–San Marcos.

45. "Pancho Villa's Last Gasp," *Texas Monthly*, 174.

46. John Eberts letter to Bob Montgomery, October 13, 1983, WSC.

47. Fred Fox letter to Bob Montgomery, October 29, 1983, WSC.

48. Ibid.

49. Bob Montgomery letter to Fred Fox, November 29, 1983, WSC.

50. David Brown letter to Bob Montgomery, January 13, 1984, WSC.

51. Fred Fox letter to Brigadier M. F. Hobbs, May 15, 1984, WSC.

52. Bob Montgomery letter to Fred Fox, January 16, 1984, WSC.

CHAPTER FOUR

1. Skaaren letter to Mike Simpson, December 12, 1983, WSC. See also WAX, 26–27.

2. Mike Simpson, Author's Interview, October 28, 2004.

3. Ibid.

4. Karen Glasser reader's report for *Of East and West*, June 14, 1984, WSC.

5. Reader's report for *Of East and West*, Norman Jewison's office, ca. June 1984, WSC.

6. Tom Stempel, *Framework: A History of Screenwriting in the American Film* (Syracuse, NY: Syracuse University Press, 2000), 185.

7. Doug Wick, Author's Interview, September 19, 2014.

8. Warren Skaaren, notes on "Goldman," undated, WSC.

9. Warren Skaaren, "Notes on trip to meet Simpson and Bruckheimer," ca. 1985, WSC.

10. *Captive Hearts* script notes, July 1984, WSC.

11. Mike Simpson, Author's Interview, October 28, 2004.

12. Warren Skaaren, "Questions after May 5th Trip to Studios," 1984, WSC.

13. "From Dawn," notes on *Captive Hearts*, ca. 1984, WSC.

14. Warren Skaaren, "Re: Cap Hearts," ca. 1984, WSC.

15. Wick, Author's Interview, September 19, 2014.

16. Mike Simpson letter to Warren Skaaren, December 27, 1984, WSC.

17. Warren Skaaren, journal entry in red record book, December 16, 1984, WSC. See also WAX, 28, for longer version of above.

18. Journal entry, March 12, 1985, WSC.

19. "Writers Strike Is Over," United Press International, March 20, 1985, n.p.

20. Agreement for *Captive Hearts*, ca. 1984, WSC.

21. Journal entry, December 12, 1984, WSC.

22. "Notice of Tentative Writing Credits," *Captive Hearts*, November 22, 1985, WSC.

23. "Captive Hearts" story material list, December 11, 1985, WSC.

24. Writers Guild of America letter to Warren Skaaren, December 9, 1985, WSC.

25. Tad Friend, "Credit Grab," *The New Yorker*, October 20, 2003, 162.

26. Warren Skaaren letter to Writers Guild of America, December 11, 1985, WSC.

27. Writers Guild of America letter to Warren Skaaren, January 2, 1986, WSC.

28. Mike Simpson, Author's Interview, October 28, 2004.

29. Warren Skaaren, journal entry, May 8, 1985, WSC.

30. Christopher Connelly, "Winging It," *Rolling Stone*, June 19, 1986, 40.

31. Mike Simpson, Author's Interview, October 28, 2004.

32. Warren Skaaren telephone conversation with journalist Army Archerd, May 15, 1985, WSC.

33. Paul Attanasio, "The Twin Titans of *Top Gun*: How Don Simpson and Jerry Bruckheimer Propelled Their Idea to the Screen," *The Washington Post*, May 16, 1986, D1.

34. Michael Small, "With *Top Gun* and *Legal Eagles*, Two Long-Distance Screenwriters Make Hollywood's Big-League Draft," *People*, n.d., 68–69.

35. Don Simpson memorandum, May 6, 1984, WSC. Quoted material from Chip Proser interview, February 18, 2008, http://pwtenny.newsvine.com/_news /2008/02/18/1309263-interview-with-writer-director-chip-proser. Accessed June 17, 2009.

36. Attanasio, "The Twin Titans of *Top Gun*," *The Washington Post*, May 16, 1986, D1.

37. Warren Skaaren telephone conversation with Don Simpson, April 25, 1985, WSC.

38. Emily Yoffe, "The Man Hollywood Trusts," *Texas Monthly*, September 1989, 184.

39. Warren Skaaren telephone conversation with Jerry Bruckheimer and Don Simpson, April 24, 1985, WSC.

40. Warren Skaaren telephone conversation with Don Simpson and Jerry Bruckheimer, April 24 and April 25, 1985, WSC.

41. Warren Skaaren telephone conversation with Don Simpson and Jerry Bruckheimer, April 25, 1985, WSC. Although writer Chip Proser would tell Don Simpson biographer Charles Fleming that Skaaren was hired to replace him because he accepted a lower salary that Proser rejected, Skaaren actually was offered more money than Proser.

42. Warren Skaaren telephone conversation with Don Simpson and Jerry Bruckheimer, April 30, 1985, WSC.

43. Warren Skaaren telephone conversation with Don Simpson, Jerry Bruckheimer, Tony Scott, and Tom Cruise, May 1, 1985, WSC.

44. Warren Skaaren telephone conversation with Don Simpson, May 5, 1985, WSC.

45. Warren Skaaren telephone conversation with Tony Scott and Tom Cruise, May 5, 1985, WSC.

46. Skaaren, "The letter to the files regarding my experience on rewriting Top Gun," May 21, 1985, WSC.

47. Warren Skaaren telephone conversation with Tony Scott and Tom Cruise, May 5, 1985, WSC.

48. Skaaren, "The letter to the files regarding my experience on rewriting Top Gun," May 21, 1985, WSC.

49. Yoffe, "The Man Hollywood Trusts," 186.

50. Warren Skaaren, journal entry, May 8, 1985, WSC.

51. Warren Skaaren telephone conversation with Don Simpson, May 8, 1985, WSC.

52. Warren Skaaren telephone conversation with Jerry Bruckheimer and Don Simpson, May 17, 1985, WSC.

53. Skaaren, "The letter to the files regarding my experience on rewriting Top Gun," May 21, 1985, WSC.

54. "Memorandum of Agreement," revision dated May 21, 1985, WSC.

55. Warren Skaaren telephone conversation with journalist Army Archerd, May 15, 1985, WSC.

56. Warren Skaaren in multiple telephone conversations with Don Simpson, April and May 1985, WSC.

57. Don Simpson telephone conversation with Warren Skaaren, May 17, 1985, WSC.

58. Jerry Bruckheimer telephone conversation with Warren Skaaren, May 19, 1985, WSC.

59. Tony Scott telephone conversation with Warren Skaaren, May 19, 1985, WSC.

60. Jerry Bruckheimer telephone conversation with Warren Skaaren, April 25, 1985, WSC.

61. Audiotape recording of *Top Gun* rehearsals, June 19, 1985, WSC.

62. Yoffe, "The Man Hollywood Trusts," 187.

63. Memo from Don Simpson to Warren Skaaren, June 20, 1985, WSC.

64. Memorandum from Warren Skaaren to Don Simpson, Jerry Bruckheimer, and Tony Scott, March 8, 1986, WSC.

65. Wick, Author's Interview, September 19, 2014.

66. Paramount Pictures Corporation letter, August 12, 1985, WSC.

67. Article 16.A.3.a (3), *Screen Credits Manual*, Writers Guild of America, http://www.wga.org/subpage_writersresources.aspx?id=119. Accessed August 19, 2011.

68. Western Union telegram from Mike Simpson to Daniel Furie, August 26, 1985, WSC.

69. Grace Reiner letter on behalf of the Writers Guild of America, August 28, 1985, WSC.

70. Beverly Walker, "Limbo Land," *Film Comment*, February 1987, 35, 36.

71. Ibid.

72. David T. Friendly, "Development Game: All's Fair," *Los Angeles Times*, September 25, 1986, VI, 5.

73. Kirk Honeycutt, "Whose Film Is It Anyway?" *American Film*, May 1981, 35.

74. Stempel, *Framework*, 136, 140–142. See also *Guide to the Guild*, Writers Guild of America, West, 14–15.

75. Shawn K. Judge, "Note & Comment: Giving Credit Where Credit Is Due? The Unusual Use of Arbitration in Determining Screenwriting Credits," *Ohio State Journal on Dispute Resolution* 13.221 (1997): 233–235. See also *Guide to the Guild*, 15.

76. Judge, "Note & Comment," 236.

77. Warren Skaaren, "Statement by Warren Skaaren Regarding His Contribution to the Story and Screenplay for the Motion Picture *Top Gun*," ca. August 1985, page 2, WSC.

78. Phone conversation between Warren Skaaren, Jerry Bruckheimer, and Don Simpson, May 17, 1985, WSC.

79. "Veteran Executive Grace Reiner Departs Writers Guild After 20-Year-Plus Service," News Release, Writers Guild of America, West, November 18, 2006.

80. Phone conversation between Grace Reiner, Warren Skaaren, and Mike Simpson, October 11, 1985, WSC.

81. Ibid.

82. Typed notes by Warren Skaaren, "The Plan," n.d., WSC.

83. Paramount Pictures Corporation letter to Writers Guild of America, October 22, 1985, WSC.

84. Skaaren letter to Dawn Steel, October 28, 1985, WSC.

85. Ralph Kamen letter to Warren Skaaren, October 30, 1985, WSC.

86. "Notes from Warren Skaaren Regarding His Original Contribution to the Story and Screenplay for the Motion Picture *Top Gun*," November 10, 1985, page 1, WSC.

87. Ibid.

88. Ibid., 4.

89. Ibid., 6.

90. Mike Simpson letter to Warren Skaaren, November 22, 1985, WSC.

91. Skaaren letter to Martin Brest, January 15, 1986, WSC.

92. Stanley Kusunoki, *Rochester Post-Bulletin*, May 10, 1986, 11C.

93. Yoffe, "The Man Hollywood Trusts," 187.

94. Small, "With *Top Gun* and *Legal Eagles*," *People*, n.d., 70.

95. Chip Proser, interview, http://www.newsvine.com, February 18, 2008.

96. See Charles Fleming, *High Concept: Don Simpson and the Hollywood Culture of Excess* (New York: Doubleday, 1998).

97. "Some notes on the two screenings of *Top Gun* which I attended," WSC.

98. Ibid.

99. James Grenteg, "*Gun* Nat'l B.O.'s Top Flyer," *Variety*, June 10, 1986, 2.

100. Rex Reed, "Cruisin' the Sky in Search of McGillis," *New York Observer*, n.d., WSC.

101. Pauline Kael, "Brutes," *The New Yorker*, June 16, 1986, 119.

102. Vincent Canby, "Vintage Plotting Propels Mach II Planes in 'Top Gun,'" *New York Times*, June 8, 1986, 23, 24.

103. *MAD* magazine, December 1986, WSC.

104. Laura Landro, "Back on Top," *Wall Street Journal*, July 14, 1986, 1, 11. See also Gerald Putzer, "Paramount's 'Top Gun' '86 Rentals Champ," *Variety*, January 15, 1987, 60.

105. Tom Bierbaum, "Par Home Vid's 'Top Gun' Hits the Record Books with 2D Wave," *Variety*, March 20, 1987, 1, 43.

106. Karl Gottesfeld letter to Warren Skaaren, August, 6, 1986, WSC.

107. Letter from Daniel Furie to Warren Skaaren, March 17, 1986, WSC.

108. This amount is composed of Skaaren's profit participation checks, documented in letters and with check stubs in WSC.

109. Mike Simpson letter to Warren Skaaren, November 22, 1985, WSC.

CHAPTER FIVE

1. Tim Burton, videotape interview by Tom Giebink, ca. 1991, WSC.

2. Burton quoted in David Breskin, *Inner Views: Filmmakers in Conversation* (Boston: Faber and Faber, 1992), 326–364.

3. Tim Burton, videotape interview by Tom Giebink, ca. 1991, WSC.

4. Burton quoted in Kristine McKenna, "*Playboy* Interview," *Playboy* (August 2001): 62–64.

5. "Acclaimed Horror Writer's 'Death Collection' Goes on Display," Associated Press, October 31, 2013, n.p.

6. Notes from phone conversation with Tim Burton, March 2, 1986, WSC.

7. Notes on phone call with Eric Eisner, March 4, 1986, WSC.

8. Doug Wick, Author's Interview, September 19, 2014.

9. Tim Burton, videotape interview by Tom Giebink, ca. 1991, WSC.

10. Warren Skaaren memo and outline sent to Tim Burton, Eric Eisner, and Mark Canton, March 11, 1986, WSC.

11. Tim Burton, videotape interview by Tom Giebink, ca. 1991, WSC.

12. Notes for *Beetlejuice*, "Various Backups," WSC.

13. Tim Burton response to first draft, April 16, 1986, WSC.

14. Warren Skaaren letter to Eric Eisner, April 28, 1986, WSC.

15. Interoffice memorandum, Tim Burton to Eric Eisner, May 13, 1986, WSC.

16. Ibid.

17. Notes from discussion with Tim Burton and others, May 29, 1986, WSC.

18. Notes on phone call with David Bombyk, June 24, 1986, WSC.

19. Warner Bros. Interoffice Memorandum, July 7, 1986, WSC.

20. Burton quoted in Breskin, *Inner Views*, 328.

21. Draft letter to screenwriter Michael McDowell, n.d., WSC.

22. "Beetlejuice Credit Situation," notes from computer files, July 11, 1986, WSC.

23. Mike Simpson letter to David Bombyk, June 30, 1986, WSC.

24. Wick, Author's Interview, September 19, 2014.

25. Army Archerd, *Variety*, February 18, 1986, n.p.

26. Skaaren outline, 1985–1986, WSC.

27. Wick, Author's Interview, September 19, 2014.

28. Will Tusher, "Catherine Wyler Sr. V.P. for Prod'n," *Variety*, November 18, 1986, 12.

29. Outline by Warren Skaaren, "Flawless," ca. 1986, WSC.

30. Wick, Author's Interview, September 19, 2014.

31. Ibid.

32. Mentioned in letter accompanying financial statements ca. November 1986, WSC.

33. Letter from David Puttnam, January 20, 1987, WSC.

34. Mike Simpson, videotape interview by Tom Giebink, ca. 1991, WSC.

35. Figure based on signed agreements and check stubs, WSC.

36. Skaaren letter to Wick "twins," June 22, 1989, WSC.

37. "Meeting with Kathy O'Hara and Jeffery Jones," February 29, 1987, WSC.

38. Tim Burton, videotape interview by Tom Giebink, ca. 1991, WSC.

39. Anne Thompson, "Burton's Big Adventure," *L.A. Weekly*, April 16–21, 1988, n.p., WSC.

40. Letter from Grace Reiner, WGA, August 28, 1987, WSC.

41. Skaaren notes, ca. 1985, WSC.

42. "Opportunity '87," notes by Skaaren, WSC.

43. Bob Rynearson, Author's Interview, February 22, 2013.

44. "Opportunity '87."

45. Diane Haug, videotape interview by Tom Giebink, ca. 1991, WSC.

46. "Opportunity '87."

47. Ibid.

48. Diane Haug, videotape interview by Tom Giebink, ca. 1991, WSC.

49. All quotations from Linda Vance, videotape interview by Tom Giebink, ca. 1991, WSC. Background information from Linda Vance, Author's Interview, June 29, 2012.

50. Ibid.

51. "Opportunity '87."

52. Linda Vance, videotape interview by Tom Giebink, ca. 1991, WSC.

53. "Stuff Coming Up," therapy notes, November 24, 1987, WSC.

54. "Opportunity '87."

55. "Stuff Coming Up," therapy notes, November 24, 1987, WSC.

56. "Opportunity '87."

57. Lisa Gubernick, "The Marketing of a Movie," *Forbes*, May 30, 1988, 290, WSC.

58. "Medialog," *Starlog*, February 1988, 8.

59. "Writers Strike Chronology," *Los Angeles Times*, August 4, 1988, n.p.

60. "Opportunity '87."

61. Duan Byre, "'Beetle' Crawls to Top B.O. Spot," *The Hollywood Reporter*, April 5, 1988, 1.

62. "Box Office Charts," *Variety*, April 26, 1988, 6.

63. "Beetlejuice Profits," various documents and contracts, ca. 1988–1989, WSC.

64. Pauline Kael, "The Current Cinema," *The New Yorker*, April 18, 1988, 120.

65. Burton quoted in Susan King, "So good, he's frightening," *Los Angeles Herald Examiner*, April 5, 1988, n.p.

66. Roger Ebert, "House of the Nearly Deads," *New York Post*, March 30, 1988, n.p.

67. Copy of newspaper review annotated by Skaaren, Janet Maslin, "Ghosts vs. the Living in 'Beetlejuice,'" *New York Times*, March 30, 1988, C18, WSC.

68. Copy of newspaper review annotated by Skaaren, Kevin Phinney, "Inven-

tive Ideas Frittered Away in 'Beetlejuice'," *Austin American-Statesman*, April 1, 1988, C8, WSC.

69. Thompson, "Burton's Big Adventure," WSC.

70. David Edelstein, "Mixing Beetlejuice," *Rolling Stone*, June 2, 1988, 51.

71. Note from Bonni Lee with copy of "Spittlejuice," Mort Todd and John P. Severin, "Spittlejuice," *Cracked*, July 1988, WSC.

72. "Opportunity '87."

73. Skaaren letter to Helen Skaaren, June 21, 1988, WSC.

74. Thompson, "Burton's Big Adventure," WSC.

75. Draft letter to screenwriter Michael McDowell, ca. 1986, WSC.

CHAPTER SIX

1. Linda Vance, videotape interview by Tom Giebink, ca. 1991, WSC. Also, Linda Vance, Author's Interview, June 29, 2012.

2. Anne Thompson and Marilyn Johnson, "The Making of the Ultimate Sequel," *Premiere*, July/August 1987, 49.

3. Nina Darnton, "At the Movies," *New York Times*, December 5, 1986, C8.

4. Aljean Harmetz, "What Makes Hollywood Bid Big for a Hot Novel," *New York Times*, February 8, 1987, II: 1.

5. Shawn Judge, "Note & Comment: Giving Credit Where Credit Is Due? The Unusual Use of Arbitration in Determining Screenwriting Credits," *Ohio State Journal on Dispute Resolution* 13.221 (1997): 221.

6. Linda Vance, videotape interview by Tom Giebink, ca. 1991, WSC.

7. Thompson and Johnson, "The Making of the Ultimate Sequel," 49.

8. Memorandum from David Kirkpatrick, February 24, 1986, WSC.

9. Anne Thompson, "LA Clips: Heartbeat's Really Racing," *Globe and Mail* (Canada), August 29, 1986, D5.

10. Larry Ferguson draft, *Beverly Hills Cop II*, 61, WSC.

11. Ferguson letter to D. Simpson and J. Bruckheimer, September 29, 1986, "Exhibit L" in *Ferguson v. Writers Guild of America, West*, WSC.

12. "Ferguson Draft, *Beverly Hills Cop II*," ca. October 1986, WSC.

13. Skaaren, "My Outlines Cop II," WSC.

14. Skaaren, "Statement Regarding the Contributions" for *Beverly Hills Cop II*, ca. 1987, WSC.

15. Ibid.

16. Skaaren memorandum to D. Simpson, J. Bruckheimer, T. Scott, and M. London, October 17, 1986, WSC.

17. *Cop II* script notes, October 11, 1986, and October 18, 1986, WSC.

18. "Page changes," December 29, 1986, WSC.

19. Highlighted outline, *Indiana Jones and the Temple of Doom*, WSC.

20. Notes of meeting with Michael Douglas, January 21–22, 1987, WSC.

21. William Morris Agency deal memorandum and contract, January 19, 1987, and subsequent contract revisions through March 1987, WSC.

22. Notes on meetings and outline details, "*Crimson Eagle* Research," ca. February 1987, WSC.

23. Skaaren memorandum to Michael Douglas, February 19, 1987, WSC.

24. Notes on trip to Los Angeles, February 11–13, 1987, WSC.

25. Skaaren statement to WGA concerning *Beverly Hills Cop II* arbitration, ca. March 1987, "Arbitration materials, February to April 1987," WSC.

26. Judge, "Note & Comment," 238.

27. "Crimson Eagle Character Notes," March 9, 1987, WSC.

28. Paramount Pictures, letter and list of story materials, March 10, 1987, and Skaaren letter to Grace Reiner, March 12, 1987, WSC.

29. Skaaren telegram to Helen Skaaren, March 25, 1987, WSC.

30. Hong Kong transcription, Tape 1, WSC.

31. Hong Kong transcription, Tape 2, WSC. See also "Crimson Eagle Research," WSC.

32. Skaaren telegram to Michael Douglas, March 30, 1987, WSC.

33. Letter to D. Huang, April 8, 1987, WSC.

34. David Kirkpatrick memorandum, February 24, 1986, WSC.

35. Skaaren letter to Grace Reiner, WGA, April 12, 1987, WSC.

36. Judge, "Note & Comment," 242.

37. *Screen Credits Manual*, Writers Guild of America, West, and Writers Guild of America, East, 13–14.

38. Writers Guild of America letter to Skaaren, April 28, 1987, WSC.

39. Mike Simpson letter to David Held, Paramount Pictures, April 28, 1987, WSC.

40. Warren Skaaren letter to Nikki Grasso, April 22, 1987, WSC.

41. "Notes on Revised Beats," Susan Braudy and Robert Singer to Michael Douglas, May 5, 1987, WSC.

42. Skaaren letter to Tony Scott, May 14, 1987, WSC.

43. Tony Schwartz, "The Emotion of Triumph," *Premiere*, July/August 1987, 55.

44. "Par, Murphy Golden Pair," *Variety*, May 28, 1987, 1. Opening weekend statistics, Box Office Mojo, http://www.boxofficemojo.com/movies/?id=beverlyhillscop2.htm. Accessed February 4, 2015. See also Todd McCarthy, "Arresting 'Cop 2' B.O. Tally," *Variety*, May 27, 1987, 1.

45. Janet Maslin, "Murphy in Cop II," *New York Times*, May 20, 1987, C28.

46. Hal Hinson, "Cop II Forced; Frenzy and Desperation Mar Murphy's Sequel," *The Washington Post*, May 21, 1987, D1.

47. Roger Ebert, "Beverly Hills Cop II," *Chicago Sun-Times*, May 20, 1987, http://www.rogerebert.com/reviews/beverly-hills-cop-ii-1987. Accessed February 5, 2015.

48. Vance, Author's Interview, July 2012.

49. Mike Simpson mailgram to Jerry Bruckheimer and Don Simpson, May 29, 1987, WSC.

50. Brian Walton, executive director of the Writers Guild, as quoted in Roderick Mann, "Vidal Sues to Get Credit on 'Sicilian,'" *Los Angeles Times*, February 14, 1987, http://articles.latimes.com/1987-02-14/entertainment/ca-2975_1_gore-vidal. Accessed February 6, 2015.

51. Ibid.

52. Judge, "Note & Comment," 246.

53. Nicholas Meyer document detailing testimony, ca. July 1987, WSC.

54. Leslie Dixon document detailing testimony, ca. July 1987, WSC.

55. Warren Skaaren letter to Gary Feess, Jones Day attorney, July 15, 1987, WSC.

56. Roderick Mann, "Vidal Sues to Get Credit."

57. See, for example, "Vidal Sues WGA for 'Sicilian' Credit," *Variety*, February 18, 1987, 3, 44; *Hollywood Reporter*, May 21, 1987; and "L.A. Ruling Favors Vidal in WGA/Sicilian Suit," *Variety*, November 11, 1987, 6.

58. Skaaren letter to Gary Feess, July 15, 1987, WSC.

59. Vance quoted in WAX, 59.

60. Skaaren to Michael Douglas, October 15, 1987, WSC.

61. Gary Feess letter to Skaaren, October 28, 1987, WSC.

CHAPTER SEVEN

1. Lucy Fisher to Warren Skaaren, August 29, 1988, WSC.

2. Louis Black, "Adventures in Screenwriting," *Austin Chronicle*, August 11, 1989, n.p.

3. All quotes from Tom Giebink's videotape interview with Mike Simpson, ca. 1991, WSC.

4. *Daytona* details, Warren Skaaren, *Days of Thunder* Statement of Contribution, May 1990, WSC.

5. Marc Cooper, "Two Angry Men," *Premiere*, January 1988, 48–50.

6. Margaret Heidenry, "When the Spec Script Was King," *Vanity Fair*, March 2013, 285.

7. Letter, Paramount Pictures, March 30, 1988, WSC.

8. Skaaren fax to Sara Staebell at Jones Day, July 8, 1988, WSC.

9. Warren Skaaren fax to George Kirgo, WGA president, September 27, 1988, WSC.

10. Ibid.

11. Kimberly Owczarski, "*Batman*, Time Warner, and Franchise Filmmaking in the Conglomerate Era," unpublished dissertation, University of Texas at Austin (2008), 107.

12. Michael Sragow, "Scripter Unmasked," *San Francisco Examiner*, August 27, 1989, E1; Lisa Henson memo to Mike Simpson, September 28, 1988, WSC.

13. Skaaren, "Datebook Diary Batman," ca. September 1988, WSC.

14. Owczarski, "*Batman*, Time Warner, and Franchise Filmmaking," 109.

15. "Hush-Hush 'Batman' Wraps Shooting; $30-Mill's the Talk," *Variety*, ca. February 1989, n.p.

16. Owczarski, "*Batman*, Time Warner, and Franchise Filmmaking," 111.

17. "BATMAN—Warren Skaaren" memo, Patti Connolly letter to Mike Simpson, August 31, 1988, WSC.

18. Owczarski, "*Batman*, Time Warner, and Franchise Filmmaking," 110. See also Skaaren, handwritten notes for September 1, 1988, meeting, WSC.

19. "Hamm's third draft," dated February 29, 1988, with Warren Skaaren's notes ca. August 30, 1988, WSC.

20. Notes on Tim Burton phone call, "Batman," September 3, 1988, WSC.

21. "Meeting Notes 9/1/88," WSC.

22. Ibid.

23. Bob Kane letter to Warren Skaaren, September 11, 1988, WSC.

24. "A Bad Idea," Skaaren fax to Tim Burton, September 12, 1988, WSC.

25. "Outline of Acts I and II," fax to Tim Burton, September 4, 1988, WSC.

26. Studio notes in response to *Batman* outline, September 7, 1988, WSC.

27. *Shadow of the Batman*, nos. 1–5, Steve Englehart et al., 1985–1986, WSC.

28. "Letter to T. Burton, J. Peters, et al.," September 22, 1988, WSC.

29. Carol Bahoric, "Screenplay Comparison Notes," September 16, 1988, WSC.

30. "Letter to T. Burton, J. Peters, et al.," September 22, 1988, WSC.

31. "Batman—Notes on 2nd Draft," Guber-Peters to T. Burton, W. Skaaren, September 27, 1988, WSC.

32. Joe Morgenstern, "Tim Burton, Batman, and the Joker," *New York Times Magazine*, April 9, 1989, 45.

33. Hilary de Vries, "'Batman' Battles for Big Money," *New York Times*, February 5, 1989, 19.

34. Quotes and other detail, Skaaren's handwritten notes and transcriptions, WSC.

35. Ibid.

36. Notes, meeting with Robert Wuhl, October 6, 1988, WSC.

37. Notes, meeting with Mark Canton, Jon Peters, et al., October 7, 1988, WSC.

38. "Sean, 3:15," n.d., WSC.

39. Owczarski, "*Batman*, Time Warner, and Franchise Filmmaking," 112. Handwritten notes, October 3, 1988, WSC.

40. Walter Kaufmann, ed. and trans., *The Portable Nietzsche* (New York: Penguin Books, 1977), 518.

41. Skaaren letter to Ted Flicker, October 13, 1988, WSC.

42. Transcription of meeting with Jerry Bruckheimer, Don Simpson, and Tom Cruise, September 7, 1988, WSC.

43. Daytona Conference Call, December 9, 1988, WSC. See also Skaaren's *Days of Thunder* Statement of Contribution sent to the Writers Guild of America as part of the film's arbitration proceedings, May 1990, WSC.

44. Daytona Conference Call, December 9, 1988, WSC.

45. Skaaren, *Days of Thunder* Statement of Contribution, May 1990, WSC.

46. Nancy Griffin and Kim Masters, *Hit and Run: How Jon Peters and Peter Guber Took Sony for a Ride in Hollywood* (New York: Simon & Schuster, 1996), 169.

47. Letter to Ted Flicker, October 31, 1988, WSC.

48. Letter to Mary Sean Young, November 10, 1988, WSC.

49. Kathleen A. Hughes, "Fans of Batman Fear the Joke Is on Them in a H'wood Epic," *Wall Street Journal*, November 29, 1988, 1, A5.

50. "Batman" fax to Mike Simpson, November 28, 1988, WSC.

51. Fax to Sally Burmester, WGA Screen Credits Coordinator, March 7, 1989, WSC. See also Griffin and Masters, *Hit and Run*, 171.

52. Notes for Kim Basinger, n.d., WSC.

53. Skaaren notes ca. December 1989, WSC. See also Griffin and Masters, *Hit and Run*, 169.

54. Fax to Sara Staebell and John Lee at Jones Day, November 1, 1988, WSC.

55. Fax to Sally Burmester, WGA Screen Credits Coordinator, March 7, 1989, WSC. See also Skaaren, *Batman* Statement of Contribution, March 1989, page 2, WSC.

56. Griffin and Masters, *Hit and Run*, 171.

57. Fax to Tim Burton, Jon Peters, Mark Canton, and Chris Kenny, January 10, 1989, WSC.

58. Skaaren, *Batman* Statement of Contribution, March 1989, page 1, WSC.

59. Fax to Sally Burmester, WGA Screen Credits Coordinator, March 7, 1989, WSC.

60. Mike Simpson telegram, April 18, 1989, WSC.

61. Griffin and Masters, *Hit and Run*, 170–171.

62. Jack Kroll, "Return to Gotham City," *Newsweek*, January 23, 1989, 68–69.

63. "Batman's Back," *20/20*, June 1989, http://www.batman-on-film.com/Batman-75_B89_20-20-B89-feature.html. Accessed April 1, 2015.

64. Mike Simpson fax to Warren Skaaren, May 16, 1989, WSC.

65. Hamm quoted in Howard A. Rodman, "They Shoot Comic Books, Don't They?" *American Film*, May 1989, 39.

66. Details of May 1989 trip described in memos, notes, and photos in WSC.

67. Christopher Rosen, "This Is What the Batman Premiere Looked Like in 1989," *The Huffington Post*, June 23, 2014, http://www.huffingtonpost.com/2014/06/23/batman-anniversary_n_5523030.html. Accessed April 3, 2015.

68. Doug Wick, Author's Interview, September 19, 2014.

69. Telegrams from Norman Brokaw, June 20, 1989; Leonard Hirshan, June 20, 1989; Jim Crabbe, June 20, 1989; and Carol Yumkas, June 21, 1989, WSC.

70. Griffin and Masters, *Hit and Run*, 172–173.

71. Fax from Richard Shiff and Doug Wick, June 24, 1989, WSC.

72. Ibid. See also Claudia Eller, "U.S. Goes Batty: Dark Knight Has Super-heroic $42 Mil Debut," *The Hollywood Reporter*, June 26, 1989, 1.

73. "Batman," *Variety*, June 13, 1989, n.p.

74. Mary Cantwell, "When a Full-Grown Woman Becomes 10 Again," *New York Times*, June 30, 1989, n.p.

75. Pauline Kael, "The City Gone Psycho," *The New Yorker*, July 10, 1989, 85.

76. Michael Sragow, "Scripter Unmasked," *San Francisco Examiner*, August 27, 1989, E1.

77. Skaaren quoted in Griffin and Masters, *Hit and Run*, 173.

78. Jane Sumner, "Rescuing the Dark Knight," *Dallas Morning News*, July 6, 1989, 5C–6C.

79. Owczarski, "*Batman*, Time Warner, and Franchise Filmmaking," 117, n. 43.

80. Herb Sleeper, Author's Interview, May 2012.

81. Details about Skaaren's activities and correspondence in the summer of 1989 can be found in WSC.

CHAPTER EIGHT

1. Emily Yoffe, "The Man Hollywood Trusts," *Texas Monthly*, September 1989, 120.

2. Ibid., 122.

3. Skaaren's personal notes, "The change in August 1989," WSC.

4. Skaaren quoted in Kevin Phinney, "Death of a Screenwriter," *Premiere*, March 1991, 99.

5. "BJ2 Notes," n.d., WSC.

6. Skaaren's personal notes, "The change in August 1989," WSC.

7. Phinney, "Death of a Screenwriter," 98.

8. Skaaren's personal notes, "At the screenwriter's seminar," October 24, 1989, WSC.

9. Skaaren quoted in Pat Jankiewicz, "The Dark Knight Revised," *Comics Scene*, no. 14 (1990), 51.

10. Notes on moving parents into Charter House, November 22, 1989, WSC.

11. Deal memos and contracts for "Beetlejuice in Love," ca. October and November 1989, WSC. See also Skaaren's personal notes, "The Beet 2 Final Fiasco," October 20, 1989, WSC.

12. Typed outline, "Beetlejuice in Love," notes from Geffen meeting, December 1989, WSC.

13. See *Opera News*, October 1989; Donal Henehan, "Back for the Brink Once More," *New York Times*, December 10, 1989, 31; and assorted articles, WSC.

14. Fan letter from Dena Price, sent with Denise Di Novi letter, WSC.

15. Assorted notes, "Beetlejuice in Love," ca. November and December 1989, WSC.

16. Phinney, "Death of a Screenwriter," 99.

17. *Days of Thunder* Statement of Contribution, May 1990, WSC.

18. Jeffrey Ressner, "On 'Thunder' Road with Tom Cruise," *Rolling Stone*, July 12–July 26, 1990, 54.

19. Linda Vance, Author's Interview, July 2012.

20. Ressner, "On 'Thunder' Road with Tom Cruise," 54.

21. "Goals 12/89," WSC.

22. Skaaren letter to Helen Skaaren, January 4, 1990, WSC.

23. Undated journal entry ca. December 1, 1989, WSC.

24. "Journal 1990," WSC.

25. George Papajohn, "Hollywood's Mr. Fix-It," *Chicago Tribune*, March 6, 1990, 1, 2.

26. "Best Lines of 1989," *Premiere*, February 1990, 82.

27. Skaaren as told to Gene Stone, "How to Write a Screenplay," *Mirabella*, January 1991, 54.

28. "Journal 1990," WSC.

29. Skaaren's personal notes, "The change in August 1989," WSC.

30. Entry dated January 9 in "Journal 1990," WSC.

31. *Beetlejuice in Love*, ninety-seven-page screenplay, ca. April 1990, WSC.

32. WAX, 57.

33. Pat Jankiewicz, "The Dark Knight Revised," 51.

34. Julie Jordan, videotape interview by Tom Giebink, ca. 1991, WSC.

35. In a profile about Tom Cruise and the film, Towne claimed that he took inspiration for this character from late NASCAR driver Tim Richmond's real-life romance with an ophthalmologist. See Ressner, "On 'Thunder' Road with Tom Cruise," 54–55. In the time since Skaaren had worked on the script, Cruise had begun dating actress Nicole Kidman, and her casting in the role may have affected changes to the part as well.

36. Letter from the Writers Guild of America, April 26, 1990, WSC.

37. Will Tusher, "'Thunder' Script Credit Clouded," *Variety*, May 8, 1990, 19.

38. Will Tusher, "'Thunder' Writers Charge Credit Plunder," *Variety*, May 9, 1990, n.p.

39. *Days of Thunder* Statement of Contribution, May 1990, WSC.

40. Ibid.

41. Army Archerd, "Just for Variety," *Variety*, September 17, 1990, 2.

42. *Days of Thunder* Statement of Contribution, May 1990, WSC.

43. "'Days of Thunder' Almost Stalled in Production," *Sarasota Herald-Tribune*, June 30, 1990, 8E.

44. Various drafts of Skaaren's Writer's Agreement for *Days of Thunder* exist, but the final version was signed on December 21, 1988. See letter from attorneys for

Jerry Bruckheimer and Don Simpson, dated December 21, 1988, for final language about profit participation, WSC.

45. *Days of Thunder* earned $15.4 million on its opening weekend. Box office figures from "Box Office Mojo," http://www.boxofficemojo.com/movies/?id=daysof thunder.htm. Accessed May 14, 2015.

46. Julie Jordan, videotape interview by Tom Giebink, ca. January 1991, WSC.

CONCLUSION

1. Diane Haug, videotape interview by Tom Giebink, ca. 1991, WSC.

2. *Beetlejuice in Love*, bound first draft, July 10, 1990, WSC.

3. Linda Vance, videotape interview by Tom Giebink, ca. 1991, WSC.

4. Ibid.

5. Ibid.

6. Ibid. See also Amon Burton, videotape interview by Tom Giebink, ca. 1991, WSC.

7. Linda Vance, videotape interview by Tom Giebink, ca. 1991, WSC.

8. Ibid.

9. Linda Vance, Author's Interview, June 29, 2012.

10. Linda Vance, videotape interview by Tom Giebink, ca. 1991, WSC.

11. Julie Jordan, videotape interview by Tom Giebink, ca. January 1991, WSC.

12. Ibid.

13. Brian Connors, videotape interview by Tom Giebink, ca. 1991, WSC.

14. Linda Vance, videotape interview by Tom Giebink, ca. 1991, WSC.

15. Lee Walker, videotape interview with Amon Burton by Tom Giebink, ca. 1991, WSC.

16. Julie Jordan, videotape interview by Tom Giebink, ca. January 1991, WSC.

17. Journal entry, ca. September 1990, WSC.

18. "Agenda October/November 1990," WSC.

19. Linda Vance, Author's Interview, June 29, 2012.

20. Mike Simpson, Author's Interview, October 28, 2004.

21. Brian Connors, videotape interview by Tom Giebink, ca. 1991, WSC.

22. Bob Rynearson, Author's Interview, February 22, 2013.

23. Journal entry, October 7, 1990, WSC.

24. Kaye Connors, Author's Interview, April 11, 2014.

25. Anonymous.

26. Linda Vance, videotape interview by Tom Giebink, ca. 1991, WSC.

27. Jerry Hall, Author's Interview, December 12, 2003.

28. Linda Vance, videotape interview by Tom Giebink, ca. 1991, WSC.

29. Julie Jordan, videotape interview by Tom Giebink, ca. 1991, WSC.

30. Kaye Connors, videotape interview by Tom Giebink, ca. 1991, WSC.

31. Diane Haug, videotape interview by Tom Giebink, ca. 1991, WSC.

32. Ibid.

33. Ibid.

34. Ibid.

35. Julie Jordan, videotape interview by Tom Giebink, ca. 1991, WSC.

36. Mike Simpson, Author's Interview, October 28, 2004.

37. Skaaren letter to Amy Burton, February 2, 1990, WSC.

38. Brian Connors, videotape interview by Tom Giebink, ca. 1991, WSC.

39. Diane Haug, videotape interview by Tom Giebink, ca. 1991, WSC. See also Kaye Connors, Author's Interview, April 11, 2014.

40. Kaye Connors, Author's Interview, April 11, 2014.

41. Julie Jordan, videotape interview by Tom Giebink, ca. 1991, WSC.

42. Kaye Connors, videotape interview by Tom Giebink, ca. 1991, WSC.

43. Heloise Gold, videotape interview by Tom Giebink, ca. 1991, WSC.

44. Diane Haug and Kaye Connors, videotape interviews by Tom Giebink, ca. 1991, WSC. See also Linda Vance, Author's Interview, July 2012, and WAX, 61.

45. Linda Vance, Author's Interview, July 2012.

46. Gene Stone, "How to Write a Screenplay," *Mirabella*, January 1991, 54.

47. *Ferguson v. Writers Guild of America, West*, Casebriefs, ca. 1991, http://www.casebriefs.com/blog/law/civil-procedure/civil-procedure-keyed-to-yeazell/resolution-without-trial/ferguson-v-writers-guild-of-america-west/. Accessed October 28, 2011.

48. Mike Simpson, videotape interview by Tom Giebink, ca. January 1991, WSC.

49. Tim Burton, videotape interview by Tom Giebink, ca. January 1991, WSC.

Select Bibliography

Ansen, David, and Peter McAlevey. "The Producer Is King." *Newsweek*. May 20, 1985: 84–87.

Arnheim, Rudolf. "Who Is the Author of a Film?" *Film Culture* 4.1 (1958): 11–13.

Attanasio, Paul. "The Twin Titans of 'Top Gun.'" *Washington Post*. May 16, 1986, D1, D3.

Azlant, Edward. "Screenwriting for the Early Silent Film: Forgotten Pioneers, 1897–1911." *Film History* 9.3 (1997): 228–256.

Beauchamp, Cari. *Without Lying Down: Frances Marion and the Powerful Women of Early Hollywood*. New York: Lisa Drew/Scribner, 1997.

Becker, Ernest. *The Denial of Death*. New York: Free Press Paperbacks, 1973.

Boon, Kevin Alexander. *Script Culture and the American Screenplay*. Detroit: Wayne State University Press, 2008.

Bordwell, David. *The Way Hollywood Tells It: Story and Style in Modern Movies*. Berkeley: University of California Press, 2006.

Bordwell, David, Janet Staiger, and Kristin Thompson. *The Classical Hollywood Cinema: Film Style and Mode of Production to 1960*. New York: Columbia University Press, 1985.

Burton, Tim. *Burton on Burton*. Boston: Faber & Faber, 1995.

Carson, Diane, ed. *John Sayles: Interviews*. Jackson: University Press of Mississippi, 1999.

Cirile, Jim. "WGA Arbitration: The Good, the Bad, and the Ugly." *Stormfront Blog*. http://coverageink.blogspot.com/2010/12/wga-arbitration-good-bad-and-ugly.html.

Connelly, Christopher. "Fast Track." *Premiere*. July 1988: 42–44, 50.

Conor, Bridget. "'Everybody's a Writer': Theorizing Screenwriting as Creative Labour." *Journal of Screenwriting* 1.1 (2010): 27–43.

Corliss, Richard. *Talking Pictures: Screenwriters in the American Cinema, 1927–1973*. Woodstock, NY: Overlook, 1974.

Crofts, Stephen. "Authorship and Hollywood." *Wide Angle* 5.3 (1983): 16–22.

Dunne, John Gregory. *Monster: Living Off the Big Screen.* New York: Random House, 1997.

Field, Syd. *Screenplay: The Foundations of Screenwriting.* New York: Delacorte, 1982.

Fine, Richard. *Hollywood and the Profession of Authorship, 1928–1940.* Ann Arbor: UMI Research Press, 1985.

Fleming, Charles. *High Concept: Don Simpson and the Hollywood Culture of Excess.* New York: Doubleday, 1998.

Fraga, Kristian, ed. *Tim Burton: Interviews.* Jackson: University Press of Mississippi, 2005.

Fragale, Jim. "How to Write a Hit Movie, Or Who Is Syd Field and Why Does Everybody Own His Books?" *Creative Screenwriting* 1.4 (Winter 1994): 119–125.

Friend, Tad. "Credit Grab." *The New Yorker.* October 20, 2003, 160–169.

Friendly, David T. "Development Game: All's Fair." *Los Angeles Times.* September 25, 1986, 1, 4.

Goldman, William. *Adventures in the Screen Trade: A Personal View of Hollywood and Screenwriting.* New York: Warner Books, 1983.

Griffin, Nancy, and Kim Masters. *Hit and Run: How Jon Peters and Peter Guber Took Sony for a Ride in Hollywood.* New York: Simon & Schuster, 1997.

Heidenry, Margaret. "When the Spec Script Was King." *Vanity Fair.* March 2013: 284–292.

Honeycutt, Kirk. "Whose Film Is It Anyway?" *American Film.* May 1981: 34–38, 70.

"How Hollywood Writers Arbitrate." *Variety.* July 7, 1965.

Howard, Sidney. "The Story Gets a Treatment." In *We Make the Movies*, edited by Nancy Naumburg, 32–52. New York: W. W. Norton, 1937.

Hoyt, Eric. "Writer in the Hole: *Desny v. Wilder*, Copyright Law, and the Battle Over Ideas." *Cinema Journal* 50.2 (2011): 21–40.

Hutcheon, Linda. *A Theory of Adaptation.* New York: Routledge, 2012.

Judge, Shawn K. "Note & Comment: Giving Credit Where Credit Is Due? The Unusual Use of Arbitration in Determining Screenwriting Credits." *Ohio State Journal on Dispute Resolution* 13.1 (1997) 221–262.

Kael, Pauline. "Circles and Squares." In *Film Theory and Criticism: Introductory Readings*, edited by Gerald Mast and Marshall Cohen, 541–552. New York: Oxford University Press, 1985.

King, Geoff. *New Hollywood Cinema: An Introduction.* New York: Columbia University Press, 2002.

Kipen, David. *The Schreiber Theory: A Radical Rewrite of American Film History.* Hoboken, NJ: Melville House, 2006.

Macor, Alison. *Chainsaws, Slackers, and Spy Kids: Thirty Years of Filmmaking in Austin, Texas.* Austin: University of Texas Press, 2010.

Maras, Steven. *Screenwriting: History, Theory, and Practice.* London: Wallflower, 2009.

McGilligan, Patrick, ed. *Backstory 1: Interviews with Screenwriters of Hollywood's Golden Age*. Berkeley: University of California Press, 1986.

———. *Backstory 2: Interviews with Screenwriters of the 1940s and 1950s*. Berkeley: University of California Press, 1991.

———. *Backstory 3: Interviews with Screenwriters of the 1960s*. Berkeley: University of California Press, 1997.

———. *Backstory 4: Interviews with Screenwriters of the 1970s and 1980s*. Berkeley: University of California Press, 2006.

McMahan, Alison. *The Films of Tim Burton: Animating Live Action in Contemporary Hollywood*. New York: Continuum, 2005.

Mehring, Margaret. *The Screenplay: A Blend of Film Form and Content*. Boston: Focal, 1990.

Millar, Jeff. "Warren Skaaren, Movie Mogul." *Texas Monthly.* July 1973: 60–62.

Nelmes, Jill. "Some Thoughts on Analysing the Screenplay, the Process of Screenplay Writing, and the Balance Between Craft and Creativity." *Journal of Media Practice* 8.2 (2007): 107–113.

Nichols, Dudley. "The Writer and the Film." In *Twenty Best Film Plays*, edited by John Gassner and Dudley Nichols, xxxi–xl. New York: Crown, 1977.

Norman, Marc. *What Happens Next: A History of American Screenwriting*. New York: Harmony, 2007.

Pearson, Roberta, and William Uricchio, eds. *The Many Lives of the Batman: Critical Approaches to a Superhero and His Media*. New York: Routledge, 1991.

Phinney, Kevin. "Death of a Screenwriter." *Premiere.* March 1991: 98–99.

Price, Steven. *The Screenplay: Authorship, Theory, and Criticism*. Basingstoke, U.K.: Palgrave McMillan, 2010.

Ross, Murray. *Stars and Strikes: Unionization of Hollywood*. New York: Columbia University Press, 1941.

Sarris, Andrew. "Notes on the Auteur Theory in 1962." In *Film Theory and Criticism: Introductory Readings*, edited by Gerald Mast and Marshall Cohen, 527–540. New York: Oxford University Press, 1985.

Schwartz, Nancy Lynn. *The Hollywood Writers' Wars*. New York: Knopf, 1982.

Scott, Ian. *In Capra's Shadow: The Life and Career of Screenwriter Robert Riskin*. Lexington: University Press of Kentucky, 2006.

Screen Credits Manual. Los Angeles: Writers Guild of America, West, 1984.

Screen Credits Manual. Los Angeles: Writers Guild of America, West, 2010.

Shone, Tom. *Blockbuster: How Hollywood Learned to Stop Worrying and Love the Summer*. New York: Free Press, 2004.

Staiger, Janet. "Blueprints for Feature Films: Hollywood's Continuity Scripts." In *The American Film Industry*, edited by Tino Balio, 173–192. Madison: University of Wisconsin Press, 1985.

Steel, Dawn. *They Can Kill You . . . But They Can't Eat You*. New York: Pocket Books, 1993.

Stempel, Tom. *Framework: A History of Screenwriting in the American Film*. Syracuse, NY: Syracuse University Press, 2000.

Sternberg, Claudia. *Written for the Screen: The American Motion-Picture Screenplay as Text*. Tübingen, Germany: Stauffenburg, 1997.

Taylor, Thom. *The Big Deal: Hollywood's Million-Dollar Spec Script Market*. New York: William Morrow, 1999.

Thompson, Kristin. *Storytelling in the New Hollywood: Understanding Classical Narrative Technique*. Cambridge: Harvard University Press, 1999.

Truffaut, Francois. "A Certain Tendency in the French Cinema." In *Movies and Methods: Volume 1*, edited by Bill Nichols, 224–237. Berkeley: University of California Press, 1976.

Vale, Eugene. *The Technique of Screen and Television Writing*. Englewood Cliffs, NJ: Prentice-Hall, 1982.

Vidal, Gore. "Who Makes the Movies?" *The New York Review of Books*. November 25, 1976, 35–39.

Walker, Barbara. "The Majors: Limbo Land." *Film Comment* 23.1 (1987): 34–40.

Waxman, Natasha. *Warren Skaaren, Screenwriter: His Life, Films, and Letters*. Austin: Harry Ransom Humanities Research Center, University of Texas, 1991.

Wheaton, Christopher D. "A History of the Screen Writers' Guild (1920–1942): The Writer's Quest for a Freely Negotiated Basic Agreement." PhD diss., University of Southern California (Communications-Cinema), 1973.

Wyatt, Justin. *High Concept: Movies and Marketing in Hollywood*. Austin: University of Texas Press, 1994.

Yoffe, Emily. "The Man Hollywood Trusts." *Texas Monthly*. September 1989: 120–123, 184–187.

Index

ABC Television, 62, 169

Academy of Motion Picture Arts and Sciences, 47, 100

Ackland-Snow, Terry, 155

Adventures in the Screen Trade: A Personal View of Hollywood and Screenwriting (book), 83

Against All Odds (1984), 185

Agnes of God (1985), 117

AIP, 71

Akers, Fred, 69

Ali, Muhammad, 70

Allen, Herbert, 32

Allen, Jay Presson, 178

All in the Family (TV; 1971–1979), 134

American Film (magazine), 170

"American Gothic" (painting), 110

Andy Warhol's Frankenstein (1973), 52, 55

Aniston, Jennifer, 44

Archerd, Army, 95, 96, 117, 126, 186

Atherton, William, 47

Atlanta International Film Festival, 48

Austin, Texas, 37, 39–40, 46, 62, 81, 145

Austin Symphony, 66

authorship, 8, 9–10, 86, 143, 147, 152, 168

Bach, Danilo, 133

Bad Company (1972), 42

Bahoric, Carol, 159, 160

"Ballad of East and West, The" (poem), 75

Ballard, Lucien, 43

Bang the Drum Slowly (1973), 61

Barney Miller (TV; 1974–1982), 63

Basinger, Kim, 153, 165, 167, 168, 169

Batman (1989), 4, 7, 25, 120, 190; box office, 171–173; budget, 151, 154, 161, 166, 169; casting, 155–156; crew, 154–155, 161–162; critical reception, 169–170, 171–173, 182; development, 153–154, 156–161; fan protests, 165–166; premiere, 170–171; production, 163, 165–167; rehearsals, 161–163; screen-credit arbitration, 167–169; trailer, 169

Beetlejuice (1988), 7, 25, 133, 136, 162, 202; animated TV series, 129; box office, 126–127, 129; critical reception, 125, 127–128; development, 111–113; production, 120, 138; screen-credit arbitration, 115–116, 120–121, 129–130; test screenings, 125

Beetlejuice in Love (unproduced screenplay), 13, 129, 176–184, 194, 199, 202

Beetlejuice 2, 177, 179–180. See also *Beetlejuice in Love*

Beiersdorf, Fred, 56

Belafonte, Harry, 7

Benji (1974), 64

Benson, Robbie, 71

Benton, Robert, 42

Beresford, Bruce, 75, 81–82

Besman, Michael, 156

Beverly Hills Cop (1984), 100, 131, 133, 155

Beverly Hills Cop II (1987), 4, 7–8, 10, 109, 153, 155; box office, 144–145; critical reception, 144–145; development, 131–133; production, 136; screen-credit arbitration, 133, 138–140, 142–143, 147–149, 151–152. See also *Ferguson v. Writers Guild of America, West*

Beverly Hills Security Guard, 134. See also *Beverly Hills Cop II*

Bigley, Ivan, 63–65

Black Stallion, The (1979), 62

Bloch, Paul, 174

Bludhorn, Charles, 62

Bly, Robert, 65

Bodine, Geoff, 164

Bombyk, David, 114–115, 116

Bonfiglio, Lois, 117, 118

Bonnie and Clyde (1967), 42

Booker, Diane, 45–46

Boorstin, Paul, 84, 86–88

Boorstin, Sharon, 84, 86–88

Born on the Fourth of July (1989), 165

Bozman, Ron: at Rice University, 31, 33, 39; and *The Texas Chain Saw Massacre*, 48, 49, 53–55, 63; Warren Skaaren's friendship with, 13, 22, 24; and Warren Skaaren's memorial, 1–3

Braudy, Susan, 144

Breakaway (1978), 63–67

Breaker Morant (1980), 75, 81

Brest, Martin, 107, 132

Brian's Song (TV movie; 1971), 70

Bridger, Bobby, 3, 7, 62, 65–66, 67

Bridges, Jeff, 42

Brokaw, Norman, 171

Brolin, James, 171

Brown, David, 47, 78–79

Brown, Harold, 186

Broyles, Bill, 38

Bruckheimer, Jerry, 5, 6, 15–16, 89; and *Beverly Hills Cop*, 131–132; and *Beverly Hills Cop II*, 131–136, 144–145; and *Days of Thunder*, 151, 164, 170, 174; and Don Simpson, 15–16, 88; and *Top Gun*, 88–89, 92, 94–95, 107–108

Bryanston Distribution, Inc., 52–60

Burmester, Sally, 168

Burton, Amy, 199

Burton, Tim: background of, 110–111; and *Batman*, 151, 153–156, 158–163, 165, 167, 168; and *Beetlejuice*, 111–116, 119–120, 128; and *Beetlejuice in Love*, 176, 177, 179–180, 184, 188; on Warren Skaaren, 110, 111, 112, 113, 120; and Warren Skaaren's death, 203; on writers and development, 111

Burton, W. Amon, 2, 24, 75, 122, 175; and Warren Skaaren's cancer (1987), 123; and Warren Skaaren's cancer (1990), 12, 190–191, 193, 198, 201

Butch Cassidy and the Sundance Kid (1969), 40

Campbell, Joseph, 180

Canby, Vincent, 108

Cannes Film Festival, 58, 96

Canton, Mark: and *Batman*, 154–156, 158–160, 162, 165–166, 170–171; and *Beetlejuice*, 112, 115

Cantwell, Mary, 172

Captive Hearts, 83–88. See also *Fire with Fire*

Carl, Carlton, 41

Carroll, Larry, 38, 49, 50

Casablanca FilmWorks Ltd., 153

Cash, Jim, 88–91, 95, 99, 100, 102, 104–107, 145

Central Intelligence Agency (CIA), 139

Challenger Space Shuttle, 107–108

Chariots of Fire (1981), 82

Charlie's Angels (TV; 1976–1981), 138
Chassman, Leonard, 100
Chicago Sun-Times (newspaper), 145
Chimes at Midnight (1965), 161–162
Chinatown (1974), 157
Christine (novel), 84
Cleng Peerson (unproduced screen-play), 19
Cocktail (1988), 151
Colby, Loyd, 65
Colombo, Joseph, 52, 53, 56
Color of Money, The (1986), 151
Color Purple, The (1985), 117
Columbia Pictures, 99, 118
Conforte, Ruth, 71
Connolly, Derek, 9
Connors, Brian, 12, 192, 193, 194, 196, 199, 200
Connors, Kaye, 12, 24, 192, 194, 195, 196, 201
Copeland, Stewart, 180
Coppola, Francis Ford, 44, 132
Crabbe, Jim, 171
Cracked (magazine), 128
Craven, Garth, 126
Creek Theatre, 65
Crimson Eagle (unproduced screen-play), 137–141, 143, 146, 148, 151, 176
Cruise, Tom, 11, 116; and *Days of Thunder*, 151, 163–167, 170, 181, 184–186; and *Top Gun*, 15–16, 80, 89–90, 92–95, 97–98, 102, 107; and Warren Skaaren, 5–6
Cullen, Charlie, 40

Dal-Art, 56
Dallas (TV; 1978–1991), 71, 72, 158
Dallas Morning News (newspaper), 173
Daniel, Sean, 179, 180
Dante, Joe, 64
Dark Knight Returns, The (graphic novel series), 154
D'Artique, John, 170

Davis, Joy O'Dil, 42, 45
Dawson, Gordon, 43, 45, 63
"Day-O" (song), 7
Days of Thunder (1990), 6; box office, 186; conflicts, 164–165, 173, 181; development, 151, 163–164, 166, 167, 170, 174; and Robert Towne, 181–182; screen-credit arbitration, 184–186, 199; and Tom Cruise, 151, 164, 165
Daytona, 151, 163–164. See also *Days of Thunder*
DC Comics, 154, 157
Dead Poets Society (1989), 171
Decorah, Iowa, 18, 19
Deep, The (1977), 155
Deep Throat (1972), 46, 52–53, 55–56, 58–59, 71
de Menil, Dominique, 30, 39
de Menil, John, 30, 39
Denial of Death, The (book), 1, 5, 111, 113, 178
De Niro, Robert, 156
development, 9–10, 82, 87, 100, 132, 147
Diller, Barry, 62, 134
Di Novi, Denise, 180
Divergent (2014), 83
Dixon, Leslie, 146, 148
Douglas, Diandra, 6
Douglas, Kirk, 137
Douglas, Michael, 5–6, 122, 136–139, 142–143, 146, 148, 151
Dowden, W. S., 35
Downey, Robert, Jr., 171
Downs, Bill, 68, 70–72
Dunaway, Faye, 91
Dune (1984), 161

East West Center, 124
Easy Money (1983), 120
Easy Rider (1969), 40
Ebert, Roger, 127, 145
Eberts, John D., 77
Edwards, Anthony, 94, 98, 102, 178

Eggshells (1969), 47–48
Eisner, Eric, 112–115, 179–180
Eisner, Michael, 89
"Elegy Written in a Church Courtyard" (poem), 166
Elfman, Danny, 169
Encino Press, 50, 51, 61
Epps, Jack, Jr., 88–91, 95, 99, 100, 104–106, 107, 145
Esquire (magazine), 80
E. T. (1982), 180
Evans, Bill, 122
Evans, Robert, 44
Excalibur (1981), 161

Fantasy Island (TV; 1977–1984), 138
Fatal Attraction (1987), 147, 148
Feess, Gary, 146, 147, 149, 152
Fehr, Grant, 63
Ferguson, Larry, 132, 134–135, 138–139
Ferguson v. Writers Guild of America, West (1991), 142–143, 146–148, 152–153, 167, 202
Ferris Bueller's Day Off (1986), 120
Few Grains of Rice, A, 75. See also *Of East and West*
Field of Dreams (1989), 171
Film Advisory Board, 67
Film Center Building, 54, 56, 70
Film Texas!, 45, 50
Finger, Bill, 157
Fire with Fire (1986), 83–86, 87–88, 106, 115–116
First Wives Club, The (1996), 117
Fisher, Lucy, 150, 151, 153–154, 171
Flashdance (1983), 83, 88
Flawless (unproduced screenplay), 112, 117–118, 119, 143
Flicker, Ted, 63, 163
Flying Boy, The: Healing the Wounded Man (book), 126
Fonda, Jane, 112, 117–119, 133, 136
Fonda Films, 117, 118

Foote, Horton, 82, 178
Footloose (1984), 83
Foster, David: and *The Getaway*, 43–44, 47; and *The Texas Chain Saw Massacre*, 51–52, 55, 59–60, 61
Fox, Christine, 90
Fox, Fred, 73–74, 77–79
Fox, Jim, 122
Fox, Robert, 122, 123
Fox Westwood Village, 170
FPS, Inc., 71–73, 77, 80, 84–85, 104, 158, 175
France, Michael, 8
Frankfurt, Garbus, Klein & Selz, 54
Frazier, Joe, 70
Freddie (unproduced screenplay), 60, 68–71
Friend, Tad, 9
Full Metal Jacket (1987), 161
Furst, Anton, 161–162, 169, 172, 182

Gaghan, Stephen, 9–10
Geffen, David, 115, 116, 179, 188
Geffen Company, 112–115, 125, 129, 177, 179, 184, 202
Gems, Jonathan, 179
Getaway, The (1972), 43–45, 46
Ghostbusters (1984), 117
Ghostbusters II (1989), 171, 173
Gibbins, Duncan, 86
Giebink, Tom, 12, 24, 27, 199
Giler, David, 138
Girard, Stephen, 71, 72
Glass & Caylor, 55
Glasser, Karen, 82
Godfather, The (1972), 44, 52, 54, 56
Gold, Heloise, 3, 201
Goldberg, Leonard, 138
Goldberg, Whoopi, 117
Goldcrest Films and Television Limited, 77
Goldman, William, 83
Gordon, William, 34

Gould, Blake, 123, 124, 189, 191, 192
Graham, Margery, 76
Griffin, Nancy, 173
Griffith, Melanie, 171
Guber, Peter, 153, 154, 160, 162, 171
Guc, David, 137
Guest, Don, 43
Guinn, Bill, 3

Hagman, Larry, 72
Hall, Jerry, 36; and *The Texas Chain Saw Massacre*, 38–39, 49; and the Texas Film Commission, 40–42; Warren Skaaren's friendship with, 60, 85, 195–196
Hallingdal, Norway, 17
Hamm, Sam, 154, 170–172, 182
Hancock, John, 61
Haney, Richard, 50
Hanson, Curtis, 154
Harrison, George, 128
Hart to Hart (TV; 1979–1984), 138
Hassanein, Richard, 70
Hawg, Diane, 12, 24, 123, 188, 196–198, 200
Hawn, Goldie, 46, 47
Heisters, The (1965), 47
Hendrick, Rick, 163
Henkel, Kim, 47–51, 55, 57, 58
Henson, Lisa, 115, 154, 156, 157, 158, 159, 160
Hickson, Julie, 154
Highlander (1986), 132
High Sierra (1941), 43
Hinojosa, Tish, 198
Hinson, Hal, 145
Hoffman, Dustin, 107
HolliBalance Well-Being Center, 123
Home Box Office (HBO), 70
Honey, I Shrunk the Kids (1989), 171
Hooper, Tobe, 38–39, 47–51, 55
Hoover, J. Edgar, 63
Howorth, Ted, 43

Huang, David, 140–142
Hughes, Eric, 184–185
Hulk, The (2003), 8

IBM, 22, 25
Ice Castles (1978), 71
Ince, Thomas, 161
Indiana Jones and the Last Crusade (1989), 173
Indiana Jones and the Temple of Doom (1984), 137
Inman, John, 66
I Play to Win (book), 69

Jaffe, Andrea, 174
Jamail, William, 68
Jaws (1975), 78
Jeffers, Bill, 5
Jenkins, Dan, 132, 133–134, 138, 148, 149, 167
Jewel of the Nile, The (1985), 122, 136–137
Jewison, Norman, 82
John Marshall High School, 25–26, 173
Johnson, Ben, 47
Johnson, Don, 170
Jolie, Angelina, 44
Jones, Dan, 124
Jones, Day, Reavis & Pogue, 146
Jones, Jeffrey, 120
Jordan, Julie: astrological prediction and Warren Skaaren, 187; on Warren Skaaren, 11, 13–14, 177, 187, 192; and Warren Skaaren's cancer (1990), 187, 190–194, 196; Warren Skaaren's final conversation with, 198, 200; Warren Skaaren's first meeting with, 176
Judge, Shawn K., 10
Jung, Carl, 180
Junior Bonner (1972), 43
Jurow, Martin, 42, 68
Jurassic World (2015), 8–9

Kael, Pauline, 108, 127, 172
Kafka-Wagner, Sherry, 4
Kamen, Ralph, 105
Kamen, Stan, 81
Kane, Bob, 153, 154, 157–158
Katzenberg, Jeffrey, 6, 83, 89, 100
Kaufmann, Walter, 163
Keaton, Diane, 202
Keaton, Michael: and *Batman*, 153, 155, 157, 162, 165, 166, 169; and *Beetlejuice*, 127, 180
Keats, John, 202
Keitel, Harvey, 156
Kempley, Rita, 127
Kett, Mary, 12, 194, 200
Killing Fields, The (1984), 78
Kilmer, Val, 92, 97, 98, 102, 136
King, Stephen, 84
Kipling, Rudyard, 75
Kirgo, George, 153
Kirkpatrick, David, 96, 134, 142
Klein, Arthur, 54, 57–60, 62, 67
Klein, Dennis, 132, 134, 138
Kooris, Richard, 50
Kotlowitz, Steve, 99, 104
Kroll, Jack, 169
Kubrick, Stanley, 161
Kuhn, Robert, 58–59

Lam, John, 141
Lansing, Sherry, 16
Last Picture Show, The (1971), 42
Leatherface, 38, 48–49. See also *Texas Chain Saw Massacre, The*
Lee, Bonni, 128
Lee, Bruce, 52
Lee, John, 126
Lee, Robert E., 77
Lehman, Ernest, 178
Levett, Valerie, 168
"life squad," 193–197, 201
Lillie and Beck (unproduced screenplay), 112, 116–117, 150

Lloyd, Euan, 77
Logan, Richard, 50
Long, Shelley, 119
Longley, Joe, 50
Love Boat, The (TV; 1977–1987), 128
Love Story (1970), 44, 52, 70
Lovett, H. Malcolm, 31, 32, 35
Lucchesi, Gary 146

MAB, 50, 55
MacGraw, Ali, 43, 44
macrobiotics, 123, 124, 148, 192
MAD (magazine), 108
"Maggs, the 10,000 Year Old Woman," 3
Main LaFrentz & Co., 57
Malden, Karl, 42
Mancuso, Frank, 134
Mankiewicz, Joseph L., 154
Mankiewicz, Tom, 154
Mann Bruin Theatre, 170
Mann's Chinese Theatre, 144
Man Who Skied Down Everest, The (1975), 66
Mary Hartman, Mary Hartman (TV; 1976–1977), 134
Mask of Zorro, The (1998), 8
Maslin, Janet, 127, 145
Masters, Kim, 173
Masterson, William H., 32–35
Masterson Affair, 32–35, 41
Mayo, Charles, 20
Mayo, William, 20
Mayo, William Worrall, 20
Mayo Clinic, 4, 20, 25, 178
McDowell, Michael, 111–113, 115–116, 120–121, 125, 127, 130, 202
McGillis, Kelly, 90, 96, 98, 102, 178
McKeown, Charles, 167–169
McQueen, Steve, 43–44, 81, 94
MD Anderson Cancer Center, 13, 68, 190, 192, 194, 195
Medavoy, Mike, 43
Meddings, Derek, 155

Meyer, Nicholas, 146–148
MGM Studios, Inc. (Metro-Goldwyn-Mayer), 61, 71
Midler, Bette, 119
Midnight Express (1978), 74, 153–154
Miller, Frank, 154
Minimum Basic Agreement (MBA), 100–101
Mirabella (magazine), 202
Mission: Impossible (TV; 1966–1973), 138
Miura, Yuichiro, 66
Mod Squad (TV; 1968–1973), 63
Mona Lisa (painting), 157
Montgomery, Bob, 77–79
Moore, Demi, 96
Morning After, The (1986), 117
Motion Picture Association of America, 178
Murphy, Eddie, 16, 95, 153; and *Beverly Hills Cop II*, 131–136, 142–145, 147, 148, 167

Nardino, Gary, 85–86
National Association of Theatre Owners of Texas, 40
Never Cry Wolf (1984), 154
Nevins, Sheila, 70
Newman, David, 42
Newman, Paul, 151
New Mexico Motion Picture Industries Committee, 40
Newsweek (magazine), 169
New West (magazine), 84, 86
New York Observer (newspaper), 108
New York Post (newspaper), 127
New York Times (newspaper), 145, 172
New Yorker (magazine), 127
Nicholson, Jack: and *Batman*, 153, 154, 162, 163, 166, 167, 168, 169, 171, 172; and Warren Skaaren, 150, 156–157, 181, 182
Nietzsche, Frederick, 156, 163
Nixon, Richard, 68

Noo, Gregory, 140–141
North by Northwest (1959), 178

O'Connor, Sandra Day, 76
Odd Couple, The (TV; 1970–1975), 134
Of East and West (unproduced screenplay), 73–78, 80–82, 118, 126, 161
Office of Strategic Services (OSS), 139
Officer and a Gentleman, An (1982), 100, 164
O'Hara, Catherine, 120
On Golden Pond (1981), 117
Osmond Television, 71
Outrageous Fortune (1987), 119

Pakula, Alan, 85
Palance, Jack, 156
Paramount Decrees, 41
Paramount Pictures, 6, 41, 42, 44, 52, 61–62; and *Beverly Hills Cop II*, 134, 138, 142–146, 152–153, 164; and *Days of Thunder*, 184–185; and *Fire with Fire*, 83, 85–87; and *Top Gun*, 15–16, 88–89, 94–96, 99–100, 105, 107, 108
Paramount Theatre, 1, 3, 7, 66, 67
Parker, Sarah Jessica, 171
Parsley, Bill, 38–39, 40–41, 48–51, 55, 58–59
Pattern Language, A (book), 5, 76, 193
Peckinpah, Sam, 43–44, 45, 94
Penthouse (magazine), 80
Peraino, Anthony "Big Tony," 52, 55, 58–59
Peraino, Joseph C. "The Whale," 52, 55, 58–59
Peraino, Louis "Butchie," 52–59, 70–71
Perry, Lou, 52. *See also* Peraino, Louis "Butchie"
Peter, Paul, and Mary: The Song Is Love (1970), 47
Peters, Jon, 153–154, 156, 158–160, 162, 166–169, 171, 173
Petrie, Daniel, Jr. 133

Petty, Dan, 42
Peyton Place (TV; 1964–1969), 63
Pfeiffer, Michelle, 165
Pfeiffer, Paul, 33
Phillips, Bill, 84–88
Phillips, Julianne, 96
Phinney, Kevin, 127, 176, 178
Phoenix, River, 171
Photoplay (magazine), 43
Piccolo, Brian, 69, 70
Pie in the Sky (P.I.T.S.), 50, 55
Pinewood Studios, 161–162, 165, 167, 169
Pitt, Brad, 44
Pitzer, Kenneth, 31
Poe, Edgar Allan, 166
Polk, James, 139
Polygram, 153
Pope, Joe, 71
Portable Nietzsche, The (book), 163
Premiere (magazine), 7, 88, 144, 152, 182
President's Analyst, The (1967), 63
Prime of Miss Jean Brodie, The (TV; 1978), 77, 178
Production Code, 41
Proser, Chip, 16, 90–92, 95, 99, 100, 102, 107
Pulitzer Prize (unproduced screenplay; 1984), 154
Puttnam, David, 74, 77, 78, 80, 118–119
Pyle, Chuck, 66

Quarve & Anderson, 16, 20, 21, 28
Quorum Club, The, 38–39, 49

Radford School for Girls, The, 76
Rae, Douglas, 77
Raggedy Man (1981), 62–63
Raggedy Man, The (screenplay), 61–62, 64
Rain Man (1988), 107, 151
Random House, 80
Rank, J. Arthur, 161
Rauk, Edward, 18–19

Rauk, Hans Knudtson, 17–18
Rauk, Kay, 18
Rauk, Ole, 18
Rauk, Pauline (Pederson), 18
Rauk, Sigrid, 17
Reed, Rex, 108
Reiner, Grace, 99, 103–104, 105, 106, 121, 140, 142
Reisenbach, Sandy, 128
Return of the Dragon (1974), 52, 53, 55
Rice University, 1, 25, 27–28, 94; Coat and Tie Rebellion, 33–35; history of, 28–29; Institute for the Arts, 30; K. Pitzer's resignation from, 31; Masterson Affair, 32–35, 41; presidential search process (1968–1969), 31–32; The Rice Coffee House (Corner of the Dreaming Monkey), 30
Richards, Ann, 40
Richardson, Sallye, 49
Richmond Art Forum, 30
Righteous Brothers, 16, 98, 107
Ringwood, Bob, 161
Risky Business (1983), 88
Roberts, Michael, 96
Robinson, Jerry, 159
Rochester, Minnesota, 4, 16, 19, 21, 24, 26–27, 29, 65, 129, 173, 198; history and growth of, 20, 22
Rochester Community and Technical College, 27. *See also* Rochester Junior College
Rochester Junior College (RJC), 27, 29
Rockford Files, The (TV; 1974–1980), 10
Rock Prairie, Minnesota, 17
Rogers, Mimi, 170
Rogers & Cowan, 174
Rolling Stone (magazine), 128, 181
Romancing the Stone (1984), 6, 136, 140
Rosenberg, Mark, 117
Ross, Steve, 171
Rossellini, Roberto, 30
Royal, Darrell, 67

Ruddy, Al, 56

Ryan, Meg, 98, 102

Ryder, Winona, 171, 179

Rynearson, Bob, 21–22, 23–24, 25, 27; and Warren Skaaren's cancer (1987), 122–123; and Warren Skaaren's cancer (1990), 195; Warren Skaaren's first meeting with, 21

Rynearson, Ed, 128

Saint Marys Hospital, 20, 21

San Francisco Examiner (newspaper), 172

Sass, Ronald, 29

Sawyer, Beverly, 86

Sayers, Gayle, 70

Schamus, James, 8

Schwarzenegger, Arnold, 156

Scott, Tony: and *Beverly Hills Cop II*, 132, 136, 144–145; and *Top Gun*, 16, 92–94, 96–97, 107

screen-credit arbitration: definition of, 9–11; and 50 percent rule, 103; process of, 8, 10–11, 87; and Statement of Contribution, 87, 100; and 33 percent rule, 103, 143, 146–147;

Screen Credits Manual, 102, 105, 106, 142, 143

"screenplay by" credit, 99

screenplay credit, assignation of, 10, 100–101

script doctoring, 82, 147

Season of '69, The (unproduced screenplay), 67–68. See also *Freddie*

Seekers of the Fleece/Lakota, 65

Sellars, Peter, 180

Selz, Tom, 54, 57, 58, 59

Semel, Terry, 153, 156, 158–160, 171

Shadow of the Batman (comic book), 159

Shagan, Steve, 8, 146

Sherrod, Blackie, 68–69

Shootout Films, 50

Shrake, Bud, 132, 133–134, 138, 148, 149, 167

Sicilian, The (1988), 8, 146, 152

Silence of the Lambs, The (1991), 1

Simpson, Don, 5; and *Beverly Hills Cop*, 131–132; and *Beverly Hills Cop II*, 131–136, 144–145; and *Days of Thunder*, 151, 164–165, 170, 174; on development, 132; and Jerry Bruckheimer, 15–16, 88; and Tom Cruise, 92; and *Top Gun*, 88–89, 91, 93–98, 107–108; and Warren Skaaren, 91, 107, 131, 175

Simpson, Mike: background of, 5, 80–81; and *Batman*, 6–7, 151, 155, 169, 170; and *Beetlejuice*, 7, 112; and *Beetlejuice in Love*, 202; and *Beverly Hills Cop II*, 137, 145; and *Top Gun*, 83, 106, 109; and Warren Skaaren's cancer (1990), 3, 194

Singer, Robert, 144

Skaaren, Clyde (cousin), 17, 19, 24

Skaaren, Helen Griffin (wife), 1, 3, 31; and dating Warren Skaaren, 31; and early marriage to Warren Skaaren, 45–46; education of, 31, 37; and separation from Warren Skaaren, 3, 13, 22, 151, 176–177, 182; and *Top Gun*, 93, 98; and Warren Skaaren's cancer (1987), 122, 195; and Warren Skaaren's cancer (1990), 187, 190–191, 195, 198, 200; and Warren Skaaren's foster children, 1, 46; and wedding to Warren Skaaren, 36

Skaaren, Julius (uncle), 17, 28

Skaaren, Lewis (uncle), 17

Skaaren, Morris (father), 20, 21, 178, 198; ancestry of, 16–17, 18; and Pearl Skaaren's marriage, 19–20, 129; and relationship with Warren Skaaren, 23, 111, 129, 178–179

Skaaren, Pearl Rauk (mother), 22, 178–179, 201; ancestry of, 17–18; and marriage to Morris Skaaren, 19–20, 22,

Skaaren, Pearl Rauk (*continued*)
129; mental health of, 19–20; and relationship with Warren Skaaren, 23–24, 111, 129, 178–179; and Warren Skaaren's birth, 21; and Warren Skaaren's final visit, 198

Skaaren, Warren: adolescence of, 23–27; in Austin, Texas, 90–91; awards won by, 26–27, 28, 35; and *Batman*, 120, 150–151, 154–163, 165–167, 171, 173–174, 177; and *Beetlejuice*, 111–116, 120, 126–127, 129–130; and *Beetlejuice in Love*, 176–181, 188, 202; and *Beverly Hills Cop II*, 131–136, 138–140, 142–143, 146–149, 152–153, 167; and Bill Wittliff, 61–63; birth of, 21; and Bob Kane, 157–158; and *Breakaway*, 63–67; and cancer (1987), 122–125, 148–149, 182; and cancer (1990), 187, 188–200; childhood of, 21–27; and childhood "visitation," 24–25; and *Crimson Eagle*, 137–141, 143, 146–148; and Dawn Steel, 83, 88–89, 105; and *Days of Thunder*, 151, 163–164, 170, 181, 182, 186, 231n35; death of, 200–202; and Don Simpson, 90, 96, 107; family history of, 16, 19, 21–22; and *Fire with Fire*, 83–88; and *Flawless*, 112, 117–119, 143; and FPS, Inc., 71–73; and *Freddie*, 67–72; and Helen Skaaren, 1, 31, 36, 37, 46, 121, 125, 129, 176, 177, 187, 195, 198; and Jack Nicholson, 156–157, 163; and Warner Bros. job opportunity, 119; and Julie Jordan, 176–177, 187, 190–194, 196, 198, 200; and Kim Basinger, 166–167; and Larry Ferguson, 143, 146, 152–153, 167; and *Lillie and Beck*, 85, 99, 112, 116; and Linda Vance, 131, 133; and Lucy Fisher, 120, 150, 154, 171; memorial for, 1–7, 11–12; and Michael Douglas, 136–138, 142; and Mike Simpson, 80–81, 106, 109; and Morris Skaaren, 23, 111, 129, 178–179; and music, 26, 128; and *Of East and West*, 73–79, 80–82; and Office of Texas Governor, career with, 36–37, 39–40; and Pearl Skaaren, 23–24, 111, 129, 178–179; and relationships with women, 12–13, 18, 27, 45–46, 124–125, 177, 182–183; and Rice University, 29–30, 32–35; and Rochester Junior College (RJC), 27–28; and screen-credit arbitration, *Batman*, 167–169; and screen-credit arbitration, *Beetlejuice*, 115–116, 120, 129–130; and screen-credit arbitration, *Beverly Hills Cop II*, 133, 138–140, 142–143, 146–149, 152–153, 167; and screen-credit arbitration, *Top Gun*, 99–100, 101–106; screenwriting and script doctoring approach of, 69, 75–76, 91, 175, 182, 202; and Sean Young, 162, 165; and The Skaaren Corporation, 50–51, 62; and *Spooks*, 63, 84, 117; and *The Texas Chain Saw Massacre*, 39, 48, 51–55, 56–60; and the Texas Film Commission, 39–45, 50–51, 61; and Tim Burton, 110, 183–184; and Tom Cruise, 15–16, 93, 95, 151, 164; and Tony Scott, 92–93, 136, 144; and *Top Gun*, 15–16, 90–99, 105–109, 178; and Western medicine, 20; Wren Valley home of, 12, 121–122; and writers' strike (1988), 126, 128

Skaaren Corporation, The, 50–51, 62
Skaren (as alternate spelling), 17
Skerritt, Tom, 98
Slater, Christian, 171
Sleeper, Herb, 20, 25–27, 173–174
Smith, Preston, 2, 36, 38, 40–42, 45, 49
Sound of Music, The (1965), 178
Spacek, Sissy, 63
Spielberg, Steven, 47, 180

Spooks (unproduced screenplay), 63, 84, 117

Sports Illustrated (magazine), 132

Spring Grove, Minnesota, 17–19

Springsteen, Bruce, 96

Spy Who Loved Me, The (1977), 155

Squire Shop, 26, 28

Sragow, Michael, 172

Staebell, Sara, 152

Star Is Born, A (1976), 153

Stark, Ray, 161

Starlog (magazine), 125

Starting Over (1979), 85

Steel, Dawn, 6, 83–86, 88, 100, 105, 107

Steinmark, Fred, 69–70, 72

Steinmark, Freddie, 60, 67, 178

Steinmark, Gloria, 69–70, 72

Stempel, Tom, 9, 11, 82

Stewart, Donald, 184–185

Stone, Gene, 202

Stone, Oliver, 165

Sugarland Express, The (1974), 46–47, 78

Sunshine Boys, The (1975), 161

Superman (1978), 155

Superman II (1980), 155

Superman III (1983), 155

Superman IV (1987), 155

Tanen, Ned, 107, 146, 174

Tender Mercies (1983), 82

Texas A&M University, 123

Texas Chain Saw Massacre, The (1974), 5, 62, 71, 81; and Bill Parsley, 38–39, 48–49; box office, 56, 58, 59; and Bryanston Distribution, Inc., 52–59; critical reception, 58; financing, 48–49, 50; post-production, 49–50; production, 48–49

Texas Film Commission, 39–42, 50–51, 61

Texas Film Communication Commission, 41–42. *See also* Texas Film Commission

Texas Monthly (magazine), 38, 76, 80, 175

Texas Motion Picture Services (TMPS), 63

Texas State Penitentiary, 43, 44

Thomas Crown Affair, The (1968), 91

Thompson, Jim, 43

Time-Life Films, 72

To Kill a Mockingbird (1962), 178

Tommy (1975), 77

Top Gun (1986): box office, 108; critical reception, 108, development, 15–16, 88–97; pick-up scene, Officer's Club, 98, 107, 178; production, 98–99; screen-credit arbitration (final), 104–106; screen-credit arbitration (Separated Rights), 99–104; test screenings, 107–108; volleyball scene, 92, 96–97, 107, 136

Top Guns, 15, 89. See also *Top Gun*

Towne, Robert, 157, 181–182, 184–186

Townsend, Tommy, 50

Traffic (2000), 9

Treverrow, Colin, 8–9

Trip to Bountiful, The (1985), 178

Turman, John, 8

Turman, Lawrence, 61

Turner, Kathleen, 136–138, 141, 146

20th Century Fox, 16, 42, 52, 61, 71, 137

20/20 (TV; 1978–), 169–170

Two Jakes, The (1990), 157, 181

United Artists, 71

United Film Distribution Co., 70

Universal Pictures, 46, 63

University of Texas at Austin, The, 5, 40, 47, 50, 60, 67, 80, 177, 189

Valenti, Jack, 178

Vance, Linda, 3, 12–13, 145, 164, 181;

background of, 123–124; and *Days of Thunder*, 164; on "life squad," 191, 192, 193; and relationship with Warren Skaaren, 131, 133; and Warren Skaaren's cancer (1987), 124; and Warren Skaaren's cancer (1990), 187, 188–191, 195, 200–202; on Warren Skaaren's career, 145, 194; on Warren Skaaren and medicine, 124, 191
Verdict, The (1982), 178
Vertue, Beryl, 77
Vestre Slidre, Norway, 17
Vidal, Gore, 8, 146–147, 152
Villa, Pancho, 76, 80, 175
Viola, Liz, 3, 191
Viola, Tom, 3, 50
Vitello, Philip, 54
Vortex, 49, 50, 51, 55, 57

Wachs, Robert, 134, 142–143, 148
Waldman, Frank, 67–69
Walken, Christopher, 156
Walker, Beverly, 9
Walker, Lee, 24, 193, 199, 200
Walters, Barbara, 170
Warhol, Andy, 30, 52, 128
Warner Bros., 13, 41, 54, 61, 85; and *Batman*, 150, 153–159, 162–163, 165–166, 168–172, 175; and *Beetlejuice*, 111–112, 114–117, 119, 121, 125–129; and *Beetlejuice in Love*, 177, 184, 202
Washington Post (newspaper), 127, 145
Waxman, Natasha, 29, 80, 183
Way We Were, The (1973), 161
Weinstein, Paula, 85, 117
Welles, Orson, 161
Wheeler, Linda, 68, 70, 72
White Knights (1985), 185
Wick, Doug, 83, 85, 99, 112, 116–120, 136, 150, 171

Wild Basin Wilderness Preserve, 66–67, 121
Wild Bunch, The (1969), 43
Wild Geese, The (1978), 77
William Morris Agency, 3, 5, 80–81, 84, 169, 171, 198
Williams, Bryan, 33
Williams, Mike, 197
Wilson, Larry, 111, 121
Windsplitter, The (1971), 49
Wise, Robert O., 4, 27–28, 29
Witness (1985), 96
Wittliff, Bill, 61–63
Wood, Grant, 110
World Encyclopedia of Comics, The (book), 159
Worrell, Reverend John D., 36
Writers Guild of America (WGA), 87, 138, 140, 152–153; and arbitration, 8–10, 99, 100–101, 103–109, 135, 142–143, 146–148, 168, 181, 184–186, 202; author of screenplay, definition of, 10; and Policy Review Board, 142–143; writer's strike (1985), 86; writer's strike (1988), 126, 147, 152, 154, 170, 172
"written by" credit, 99

Yablans, Frank, 52, 61–62
Yates, Walter, 63–67, 73
Yoffe, Emily, 175
Young, Peter, 155, 182
Young, Sean, 153, 156, 162, 165
Yumkas, Carol, 171

Zanuck, Richard, 47, 78
Zanuck/Brown Company, The, 80
Zephro, Ted, 52, 53, 59
Zoetrope Studios, 132